GOVERNMENT SECRECY IN DEMOCRACIES

*the text of this book is printed
on 100% recycled paper*

GOVERNMENT
SECRECY
IN
DEMOCRACIES

Edited by Itzhak Galnoor

NEW YORK UNIVERSITY PRESS
New York
1977

To my mother and D. G.

LIBRARY OF CONGRESS CATALOG CARD NUMBER: 76–49772

INTERNATIONAL STANDARD BOOK NUMBER: 0–8147–2964–9

Contents

Part III   A Comparative Perspective

Editor's Preface

My own curiosity about government secrets began in the mid-sixties, when Bertram Gross and I were working on American federal budgetary reforms at Syracuse University. At the time he called my attention to the Freedom of Information Act and wondered whether it would help us to get some information from the Bureau of the Budget. It did not. We still had to use Bert's old contacts in Washington to get what we wanted. He therefore shares indirect responsibility for the conception of this book, as he first generated my interest in matters hidden from the indiscriminating eye. Subsequently I conducted a seminar on comparative government secrecy at the Hebrew University and published a number of articles on this and the broader subject of the politics of information.

I am still intrigued by what first captured my interest regarding the secret affairs of government, referred to in my concluding article as "situational secrecy." Secrecy seems to be a question of both geography and idiosyncracy. Note the quotation I found in my files from that period:

> The concept of a return to secrecy in peacetime demonstrates a profound misunderstanding of the role of a free press as opposed to that of a controlled press. The plea for secrecy could become a cloak for errors, misjudgments and other failings of government.

The speaker: Richard M. Nixon. The time: May 1961, after the Bay of Pigs fiasco (*The New York Times*, May 10, 1961). Thirteen years later, the same person, as president of the United States, declared on television: "I am not a crook" and was subsequently ousted from office for not revealing the truth.

"Secrecy is conditioned by time, place, and the distinct attributes of different systems," notes Carl Friedrich in his introduction to this volume. This stands in contrast with the tendency to separate secrecy and publicity practices from their specific political culture and social environment. Thus, British observers tend to envy the

American practice of "openness," whereas Americans tend to favor the "responsible" and discreet British system. This book does not frame the riddle, or intend to answer it, but shows that, despite the differences, democratic societies share a common attitude: Both the people's right to know and the government's privilege to conceal are axiomatically—and often grudgingly—accepted. The resulting paradox of this simultaneous acceptance is the subject of this volume.

Simply stated, the hurdle is that, given human nature and the subtlety of the political process, both of the following assumptions are probably correct: (1) If all government activities were to be conducted openly, there would still be some secrecy; (2) if all government activities were to be conducted secretly, there would still be some publicity.

The idea of assembling this book arose when I realized that the subject of government secrecy, which has been a focal point of interest in all democratic countries, has neither been researched intensively nor treated comparatively. Even the more scholarly treatments suffer from what Francis Rourke calls the "issue attention cycle": A few books and articles appear when the subject is a potent political issue and then attention fades. This book is likewise appearing at a time when secrecy is a front-page issue, but it is not about the headline-making events in the U.S.A. during the Nixon administration, or any specific scandals in other countries. Instead, the contributors to this volume have aimed at a more general inquiry into the subject. I hope that the broader perspective of this book will still be of interest when we reach our next apex in the cycle of attention given to government secrecy.

In approaching the contributors for this volume, I had one distinct bias regarding the subject. I wanted them to emphasize the *political* and *administrative* dimensions of the secrecy issue. We seem to know a considerable amount about the right to vote, to express opinions, to participate in the political process, and to contest, but very little about the practical arrangements that make these rights relevant to government affairs. What about the right to demand information on government activities in order to indicate "where the shoe pinches?" What about those citizens who meet the prerequisites of being enlightened and interested and who are still unable to find out about governmental processes?

Most publications on the subject have hitherto confined their discussions to the legality of secrecy and to the government–mass-media encounter over withholding information. Conversely, most of the contributors to this book are political scientists, and except for chapter 5, "The Information Marketplace," all the chapters have been written especially for this volume. The emphasis is on politics and on secrecy as part of the political process as viewed by sixteen authors from ten different countries. As for timeliness, most of the chapters in this book were completed by the end of 1974 and some during 1975. Secrecy in democracies might be immortal, but secrets are contemporary. The reader is invited to test the general concepts presented in this book and to fill in the latest scoop from this morning's headlines.

The book is divided into three parts. Part I, "The Context of Government Secrecy," aims at opening up a broader spectrum by tracing issues such as the people's right to know back to political philosophy and viewing them in the light of political theory, information processes, and government decision making. The chapters in part I do not share a conceptual framework. Each author pursues his own path of inquiry with no attempt on my part to compare or aggregate the results. This first part is open-ended in the sense that it portrays the rich cultural, social, and political context of the subject of government secrecy.

The chapters in part II were written on the basis of a common framework presented by the editor and refined through mutual exchanges. They share the awareness that government secrecy is a phenomenon common to all democratic systems. Taken together, these nine chapters enable us to compare at least three dimensions of government secrecy in the countries portrayed:

1. *The political culture* in each country and its probable impact on the axiomatic approach to and the deviations from the people's right to know, on suspicion of or deference to government in general, on the legitimacy of secrecy, and on the role of the mass media.

2. *The constitutional and legal provisions* that provide formal rules for secrecy and publicity and for solving conflicts between holders and requesters of government information. The topics discussed are official secrets, freedom of access, executive privilege, document classification, civil-service codes of behavior, disclosure

of evidence before the courts, censorship, and other laws affecting the mass media.

3. *The political marketplace*, where information is a resource and secrecy and publicity are the results of transactions between political actors. Here the questions are: Who really knows what, and how can one gain access to information in each country?

In addition, these chapters contain the authors' opinions regarding remedies for the current disequilibrium between secrecy and publicity and also projections of probable directions and trends. The combined result of part II is far from being a unified map of the entire terrain; rather, it depicts the broad features of government secrecy in each country and provides a basis for a comparative perspective.

Part III is my attempt to offer such a comparative perspective by asking the question: What do we know about government secrecy in democratic systems? This chapter further develops the conceptual framework along the three dimensions that served as the basis of part II. It draws upon the other chapters for comparisons as well as for tentative conclusions. Readers who are interested in the comparative aspect of government secrecy are advised to read first Carl Friedrich's introduction and my concluding chapter.

The contributors are responsible only for their respective chapters, and I am grateful for their fruitful cooperation. I take full responsibility for the possibility that the sum may be less than the parts.

I would like to thank my colleagues in the political science department of the Hebrew University, Emanuel Gutmann and David Ricci, for their comments on my articles and Max Mark and my other colleagues at the political science department of Wayne State University, where I spent a year on leave in 1973/1974, who helped me in the early stages of preparing this book. Wayne State University also provided financial support for this project, for which I am very grateful. A grant from the faculty of social sciences of the Hebrew University helped to finance the completion of the editing task and the valuable assistance of Meir Nitzan, a graduate student in the political science department. There is one person without whose efforts, enthusiasm, and patience this book would not have been published, Fay Krimper of Harper & Row. Since it is impossible to list all her contributions, I will mention just one fact: Her helping hand can be found on every page of this volume.

Finally, I apologize for not revealing more details about the ups and downs of editing a book whose authors are scattered all over the world. These matters are *really* secret.

ITZHAK GALNOOR

Jerusalem
Fall 1975

Introduction

CARL J. FRIEDRICH

In my book *The Pathology of Politics* (New York: Harper & Row, 1972) I concluded that both propaganda and secrecy are endemic to all political orders, and that these two ways of manipulating the ruled by the ruler and of influencing the ruler by the ruled resemble other pathologies of politics. I pointed out that much material illustrating the evil aspects of politics, and especially of democratic public life, has come to hand. Yet certain issues have not been significantly advanced, notable among them that of secrecy. Secrecy, and especially the confidential operations of the executive, have, however, been frequent news items. The secrecy of many things has been enhanced and the desire for publicity increased. Thus we have more information on subjects that are supposed to be secret. All states have a tendency to look upon all their actions as secret. Thus there develops an inclination to keep secret things that are generally known. As a result more controversy over the legal and moral aspects of secrecy has developed. This is not a new phenomenon. Politics has always been a fertile ground for secrecy and all the evils that accompany it.

In the United States, the Vietnam War, the publication of the Pentagon Papers, and Watergate have shown that secrecy can be a tool of politics. Such events may cause even more secrecy, and the result is often that democratic states are plagued by accusations and counteraccusations.

I had hoped to introduce much of the material pertaining to the pathology of politics. This hope was only partly fulfilled. Even the frequent appeal to secrecy has not produced a sufficient amount of repetition. A slogan has now appeared claiming "the right to know" as the ground for public interest, and a part of the Bill of Rights. If a problem produces controversial steps by a government, a case for keeping them secret is very strong. The argument is that the public cannot form an adequate judgment on policy unless all the necessary information is made available. But it is precisely this that cannot be made available to those whose support is called for without at the same time making this information available to the enemy. This makes governmental information a risky thing, for to inform provides weapons for counterattack.

Secrecy is conditioned by time, place, and distinct attributes of different political systems. This is true not only between friend and enemy. Within the same country similar events have different informational connotations under different circumstances. The opposition can take advantage of such information, and the circumstances are correspondingly different.

We have seen quite a number of illustrations for these and related complexities. If the same event has different informational connotations in the same country, the right policy under different circumstances is a very difficult matter to determine. For example, the secrecy aspect of the Pentagon Papers and of Watergate became embroiled in the political situation in the U.S.A. in the early 1970s. This is not an unusual situation. For many reasons what happened in America is likely to happen in other democratic societies. The present world situation, and particularly global conflicts, will continue to create problems of secrecy and publicity.

This book contains many illustrations of the serious problems and the complexity of the secrecy issue in the present time. It has proven exceedingly difficult to keep secrecy matters within functional limits. Politics probably needs many dubious practices that a government seeks to hide by secrecy. In the nature of the case it is essential to challenge such secreting of governmental operations. But there cannot be any effective democractic conduct of policy, and more especially foreign policy, without such practices. Such practices need, in turn, to be challenged in order to keep them within limits. Recent events in democratic states and especially in the U.S.A. have made the effort to understand secrecy in order to restrain it even more important. The quest for a comparative study of such issues became the focus of scientific inquiry. The results are being laid out in the ensuing pages.

Most of the topics presented in this book are within what is usually considered to be the disciplinary domain of political science. The editor of this book and most of the contributors teach in political science departments. I welcome the renewed interest of political scientists in this field of inquiry. Of course, the subject itself has never ceased to be part of politics, but it has been treated mainly in legalistic terms (Official Secrecy Act in Great Britain, executive privilege in the U.S.A.). As Rourke points out in his essay about the United States, secrecy has also been part of the public "attention cycle" because of the mass media's crusade on behalf of the freedom of the press and of the people's right to know. The people's right to know is as yet ill defined, but it is a new extension of popular rights. As a result, it has become part of the democratic battle cry and for many it has become almost identical to the demand for democracy. As the essays in this book demonstrate, the legal framework for defining governmental activity in withholding and releasing information is not only highly controversial, but constantly increasing and changing under different circumstances. Secrecy and privileged information are only two dimensions of the broader political issues involved. What the law is can only be pragmatically ascertained by describing the activities involved. The question is one of ever new dimensions. What new light can political scientists shed on this subject and related issues of governmental secrecy? The impossibility of formulating hard and fast rules in answer to this question is the patent concern of the political scientist who ventures into this field. Limiting secrecy is on the agenda of most democracies. The first task is an effort to clarify the issues involved and to present a more generalized map of the "secrecy topography" in different democratic countries.

This book is an important step forward. The first six chapters indicate the wide range of related subjects. What the editor calls "the context of government secrecy," that is to say, the political environment of these phenomena, is very complex. By identifying the influence of variables such as the information revolution and symbolism, we are able to ask questions, but we are not yet in a position to predict the behavior of the political system with regard to secrecy. Nor can we categorize a given system precisely as "open" or "closed."

The first two chapters try to place current slogans about the people's right to know and human rights within political theory, especially modern liberal democratic theory. To the best of my knowledge, this is one of the first efforts to go back to our rich sources of political philosophy in order to gain insight and test their relevance to this particular issue. Further, the editor chose for special attention the impact of the information revolution, the marketplace of political information, and those generic secrets that are part of government decision making, that is, the kinds of secrets that occur "naturally." Government is in this respect to be treated like other organizations, which, under competitive conditions, protect their particular specialities. This part is enriched by a chapter on the symbolic uses of information. That words can become symbols is generally true in politics (as well as in other spheres that employ words) and has become widely acknowledged. As Galnoor tells us in chapter 5, it has become practically known and part of the arsenal of pressure groups, as well as an integral part of the decision-making process (as illustrated by Curzon in chapter 6). Symbolism has to be accounted for in any analysis of political orders. This book deals only with the context and the incidence of secrecy in democratic systems. But what is common in democratic politics is magnified and exaggerated in totalitarian politics. Much could be learned if we knew more about the political environment and the practice of secrecy in other types of regimes.

The second part of this book is a descriptive analysis of how secrecy is treated in ten democratic states. All the chapters show the relevance of the topics presented in the first part and the extent to which secrecy has become a controversial issue in many democratic systems. Moreover, the essays analyze how different democratic systems cope with the same phenomenon and the methods they have adopted. The United States is not unique; it exhibits the usual methods, such as trying to suppress news, to drown it by related data, and the like.

The parameters available for analyzing secrecy are as yet not sharp enough to develop firm comparative research, but the essays do provide a comparative perspective. For instance, problems such as executive privilege occur in different countries and are handled in similar ways. Because of the Nazi experience, the Federal Republic of Germany is especially sensitive to governmental information manipulation, and as Reese tells us, the contents of government information "crave for acclamation"; they do not promote "critical discussion." (See chapter 13.)

One problem is recurrent. Is there any attempt of public officials to release information in order to promote serious discussion? Governments in general do not believe in the wisdom of the un-identified citizen. The benefits that can sometimes occur by public discussion do not outweigh the costs of exposure, especially of what is euphemistically referred to as "premature disclosure." In small countries like the Netherlands and Israel, and in some big countries like the United States as well, information manipulation by govern-ments takes very similar forms. All the national essays deal with the legal aspects of secrecy as well as with the more political ones. It is interesting to note that the tight legal framework of public administra-tion in France is still very influential as far as secrecy is concerned (see chapter 14), while in Great Britain (see chapter 10) changes in the political environment are slowly catching up with the secrecy laws of the country. One of the most interesting aspects of this part of the book is the fact that secrecy became a primary concern of legislation and that many political systems have adopted legislative methods for dealing with it.

I hope that subsequent editions of this book will contain updating material that will teach us two additional important things: first, to what extent secrecy will remain a central and controversial issue (with all the political implications of such a phenomenon) in demo-cratic systems; second, what happened to all the legislative measures adopted recently.

The appeal to political scientists to be more concerned with in-formation problems is sound, but how to go about it is an in-formational desideratum that is unresolved. Will it be the task of the mass media to solve the problems of interpretation? This and related problems shared by the democratic systems and reviewed in these pages are no more ready to receive an answer than are other questions about our society.

It is not possible, in light of these complexities and other prob-lems, to make a clear-cut prophecy. As the concluding chapter by Galnoor suggests, we have some knowledge but we still do not know enough about government secrecy. We certainly do not know how to replace it with something better. In fact, we know little about the political circumstances that make secrecy so attractive to those who possess official information and so relevant to government conduct of public affairs, especially in modern industrialized countries. As the last chapter points out, we are not even sure whether a country is "more democratic" only because it is more "open" as far as the secrecy pathology is concerned.

In a very tentative way I conclude this introduction by pointing out the evils of repressing information. In view of this set of facts we can say that the repression of unwelcome information is subject to many of the general problems of the information. For one thing, greater freedom in making information available is likely to yield better results. Nothing in the position of governments assures the public of all desirable information. The general remedy of making a maximum of information available and the government open is likely to improve information and thus to give more satisfactory results.

PART I

The Context of Government Secrecy

1

Political Theory and the People's Right to Know

PETER DENNIS BATHORY
AND
WILSON CAREY McWILLIAMS

INTRODUCTION: AN "INFORMED" PUBLIC
AND THE POLITICAL ORDER

A recent commentator insists that "a democratic system requires a public informed about the decisions and actions of its political leaders."[1] Free and open circulation of ideas and information is defended, in other words, not as a "right of expression" belonging to the individual speaker or writer, but as an essential element of democracy derived from the public's "need to hear" what is important in political life.[2] In an increasingly influential dissenting opinion, Justice William O. Douglas wrote:

> The Press has a privileged position in our constitutional system, not to enable it to make money, not to set newsmen apart as a favored class, but to bring fulfillment to the people's right to know.[3]

Douglas has also pointed out that the "right to know" includes more than the "decisions and actions of . . . political leaders": "The ques-

1. David Wise, *The Politics of Lying* (New York: Random House, 1973), p. 219.
2. Edward J. Bloustein, "The First Amendment and Privacy: The Supreme Court and the Philosopher" (Talk presented to the New Jersey Philosophical Association, 1974), pp. 1–10.
3. Branzburg v. Hayes, 408 U.S. 665 (1972), at p. 721.

tion is whether a public *issue*, not a public official, is involved."[4] In this context, freedom of speech and of the press are not individual liberties exercised or ignored at the individual's option, but needs of the polity as a whole, and logically, civic duties commanded by a sovereign public.[5]

Earlier democratic theorists like Alexis de Tocqueville and Jean Jacques Rousseau took a similar position. They would, however, have detected the danger implicit in speaking of the public's *need for knowledge* in terms of a "right" to know. Does the public have a "right" to be ignorant or ill-informed? The question is more than academic. Conceived as elements of human nature, as "natural rights," the great freedoms are as inalienable and inescapable as human nature itself, inhering in us whether we choose (or are allowed to choose) to use them or not. In political life, however, human beings can choose, have chosen, and likely will continue to choose to give up political freedoms and even private rights and liberties, preferring new tyrannies to the uncertainties and responsibilities of democratic citizenship.[6] Providing citizens with "information" is no guarantee against such a choice.

This is only to point out that no part of a political order—and the right to know is just that—can be understood in isolation from the whole. As the great teachers of democracy warned us, no single institution and no set of formal political institutions is a sufficient condition of democracy. Any political order, and democracy more than others, depends on the values and feelings of the people; on their economic and social relationships; on their preception of the relation between themselves, their fellow citizens, and their common institutions and public life.[7] An informed public has undeniable value for a democracy, but a whole series of questions has logical priority. What is a public? What is the nature of a *democratic* public? What is the character of *this* public at this time? And what does it mean to refer to a public, once defined, as "informed?" There is more than a semantic difference, after all, between an "informed public" and "a public informed," for an "informed public" has presumably heard and learned what a "public informed" has merely been *told*.

---

4. Concurring in Rosenblatt v. Baer, 383 U.S. (1966), pp. 89 ff.
5. Bloustein, "The First Amendment and Privacy."
6. Erich Fromm, *Escape from Freedom* (New York: Rinehart, 1941).
7. Alexis de Tocqueville, *Democracy in America*, 2 vols. (New York: Vintage, 1945), 1:298 ff.

There is no one-to-one relationship between information made available and information comprehended.

In one sense, public knowledge is inseparable from the idea of the public itself. A public is not a random collection of individuals; the concept presumes some minimal awareness of commonality. Similarly, if what is public is what is common, the perception that there is a public implies a sense of what is private, uncommon, particular to groups and individuals within the polity. The public's need to hear what is essential to public affairs—whether defined in relation to "the decisions and actions of its political leaders" or to "public issues"—does not extend to *everything*. In logic, as well as in law, there is a "right to privacy" about private matters.[8] But what is the line between public and private affairs, and who decides what is relevant to public concerns and what is not?

The "people's right to know," in other words, raises the great questions of political theory, inevitably demanding a discussion of authority, political community, and civil and private liberty. Indeed, it is inseparable from the perennial riddles of political philosophy— Is political knowledge possible? Can political virtue be taught?— and the areas of concern to which they refer: political education, rhetoric, the nature of political things. And because the "right to know" is a vital issue for politics in our time, it deserves the same sense of its interwoven relation to the whole fabric of political life that was given it by the great theorists of our tradition.

DEMOCRATIC PARTICIPATION AND THE NEED TO KNOW

"The people of England regards itself as free," Rousseau argued in *The Social Contract*, "but it is greatly mistaken: it is free only during the election of members of Parliament. As soon as they are elected, slavery overtakes it, and it is nothing."[9] Democracy was far more than voting for Rousseau. Democratic citizenship demanded a regular participation in and concern for common problems that could not be ceded to anyone. Participation in deliberation was essential if the citizen was to shape the alternatives that set the conditions of political choice, at the polls and outside them; and

8. Griswold v. Connecticut, 381 U.S. 479 (1965).
9. Jean Jacques Rousseau, *The Social Contract* (New York: Everyman, 1950), p. 94.

without influence on those alternatives the citizen's freedom was at best limited, at worst, a sham. Giovanni Sartori makes a similar argument in a contemporary context: "Electoral power per se is the mechanical guarantee of the system, but the substantive guarantee is given by the conditions under which the citizen gets the information and is exposed to the pressure of opinion makers."[10] But Sartori's citizen, by Rousseau's standards, is already well on the way to political enslavement—passively "getting" information, "exposed" to the "pressure" of those who "make" opinion.

Rousseau went further in another sense. Even formal participation was not enough; statistics describing voting, attendance at meetings, subscription to political periodicals, and the like would, at best, be surface indicators of civic freedom. Rousseau insisted that the free citizen be public-spirited, that he approach public affairs with a concern for the "general good," attempting to govern his private interests and will by a "general will" that directed his mind to the good of the polity as a whole. A citizen who followed his private passions, interests, and will was in reality less than free. His psyche had already resolved to sacrifice the community, should it become necessary, to protect his private concerns. But since freedom demanded the ability to affect the great alternatives that shape human destiny, and since that ability can only be had in political community and collective action, the private man had resolved, in the last analysis, to surrender freedom in any crisis. A purely private will was a will to enslavement.

Rousseau knew that such a participant public, governing in accordance with the general will, would be all but impossible to achieve. In fact, he commented that "a real democracy is only an ideal."[11] He meant to present a standard at which all less-than-perfect democracies must aim and to insist that institutional mechanisms and procedural guarantees are always inadequate, that the substance of democracy can only be understood in relation to the people, their opinions, their beliefs, and their knowledge. Despite the increasing complexity of our political life, his analysis remains valid.

There is no need to pretend that the circumstances of our world provide the most congenial setting for democracy. Democracy is a creed born in and adapted to small states, in which time permits all

10. Giovanni Sartori, *Democratic Theory* (Detroit: Wayne State University Press, 1962), p. 74.

11. Rousseau, *Social Contract*, p. 109.

citizens to participate actively, in which each has the opportunity to address all, and in which the whole is not an airy abstraction but something we can see and "emotionally comprehend."[12] If Rousseau's Paris of the eighteenth century was lost to democracy, then surely the twentieth-century megalopolis is at least problematic. Plato had set 5,040 as the ideal population of the ideal city; Rousseau revered his speculation. In a world like our own, the guarantee of rights— and particularly the "right to know"—becomes more urgent, but it is more difficult as well.

Even in the smaller and simpler democracies of the past, it was often argued that "the many" were ignorant, inclined to be swept away by passion and to think in the short term, and hopelessly inept at the tasks that citizenship required of them. *The Federalist* sometimes remarks on the good qualities of the people, but it provides far more abundant testimony to the framers' fear of "mere democracy" and to their conviction that the public is inclined to parochiality and emotionality and is dangerously vulnerable to demagoguery. In our time, that criticism of democracy seems much more powerful. Even a friend of democracy like John Dewey argued (nearly fifty years ago, in a political environment that itself seems much simpler than our own) that "public" decisions involved an evaluation of complex and far-removed consequences quite beyond the ordinary "private" life and experience of the citizen.[13] As Sartori comments:

> Let's be honest. The average voter is called upon to make decisions on questions about which he knows nothing. In other words, he is incompetent. And decisions that each of us makes in fields in which we have no skill are obviously decisions that have been suggested by someone else, either a competent or a pseudo-competent.[14]

More than one democratic theorist has been daunted by the fact that, inevitably, we depend on experts and specialists to deal with many aspects of our world. That dependence, however, tempts us to give the expert more deference (and the citizen less respect) than he deserves. Long ago, Plato pointed out that the "art of politics" is quite distinct from the other arts, and the distance may have grown

12. Mancur Olson, *The Logic of Collective Action* (Cambridge: Harvard University Press, 1965); see also Robert Dahl and Edward Tutte, *Size and Democracy* (Stanford: Stanford University Press, 1973).
13. John Dewey, *The Public and Its Problems* (New York: Holt, 1927).
14. Sartori, *Democratic Theory*, p. 78.

even greater in our time. Increasing size and complexity have created new vistas for all human beings, demanding a political knowledge equal to an expanded world—a broader vision; a more inclusive sense of past, present, and future; a greater ability to conceive ways in which diverse factors and events can be integrated into a whole that maximizes the public good. But the same world *narrows* the relative focus of the specialist. Logically, each skill should be valued less because it is of relatively smaller consequence.

The case for democracy does not require that the citizen be familiar with all the bits and pieces of expert knowledge. He cannot be, in any case, and we do him individually and the people collectively no credit if we believe that the political claims of democracy can be maintained only by telling lies that exaggerate the ability of the citizen. Jack-of-all-trades, master of none: The maxim applies in the political as well as the mechanical arts, and in a democracy a sovereign public must be master of its own trade. The public, as the great theorists of the past knew, requires a skill qualitatively different from that of experts, a political *judgment* that enables it to know which facts are important and which are not, and to evaluate measures and men. Vindicating the "people's right to know" does not require that all specialized, private, and relatively inaccessible information be "made public." It demands, rather, that the public have access to those facts necessary for public judgment about public things, and more important, that it have the *greatest possible opportunity to learn and master the art of political judgment.*

EDUCATION AND POLITICAL JUDGMENT

That the "people's right to political education" embraces and has precedence over the "right to know" is hardly a new proposition: Free public education was defended as a preparation for public duties before it was urged as a means to private advantage.[15] Emphasis on the contribution of formal education to economic and social mobility has led us to neglect its civic functions—or, more perniciously, to assume that the latter are included in the former. At the same time, we have tended to forget that formal education, however helpful, is

15. Herbert Harris, *American Labor* (New Haven: Yale University Press, 1938).

only the tip of the iceberg and is neither a necessary nor a sufficient condition of political judgment and virtue.

In the canons of political theory, Socrates began the discussion of political education by disclaiming "any pretense to knowledge" about politics and political questions.[16] Socrates knew, however, that philosophy's critique of conventional "knowledge" can easily lead to cynicism, despair, or a self-assertive refusal to be limited or instructed. Different personalities hear with different ears. The true proposition "we do not know" is heard by those who would flee responsibility or whose confidence has been shattered as "I cannot learn"; the tyrannical soul hears only "*they* do not know."

Hence Socrates went on to insist that "training in common together" was a necessity of political judgment and virtue.[17] "In common" obviously meant more than "in the same place." It referred to an education that, from the first, emphasized shared responsibility, a training-in-community in substance as well as form. The first lesson of such a teaching is that self-sufficiency is impossible, a humbling of pride and arrogance that is undeniably perceived as painful. But such an education also aims to provide relationships of trust and emotional security that allow the individual to be valued *while* acknowledging his limitations and his ignorance. Self-righteousness becomes both impossible and unnecessary.

"Training in common together" might enable the individual to learn the political truth that the whole can be greater that the sum of its parts; that in relationship to his fellows each human being can find a strength, courage, and joy that would be lacking alone; that reciprocal dependence may be a liberation rather than a limitation. The lesson that the public good is to be preferred to the private would not, then, be merely an abstract moral precept, but a matter of habit and feeling.

It was precisely this concern for "the people's right to political education" that led many of the great teachers to defend censorship and even political deception.[18] They argued that in education what is learned is more important than what is taught, and that in political

16. Plato *Gorgias* 506A.
17. Ibid., 527D; and of philosophic virtue for that matter. The argument suggests the problem of educating a tyrant's son.
18. See Wilson Carey McWilliams, "Honesty and Political Authority," in *The Right to Know, to Withhold, and to Lie* (New York: Council on Religion and International Affairs, 1969).

education, what is said is less important than what is learned. They feared that political education would be endangered by too simplistic and too absolute an interpretation of "the right to know."

The classic defense of deception and censorship is complex, but one argument merits particular attention at this point.[19] Whatever our ultimate capabilities, the theory points out, we do not *begin* with a political judgment capable of detecting the "real nature" of policies, politicians, and political information.[20] This problem, as traditional political thought contended, is exacerbated in a democracy, where most of the citizen-sovereigns will spend only a small part of their time in political study and reflection. It was partly for this reason that Rousseau saw censorship as a "declaration of public judgment" characteristic of vital and vigorous democracies.[21]

In America, and in most modern democracies, while we have been willing to exhort each other to speak "responsibly," we have been increasingly unwilling to use state power to enforce that responsibility (and have found social sanctions increasingly ineffective in doing so). In fact, while we have grown censorious about rulers who deceive the public, we have grown permissive about political deception generally, especially, though not exclusively, where critics of the government are involved. In *New York Times Co.* v. *Sullivan,* the Supreme Court ruled that a publisher was not required to prove the truth of his assertions and that only when "actual malice" could be demonstrated would damages for libel be justified, if the object of the statements was a public official. Subsequent cases have broadened that definition to "public figures," though the Court's opinions have been divided and confused. However, there is certainly considerable support, in the Court as well as outside it, for the view that in political persuasion and debate "exaggeration, vilification, and even false statement" may be essential elements of democratic liberty. Edward J. Bloustein argues that the Court's ruling in the *New York Times* case established the principle that "the First Amendment . . . was designed to outlaw seditious libel and thereby to preserve political democracy by insuring that the sovereign people would not be silenced by those to whom they had temporarily delegated the

19. For an example, see Walter Berns, "Pornography and Democracy: A Case for Censorship," *Public Interest*, no. 22 (1971):3–24 and critical comments, pp. 25–44.

20. Plato *Republic* 10.595B.

21. Rousseau, *Social Contract*, p. 127.

power to govern." But Bloustein argues against the exception of statements where "actual malice" is involved because of "the natural tendency of heated debate to generate shading of the truth, exaggeration and outright lies which are intended, on occasion, to persuade people–sometimes for ultimately 'good' reasons—as truth cannot."[22] It must seem paradoxical that at a time when we denounce leaders who are secretive or deceptive, and when we deny to the public any right to censor communications it believes hostile or dangerous to the common good, that so many are willing to justify deceptive rhetoric and even lying as inseparable from or contributory to the "right to know." Yet perhaps we are wise.

Rousseau spoke of a democratic order composed of a small number of citizens. He did not advocate censorship in Paris, nor would he in New York.[23] Censorship could not, he argued, restore "legislation grown weak" nor could it revitalize decaying public morals. Far from attacking M. D'Alembert's theater in Paris, Rousseau saw it as a necessary evil, for "we are constrained to substitute for the true beauties, now eclipsed, little pleasurable accessories. . . ."[24] The "virtues of the theater" could not take the place of the simple and modest virtues of the good citizen. But in a decaying society, they may be the only virtues possible and the means to what limited good order such a society can create. "In a big city, the police can never increase the number of pleasures permitted too much, or apply itself too much to making them agreeable, in order to deprive individuals of the temptation of seeking more dangerous ones."[25]

Ours is a very different world from that for which censorship was advocated by the great theorists of the past, but Rousseau's picture of the censorless society can give us little comfort, especially since our own society is more luxurious, more massive, and more complex than the "big cities" Rousseau knew. Our less-than-perfect world may not permit the restraints Plato or Rousseau thought valuable,

22. New York Times Co. v. Sullivan, 376 U.S. 254 (1964); Walter Berns, "The Constitution and a Responsible Press," in *The Mass Media and Modern Democracy*, ed. H. M. Clor (Chicago: Rand McNally, 1974), pp. 113–136; Bloustein, "The First Amendment and Privacy." See also Cantwell v. Connecticut, 310 U.S. 296, 310 (1939) and Douglas's dissenting opinion in Ginzberg v. Goldwater, 396 U.S. 1049, 1051–1052 (1970).

23. Jean Jacques Rousseau, *Politics and the Arts* (New York: The Free Press, 1960).

24. Ibid., p. 47.

25. Ibid., pp. 59, 117.

but that should make our concern for political education greater, for that education defines the political meaning of any "right to know."

THE RIGHT TO KNOW AND THE DUTY TO ACT

It is one thing to speak of peoples and their rights abstractly, and quite another to translate such ideas into political practice. Speaking of the "true legislator's science," Rousseau declared:

> On the whole, the institution of the laws is not such a marvelous thing that any man of sense and equity could not easily find those which, well observed, would be the most beneficial for society. Where is the student of the law who cannot erect a moral code as pure as that of Plato's laws? But this is not the only issue. The problem is to adapt this code to the people for which it is made and to the things about which it decrees to such an extent that its execution follows from the very conjunction of these relations.[26]

A more contemporary observer, A. D. Lindsay, defended democracy as more likely to realize "the development of the human personality," which he saw as "the end of all state activity." But Lindsay went on to comment that "the making of rules or laws . . . depends on a sound judgment as to what people are prepared to do. That is not a judgment of what is ideally right but of right limited by fact."[27]

Today, nothing is more conventional than the proposition that different institutions are appropriate for different peoples at different times. Social scientists repeatedly assure us that "authoritarian" regimes—right or left—are a necessity in the "early stages of development." The relativism of most social scientists, however, presumes that increasing economic prosperity or greater political power (or the simple fact of survival) justifies a regime.[28] Our argument differs in presuming that regimes are justified by the greatest possible fulfillment of "the people's right to know." But before we can determine whether any regime or any communication advances that right, we must ask, "Does it truly inform *this* people at *this* time?"

---

26. Ibid., p. 66.
27. A. D. Lindsay, *The Modern Democratic State* (New York: Oxford University Press, 1962), p. 92.
28. Wilson Carey McWilliams, "On Political Illegitimacy," *Public Policy* 19 (1971):429–456.

In even the most "advanced" states, for example, it would be hard to argue that a barrage of technical information cast in professional jargon, however accurate, "informs" or "educates" the public. It is more likely to bore or infuriate the people, creating feelings of incompetence and resentment and encouraging citizens to turn away from political information and public life.

Political education requires an appropriate rhetoric, an art of speaking and informing. Minimally, information must be communicated in ways that are comprehensible (given the public's previous experience and education), that are interesting enough to draw public attention to public matters, and that create greater competence in *fact* as well as in feeling. These requirements cannot be defined precisely, for such a definition would be necessarily too abstract. Even that limitation, however, strengthens the more important point: that the nature of the specific audience, the character of a people, determines the rhetoric by which it must be addressed, especially if if is to be truly "informed." As Rousseau told M. D'Alembert:

> When one wishes to honor a people, it must be done after their fashion and not our own, lest, with reason, they be offended by harmful praises which, for all that they are given with good intention, nonetheless do damage to the estate, the interests or the prejudices of those who are their object.[29]

The current state of the people in America, then, is critical to an understanding of the "fashion" in which it should be addressed and to the political meaning of "the right to know." Ours is a nation in which the citizen is intellectually confused, aware of his dependence on experts in science, diplomacy, and public policy, yet baffled by them and painfully conscious of their frequent bumbling. To that intellectual dilemma is added *moral* confusion. If we act morally, we fear we will be victimized by those who do not; trust is the mark of folly, fidelity of "hang-ups" that invite betrayal. "What works," we are coming to believe, is at poles with "what is right."

Intellectual and moral confusion, the distrust of others, and the distrust of self—these problems are accentuated by the sheer mass of the public. As individuals, we are often insignificant within that mass, and at some level we are aware of and affected by that fact, even if it is too painful to admit consciously. Many, if not most, Americans

29. Rousseau, *Politics and the Arts*, p. 9.

resist passively, ceding their fraction of sovereignty to others more "skilled" than themselves, but jealously guarding their private interests and responding grudgingly, if at all, to appeals for sacrifice and public spirit. In the mass movements of the last decade, many—most notably students and racial minorities—found exhilaration in new participation and solidarity. But the great theme of those movements was the affirmation of selfhood, a claim on the attention and concern of leaders and experts, necessary as a precondition for public life but undeniably precivic and essentially private. Too often without roots and lacking a sense of time, the great protests were prone to exaggerate hopes, to a demand for immediate results, and were too likely to be "informed" in ways that were partial and simplified. The violent upshot, however valuable in concrete policies, also convinced other Americans that their fears of collective action were well founded. And leaders were confirmed in the belief that the people were either privatized, irresponsible, or both and could only be addressed covertly and through manipulation.

A growing crisis of confidence and belief, increasingly apparent "credibility gaps," mounting concern with official secrecy—all of these are cited as evidence of "government deception and the resultant loss of public trust."[30] It is, we are told, a loss that is something new, somehow the product of specific conditions and particular personalities—a comforting perspective, but a terribly misleading one. Just as the quality of secrecy may make all the difference—we did not lose faith in the government because it concealed the sailing dates of troop transports[31]—so there are vital differences in the quality of public trust. David Wise notes that "polls taken by Michigan researchers prior to 1964 showed that the level of public trust in government was consistently high."[32] But certainly, there was no lack of evidence in those years to demonstrate the existence of governmental deception and suspect secrecy. The U-2 flights and the American hand in the Castillo Armas coup in Guatemala or in the overthrow of Premier Mossadegh in Iran became public knowledge. Here, public rationalization of political leaders were left unexamined and taken at face value, and government was allowed to have its head; but by allowing themselves to be deceived, Americans contrived to

30. Wise, Politics of Lying, p. 21.
31. Berns, "The Constitution and a Responsible Press," p. 130.
32. Wise, *Politics of Lying*, p. 37.

insist that government alone bears responsibility for any bad consequences. It would seem that the passive trust of the fifties contributed
at least as much to the "shattered bond of confidence between the
government and the people" as the public revelation of governmental
deception in the sixties and seventies.

A recitation of governmental wrongdoings, while it may shatter
old illusions, is not enough, and not only because such a portrait is
one-sided. A diet of exposés may only feed the conviction that
politics is inevitably corrupt, that the citizen is powerless, and that
he will only be tricked or tainted if he becomes involved. The real
moral of the recent sorry history of American politics is that there
is no "right to be ignorant and irresponsible." All citizens are necessarily affected by and involved with politics. Withdrawal does not
protect us, nor does it excuse us; silence gives assent, and a decision
to be "uninvolved" is, consequently, a *political act* that makes us
accomplices in what is done by those in power. The public has a
"need to know," not only so that it will not be victimized, but so
that it may avoid complicity. The latter risk validates Rousseau's
observation that the right to participate in public affairs creates a
"duty to study" them.[33]

This is only to emphasize that the "right to know" is justified in
terms of the requirements of citizenship and political action, and that
knowledge about public affairs may not lead to civic activity. John
Schaar has lamented the tendency of the study of democratic politics
to center around "the role of the spectator," and he insists that
"liberty and action are virtually the same thing."[34] Rousseau would
have agreed, but this is hardly the world of Rousseau's imagined city,
and it may be difficult indeed to correlate liberty and action. Schaar
would certainly urge a point made at the beginning of this essay,
that one must understand the nature of a people before one can
understand how it will respond to political information. Even more
fundamentally, it is necessary to know whether a public exists at all
or whether, as Walter Lippmann argued half a century ago, the
people is simply a "phantom."[35] A nonexistent people can scarcely
possess a "right to know."

33. Rousseau, *Social Contract*, p. 3.
34. John Schaar, "Power and Purity," in *American Review*, no. 19 (January
1974):167.
35. Walter Lippmann, *The Phantom Public* (New York: Harcourt, Brace,
1925).

PUBLIC VALUES IN A PRIVATE WORLD

"The commonwealth (*res publica*) is the people's estate (*res populi*),"
says Scipio in Cicero's *De Republica,* and a people is not just a
gathering or throng but a "gathering united in fellowship by a common
sense of right and a community of interest."[36] Rousseau's notion of
a people was forbidding; describing the act of association, he wrote:

> Each of us puts his person and all his power in common under the
> supreme direction of the general will, and in our corporate capacity,
> we receive each member as an indivisible part of the whole. At once,
> in place of the individual personality of each contracting party, this
> act of association creates a moral and collective body. . . . Those
> who are associated in it take collectively the name of people.[37]

Contemporary American society compares badly, to say the least,
with these classic definitions of a people (and even in the past, we
probably fell short of their standard). There is even less comfort for
us in the proposition—almost universal among political theorists
until recent times—that a republic must be austere, fearing affluence
as a mortal civic disease. Even if wealth is distributed with relative
equality, the argument ran, increasing the number and complexity
of possessions requires that greater attention be paid to private affairs
and interests and less to public ones. And life in modern America
only documents that thesis.

Seeking a less exacting standard, and one more favorable to the
American system, recent democratic theorists have often appealed
to Tocqueville but unfortunately have not often troubled to study his
analysis. The patriotism of a republic, Tocqueville observed, is not
the instinctive patriotism of a monarchy, which is a "kind of religion"
acting not from reason but from "the impulse of faith and sentiment."
Republican patriotism is more founded in reason

> perhaps less generous and less ardent, but it is more fruitful and
> more lasting: it springs from knowledge; it is nurtured by the laws;
> it grows by the exercise of civil rights; and in the end, it is con-
> founded with the personal interest of the citizen. A man compre-
> hends the influence which the well-being of his country has upon his
> own; he is aware that the laws permit him to contribute to that

36. Cicero *De Republica* 2.42.
37. Rousseau, *Social Contract,* p. 15.

prosperity, and he labors to promote it, first because it benefits him, and secondly because it is in part his own work.[38]

Love for the common life, Tocqueville contended, is created by political participation, especially at the local level. It is this activity that is the foundation of the special attachment which is republican patriotism and which allows the citizen to feel that the common interest is his own and that general prosperity is his "own work."[39] This, Tocqueville indicated, was especially true of the United States, where the citizen

> learns to know the laws by participating in acts of legislation; and
> . . . takes a lesson in the forms of government from governing. The great work of society is ever going on before his eyes, and, as it were, under his hands.[40]

This fulfillment of "the people's right to political education," was, as Tocqueville saw it, an ascending spiral in which activity promoted attachment, which promoted further activity, and so on. "Political associations . . . become large free schools where all members of the community go to learn the theory of association," and the art of association is "the mother of action studied and applied by all."[41] Acting in support of a common interest, citizens are regularly encouraged to exercise their political rights; only by exercise are political rights fulfilled. At the same time, the use of rights increases respect for them. A sound democratic system depended on a political education and situation that led citizens to participate in public affairs and that taught them to exercise political rights.

Tocqueville was far from sanguine, even about America. He shared with the ancient Greek theorists and with Rousseau the conviction that communality grew best in the immediacy and familiarity of locality, that it required constant nurturance and was forever in jeopardy, and he worried that the rights of free human beings could be sustained in no other setting. In an age of mass equality, he feared, individuals become less important as "every citizen is . . . lost in a crowd and nothing stands conspicuous but the great and imposing image of the people at large."[42] The citizen cannot expect help from

38. Tocqueville, *Democracy in America*, 1:251.
39. Ibid., p. 258.
40. Ibid., p. 330.
41. Ibid., 2:125.
42. Ibid., p. 307.

his impotent and unsympathizing fellows, and for support—for his pride as well as for his material interests—

> he naturally turns his eyes to that imposing power which alone rises above the general depression. Of that power his wants and especially his desires continually remind him until he ultimately views it as the sole and necessary support of his own weakness.[43]

America, as Tocqueville saw it, was relatively insulated by its customs, its strong feelings about private rights, and its taste for local freedom; but even here, Tocqueville argued, "individual independence and local liberties will ever be the product of art," and centralization would be the natural tendency of government.[44]

The centralizing dynamic, Tocqueville pointed out, would attenuate the emotional and personal foundations of citizenship and republican patriotism, dissipating and diffusing civic zeal and, ultimately, undermining the public's will to defend its political rights. Tocqueville pictured a

> power which does not destroy, but prevents existence; it does not tyrannize but . . . compresses, enervates, extinguishes and stupefies a people, till each nation is reduced to nothing better than a flock of timid and industrious animals of which the government is the shepherd.[45]

In such a condition, there is no public, no people in the traditional sense. And Tocqueville's nightmare is similar enough to our own situation to justify some anxiety, at least, about our own political character, education, and rights.

THE PEOPLE'S DUTY TO KNOW ITSELF

How does one engage millions of people spread over thousands of square miles in political activity? Even given a will to do so, only a few can participate with the intensity and regularity that Tocqueville prescribed; even if that limitation could be overcome, we would lack the personal relationships and the sense of our individual importance that Tocqueville saw in local political life. And since localities are

43. Ibid.
44. Ibid., pp. 313, 316.
45. Ibid., p. 337.

themselves relatively weak and unstable, many have felt that alternative foreclosed to us. The most influential school in recent political science has turned to new "definitions" of democracy more "adapted" to our situation. Lacking massive citizen participation, the argument goes, we cannot rely on citizens to limit or guide leaders, and we must rely on other leaders to do so. Hence "democracy should be a polyarchy of elected elites," or "democracy ought to be a selection system of competing elected minorities."[46]

It may be that "democratic elitism" represents the closest approximation of democracy possible in twentieth-century America, though that is far from certain. History expropriates our ideas with great zest, but we need not make presents of them. Redefinitions of democracy too easily cloud the moral meaning and political substance of the term. To the extent that words affect us, they tend to deprive a people of the perception that alternatives to our present situation may be desirable. They are likely to increase complacency at a time when greater watchfulness is required, while traditional democratic theory preserves "the distress of spirit . . . and the goal to aim at."[47] At the very least, the "theory of democratic elitism" reduces the role of the people, and with it, concern to understand and protect "the people's right to know."[48]

Tocqueville's defense of "the freedom of the press" and "the people's right to know" remains an eloquent one. "When the right of every citizen to a share in the government of a society is acknowledged," he wrote, "everyone must be presumed to be able to choose between the various opinions of his contemporaries and to appreciate the different facts from which inferences may be drawn." For Tocqueville, however, this "presumption" demanded an attempt to create the political conditions under which what must be *presumed* will also be *true*.

Noting that "a newspaper . . . always represents an association that is composed of its habitual readers," Tocqueville recognized that the decentralized American press was closely tied to local communities and definite constituencies, more open to citizens and less able "to excite the passions of the multitude to their own advantage" than

46. Sartori, *Democratic Theory*, p. 126.
47. Friedrich Nietzsche, *Beyond Good and Evil*, in *The Philosophy of Nietzsche* (New York: Modern Library, 1954), p. 379.
48. Peter Bachrach, *The Theory of Democratic Elitism: A Critique* (Boston: Little, Brown, 1967).

the centralized press of Europe. The virtues of the American press were more than negative, for, without losing its roots, the press

> causes political life to circulate through all parts of that vast terri-
> tory. Its eye is constantly open to detect the secret springs of political
> designs and to summon the leaders of all parties to the bar of public
> opinion. It rallies the interests of the community round certain prin-
> ciples and draws up the creed of every party; for it affords a means
> of intercourse between those who hear and address each other with-
> out ever coming into immediate contact.[49]

Tocqueville's observations suggest that while there is a relation of reciprocal influence between press and people, it is the character of the people that determines the quality of the press, that a free press alone cannot create a free people, and that without such a people will scarcely remain free. Of course, Tocqueville valued a free press as the last hope of the oppressed within mass society, for the press was the "only means" of making an appeal to the "whole nation, and if the whole nation is deaf . . . to mankind."[50] In that context, how-ever, the free press is a weak refuge, as Tocqueville knew. As the movements of recent years reveal, "the oppressed" too often can gain access to the national media only by shocking actions, and since such actions become routine rather quickly, a process of escalation lead-ing to violence and terror can easily be set in motion. In any case, the "appeal" is reduced to slogans and symbols, too simple to con-vey complex meanings, too easily misinterpreted or misunderstood. And while it may help the oppressed to be noticed, it is almost cer-tainly infuriating to be unable to say what one truly means, for in that case, even a nation with goodwill is "deaf."

Tocqueville's defense of the "people's right to know" is funda-mentally concerned to protect the power of the people; the power of the press was only instrumental. Only when the people has the local and community life that makes participation and political education possible does the people truly "have power" and the political judgment required for knowledge and responsible action in public life.[51]

We are far from such a world. The very words *community*, *public power*, and *judgment* are strange to our political vocabulary, which

49. Tocqueville, *Democracy in America*, 1:190 ff.
50. Bachrach, *Theory of Democratic Elitism*, 2:342.
51. Tocqueville, *Democracy in America*, 1:195.

is much more familiar with terms like *isolation, impotence,* and *incompetence.* Nevertheless, while contemporary Americans value a great deal in their world, they also feel a great lack and a sense of loss of the earlier virtues of the republic. Surely it is not too much to ask of political leaders that they seek—with all the powers and resources available to us—stabler and more effective local communities and opportunities for association and stronger local media tied to the people themselves. This is a very minimal program, and political imagination will suggest other useful policies, but at least it addresses the foundations of public judgment and of the right to know. "If men are to remain civilized or to become so," Tocqueville remarked, "the art of associating together must grow and improve in the same ratio in which the equality of conditions is increased."[52] That is a central imperative for citizens and leaders in our time, and by following it, leaders would do more for "the people's right to know" than they would by any mechanical truth telling.

52. Ibid., 2:118.

2

Access to Political Knowledge as a Human Right

CHRISTIAN BAY

The right to knowledge, along with the rights to free speech and assembly, is often justified in terms of its necessity in a democratic system, much as the right to vote in free elections. My position is, to the contrary, that democratic institutions are essential prerequisites for meaningful human rights, including the right of access to all available knowledge. Optimal freedom guaranteed by rights is the end, political institutions the means.

My argument will be that there can be no general access to knowledge, even to knowledge bearing on our survival as a human race, before our social institutions become much more democratic than they are now; furthermore, that the false claim that democracy has been achieved, in the liberal-capitalist world, now presents the most formidable obstacle to advances toward realities of democracy in our part of the world.

It is necessary but not sufficient to reduce radically the national government's legal options to withhold information from the public. It is equally vital to develop better public defenses against far more pervasive, more insidious strategies of deception, practiced by every government since the dawn of civilization, but with particular zeal and efficiency in our allegedly democratic age: that is, the strategies of obfuscation of the realities of political power. Illusory knowledge can block access to realistic knowledge.

PREMISES ABOUT THE AIMS OF POLITICS

It is assumed in this chapter that the optimal protection and expansion of human rights must be the principal purpose of the political enterprise.[1] A system of government is legitimate only insofar as it serves to safeguard and expand, more so than any available alternative system, the sphere of protected liberties for every individual. A specific government policy is legitimate or not according to the same fundamental criterion, when it bears on actual or potential human rights.

In other words, the protection of human life, over time, and of the human spirit, freely developing, is the only acceptable basic aim of politics. I shall in this chapter speak of Politics I as the study of, and the practice of, policies in the service of human life, in contrast with Politics II, which will refer to the study of, or the practice of, policies that, prima facie, at least are not derived from and not justifiable in terms of Politics I.

There are at least three kinds of issues that must be resolved in order to make the kind of commitment required by Politics I practically meaningful and consequential: (1) A scheme of acceptable priorities must be developed to make sure that some people's less essential freedoms are not given precedence over other people's more essential freedoms; (2) there must be a near-universal access to relevant facts and alleged facts, and to a free discussion of their meaning and policy implications; and (3) government policies must be responsive to majority conceptions of what is true and what is just in a world of contending interests and contentious issues; however, when issues of individual or collective survival are at stake, and the best available professional knowledge is at variance with ma-

1. "Right" refers to a protected freedom. "Human right" refers to a kind of freedom that can be, and therefore must be, made available to and protected for all the people in a given society. A freedom that cannot be extended to all (say, the freedom to own a factory) is an example of a "social privilege." My argument is not that all social privileges must be abolished, but that in a free society a privilege must yield whenever it demonstrably becomes an obstacle to a fuller protection and expansion of human rights.

jority views, the government must protect life rather than follow majority opinion.

On the first issue, I have tried before to develop a general perspective on priorities among freedoms, with freedom from physical violence taking precedence over all other freedoms.[2] A "human rights approach," not a utilitarian or democratic approach, is adopted, which makes severe coercion of even a single individual a worse calamity than less severe degrees of coercion inflicted on larger numbers. The marginal individuals and groups, those who are most deprived, must always have the prior claim on political and economic redress.

In this chapter I shall deal with the second issue: the public's access to knowledge of facts and their interrelationships, and to discussions of their meaning and implications.

The third issue, about the responsiveness of governmental policies to public convictions about what the facts are, about what is just, and about their responsiveness also to professional opinion when life-and-death issues are at stake, cannot be treated within the limits of this chapter. Let me only say here that a people's political knowledge becomes "academic," in the pejorative sense of inconsequential, if the powers that be refuse to be influenced by public views and demands. On the other hand, if public opinion is callous or indifferent to the destruction of human lives, then there should be nothing sacrosanct about public opinion. If democracy had been a reality in our society today, chances are that most people would place a high value on human life. In our kind of society, it has tended to be every man for himself or every group for itself. A broader public access to factual knowledge is necessary but not sufficient to ensure a more insightful, more humane public opinion.

PLATO'S POSITION ON PHILOSOPHICAL KNOWLEDGE

The importance of access to dependable knowledge for the promotion of good government was recognized long before there was any conception of a *right* to knowledge, let alone of a whole people's right of democratic access to knowledge. Plato's Socrates was, at

2. Christian Bay, *Structure of Freedom* (1958; reprint ed., Stanford: Stanford University Press, 1970).

least in the annals of western philosophy, the first great teacher of politics, or Politics I, as I have called the subject—politics in the sense of promoting the public good by way of discovering and promoting truth and justice.

There was an important element of elitism in Socratic thought, an element retained in Aristotle and in the scholastic thought of subsequent centuries: To think wisely and rightly requires a continuing commitment to the world of thought, that is, to the study of philosophy and to the practice of the wisdom gained as well. Philosophy was founded on the dialogue; a constant questioning, a constant testing of ideas against rival formulations and insights was necessary to advance in learning. But this kind of life required leisure to an extent that in ancient and medieval times virtually barred most working people from access to knowledge or at least to political knowledge of any depth and complexity.

But the Socratic elitism went even further than this: Only lifelong students of philosophy could hope to approximate correct perspectives on the great issues of truth and justice. In the good society, therefore, the philosophers had to become kings or the king's philosophers. This elitism is radically different from modern authoritarianism with its cult of authority figures: *Unless* kings become true philosophers in Plato's sense, they are likely to be tyrants who deserve to be resisted by just citizens. For Plato invests supreme authority, not in any mortal man, but in philosophy itself.

Two further points must be made about the classical, and especially Plato's, commitment to the pursuit of political knowledge: The distinction between knowledge and mere opinion was emphasized as crucial, and dialectical argument was pointed to as the only reliable method to learn gradually how to tell what is true and just from what is merely made to seem true and just.

Socrates scorned the profession of rhetoricians in a sense roughly corresponding to the modern practice of Politics II: that is, politics in the sense of popularity contests between leaders, parties, or ideas, with positions of power the principal prizes. While he attacked rhetoric, or Politics II, he also recognized its prevalence in his own society, as in every other "open" society deficient in the cultivation of philosophy; and this left only future utopias, like his own *Republic*, as prospective domains for governments committed to true politics, or Politics I. In a relatively free city like Athens (at times) it remained possible within limits for a private citizen to practice the art and science of questioning in the spirit of Politics I. But the mass of citizens remained ignorant and ready to support Politics II–oriented demagogues, whose trade was in appearances and in short-run advantages, not in real benefits for the people.

Socrates maintained a long-term perspective and had hopes for a cumulation of political knowledge based on continuing cultivation of unfettered dialogue by the best, most committed philosophers. The first academies were inspired by him, and Plato in his own life tried to contribute political knowledge and wisdom to enlightened monarchs who asked for his services. His practical advice accomplished little, but the first academies became recognized as enclaves for the disinterested study of the public good by full-time scholars.

The notion of academic freedom was born. But in ancient Greece academic knowledge was conceived of as dialectical and related to the needs of man, while in our own world academic knowledge is most often pursued in a spirit of positivism and value-neutrality. This is a distinction that makes a profound difference, as we shall see in the last section, for the kind of political education promoted by our modern academies.

MODERN CONTRACT THEORY AND UTILITARIANISM

In what sense, if any, can every individual have a right to knowledge? The notion of individual natural rights is a modern one, pioneered by Thomas Hobbes in the seventeenth century. To be sure, there were *legal* rights in earlier centuries, especially if you owned property or held public office, particularly under the highly developed Roman system of jurisprudence. But the notion that every man qua man had natural rights was unknown; ordinary people had moral duties but not human rights.

Hobbes's overriding concern was with the problem of physical violence. He was the first modern political thinker in that he based his philosophy on the premise that governments can be justified only to the extent that they meet the most important needs of man. To him, protection against violence was need number one. His outlook was modern in a second sense as well: He undertook a careful study of human needs and propensities. In his political recommendations he wanted to take account of men as they really were, not as a philosopher, or God, would like them to be.

For Hobbes there could be no individual "right to know." He recognized hardly any absolute natural rights except one: the right to self-preservation. Even a justly condemned man had a natural right to try to cheat the executioner. According to Hobbes's didactically conceived social contract, all other initial natural rights had been sacrificed in order to safeguard, as fully as feasible, the right to protection against physical violence. On this issue Hobbes turned Socrates upside down: Socrates had insisted that no man should surrender his conscience to the state, lest he become a partner in injustice; but any man should be willing to give up his life if the state demands it. While Hobbes allowed a natural right to resist giving up one's life, regardless of circumstances, he would allow nobody a right to a private conscience or a right to knowledge about political facts.

Quite a different notion of natural rights was formulated by John Locke, and it has retained currency in liberal theory ever since. While Hobbes's Sovereign had no enforceable restrictions placed on his, or its, powers, Locke's commonwealth was emphatically based on a bilateral contract between government and people. Not only are there specific limits to what the supreme power can do (for example, it "cannot take away from any man any part of his property without his consent"); but the people have a right "to provide for themselves by erecting a new legislature" if the existing government violates the contract by subverting its aims, for example, by way of confiscating private property.[3]

It is ironic that Locke is frequently thought of as the spiritual father of American democracy, for Locke was not a democrat. He was a liberal, who championed human rights for people with property,[4] including, by implication at least, the right of access to knowledge. But this latter issue he never expanded on. Within the social contract tradition we have to go down to our own time, I believe, to the late Alexander Meiklejohn, to find a fully developed commitment to the people's right to know all the facts related to democratic government. Meiklejohn's position, as it applies to postwar American society, is particularly explicit on three issues, and cogent, if one were to accept his contractarian premises:

3. John Locke, *Two Treatises of Civil Government* (1924; reprint ed., London: J. M. Dent, 1949). See Second Treatise, #138, #220, passim.
4. See C. B. Macpherson, *The Political Theory of Possessive Individualism* (1962; reprint ed., Oxford: Oxford University Press, 1964), chapters 5 and 6.

1. There is a crucial distinction to be made between public and private issues, Meiklejohn argues: Our freedom of speech on public issues is without limits, while our right to advocacy about private or commercial matters is subject to regulations by law. The former freedom is guaranteed by the First Amendment to the Constitution, while the latter freedom is regulated by the "due process" clause in the Fifth Amendment. Under the Constitution, then, "the freedom of advocacy of incitement to action *by the government* may never be abridged. It is only advocacy or incitement to action by individuals or nonpolitical groups which is open to regulation."[5]

2. The Supreme Court's "clear and present danger" doctrine in effect annuls the First Amendment. This theory "regards the freedom of speech as a mere device which is to be abandoned when dangers threaten the public welfare. On the contrary, it is the very presence of those dangers which make it imperative that, in the midst of our fears, we remember and observe a principle upon whose integrity rests the entire structure of government by consent of the governed."[6]

3. The electorate is a fourth branch, or indeed the first branch of the government, Meiklejohn argues.[7] It is the people's responsibility to make up its minds conscientiously, on the basis of all relevant knowledge and deliberation, so that it may elect wisely when it bestows its authority, directly or indirectly, on the other branches of government. Any kind of censorship, any kind of intimidation against spokesmen for unpopular or even allegedly seditious views or organizations interferes with the proper functioning of this crucial branch of our government. To silence a member of the electorate is just as unconstitutional as it would be to silence any member of the Senate or the House on the same grounds, according to Meiklejohn's reading of the First Amendment and, more basically, according to his understanding of what an "agreement" about democratic government must mean. The

---

5. Alexander Meiklejohn, *Political Freedom: The Constitutional Powers of the People* (1948; reprint ed., New York: Harper and Brothers, 1960), p. 76.
6. Ibid., p. 76 and pp. 29–50.
7. Compare John Dewey's assertion: "As a citizen-voter each one of these persons is, however, an officer of the public. He expresses his will as a representative of the public interest as much as does a senator or sheriff" (*The Public and Its Problems* [Chicago: Swallow Press, 1927] p. 75).

citizenry, as makers of the laws, "have duties and responsibilities which require an absolute freedom"; McCarthyist oppression, for example, amounts to a "mutilation of the thinking process of the community" and clearly violates the First Amendment.[8]

The utilitarian tradition is the second important source of modern democratic theory. While neither Bentham nor James Mill was a democrat in the full sense of favoring universal suffrage, and while even John Stuart Mill for a time championed plural voting rights for some of the privileged strata, they were all strongly committed to support the right of access to knowledge for everybody who was capable of taking advantage of it. The logic of representative government required, of course, that all important political facts be in the public domain; how else could rational decisions be expected? The modern fine art of governmental secrecy "in the national interest" was still at a primitive level.

Within the liberal tradition J. S. Mill's *On Liberty* remains the most eloquent of all documents in defense of the public's right to hear as well as to speak freely. It is an optimistic, inspiring message: If only truth is left free to combat error in an open marketplace of ideas, humanity is bound to become more enlightened and better off in the long run; for the only effective way to deal with erroneous or dangerous ideas is to refute them, not to suppress them.

MILL'S FREE MARKETPLACE OF IDEAS RECONSIDERED

In the long run, as John Maynard Keynes once remarked, we are all dead.[9] This was true in Mill's time, too, but in that optimistic century only individuals were considered mortal, not nations, and certainly not all of mankind. In today's world all of mankind's life is at stake, and that "long run" could, for all that we can be sure, become awfully short. Technological developments and the virtually unrestricted pursuit of private wealth have set several global time bombs going. Unless the public realm can reassert itself soon, in

8. Ibid., pp. 76 and 109, passim. Also see Joseph Tussman, *Obligation and the Body Politic* (New York: Oxford University Press, 1960), pp. 119–121.

9. Quoted from John Maynard Keynes, "Tract on Monetary Reform," in F. A. Hayek, *The Constitution of Liberty* (Chicago: University of Chicago Press, 1960), p. 333.

defiance of private wealth, our world will soon be made uninhabitable by nuclear war; by continued population growth; by continuing industrial poisoning of air, water, and soil; or by the depletion of food and energy resources, if not by the destruction of the whole complex ecosystem on which our lives ultimately depend.[10]

I shall in the remainder of this chapter assume that some of the most urgent issues of our time are issues to which there are right and wrong answers and that, in some cases, wrong answers would be deadly and must be avoided at any cost. This fact, and it *is* a fact, must have profound implications for our thinking about liberal democracy and about people's need for and right of access to knowledge. Could Mill have written an essay resembling *On Liberty* today?

Ironically, Plato's critique of democracy as government by rhetoric, and his urging that the responsible statesman (in my terms, the champion of Politics I) must be like a physician, ready to dispense bitter medicine, seems far more directly addressed to man's predicament in our time than is Mill's argument for laissez-faire in the realm of ideas. Twenty-three centuries after Plato, and with far more experience of liberalism, Mill had not caught up with Plato's insight that simpleminded ideas tend to drive off more complex, more adequate ones in an open marketplace of ideas, just as, according to Gresham's law, cheap money drives off good money.

Even if our systems were democratic the (heavy costs of this myth will be discussed below), we could not for long afford the continuing luxury of national policies being determined by majorities at election times acting as umpires between contending interest groups. As Rousseau saw so clearly in another troubled age, while hucksterism and sectional rivalries between private interests dominate the economic life of a nation, no amount of democratic procedures can produce policies in harmony with a knowledgeable conception of the public interests. The trouble with liberal democracy is not just that it must fail to provide responsible leadership to represent our common interest in survival; the deeper trouble is that it discourages even the search for responsible leadership, since it views politics as an eternal contest between groups of limited vision and makes believe that all is well as long as the "rules of the game" are observed.

10. See Robert L. Heilbroner's sober assessment in his book *The Human Prospect* (New York: W. W. Norton, 1974).

Mill was in error in his assumptions about the nature of the British marketplace of ideas, just as the Manchester liberals misjudged the propensities of the marketplace of commodities: Neither of the two outlooks acknowledged the fact that equality in any marketplace perishes quickly. Each victory tends to strengthen one competitor and weaken others for future contests; growing trends toward lopsidedness and unfair advantage are inescapable, and monopoly or oligopoly is the normal end state as decades and generations go by, for ideas as well as commodities. Just as the little firms so close to Adam Smith's heart now survive, if at all, in utter dependency on large corporations, so the little magazines on the Left linger on, if at all, in the shadow of the mass media and have no chance to win power in a marketplace of ideas governed by the big moneyed interests.

In appearance the public's access to knowledge is well looked after in our society, with the newspapers bulkier than ever, the magazines slicker, and the color TV sets brighter year by year. Facts are available in overflow. What is rarely available to most citizens are coherent contexts for the information they receive, let alone alternate perspectives on their rich diet of facts—alternate visions of how our society, or the world, ought to be organized. Only "extremists" discuss such issues, and most people are effectively vaccinated against ideas and persons that the media associate with "extremism."

While the appearances of public knowledgeability leave nothing to be desired in the modern liberal states, the agendas of public discussion, and their terms of reference, tend to be tightly controlled by minorities of the powerful. This is a broader problem than the issue of secrecy as a protective device for governments in power, an issue with which other contributors to this volume will be concerned. If we are to make advances against this virtual oligopoly power over our allegedly free marketplace of ideas, we must seek new avenues and approaches to political education; but first of all we must learn to recognize the enormous harm we do if we continue to acquiesce in, or fail to oppose more vigorously, the conventional liberal myth of democracy achieved.

THE MYTH OF DEMOCRACY AS AN OBSTACLE TO PEOPLE'S ACCESS TO POLITICAL KNOWLEDGE

In a critical commentary on the *Leviathan*, Bertrand Russell remarks that governments "would be worse than they are if Hobbes's submissive attitude were universally adopted by subjects."[11] In the modern liberal states, the citizenries have been rendered dangerously submissive by way of a number of mutually supporting political myths, the crucial one being what I like to call "the democratic make-believe":[12] the belief that every person has an opportunity to influence government policy and, consequently, the belief that outcomes of elections represent the majority's will and mandate, so that properly enacted laws and public policies are thereby rendered legitimate and entitled to obedience.

A corollary assumption is that a people has the kind of government it deserves; that, in other words, it is your fault and mine if "our democratically elected government" pursues outrageous policies. We must therefore go along, even to war if necessary, until we can develop enough political strength to throw the rascals out. My argument here will be, not that the liberal assumptions about democracy achieved are false, which they are,[13] but that they do much harm: They obfuscate the realities of politics so that the citizenry is deprived of meaningful knowledge and thereby is rendered politically impotent.

My quarrel is not with our electoral institutions, which are vastly preferable to the worse shams of military or one-party rule.[14] Our system permits open attempts at dialogue and even an occasional democratic victory at local levels. Dissenters are afforded some protection under the same laws whose legitimacy they feel free to question. The point is to avoid being taken in by the liberal demo-

11. Bertrand Russell, *History of Western Philosophy* (1946; reprint ed., London: Allen & Unwin, 1948), p. 578.

12. Christian Bay, "Foundations of the Liberal Make-believe," *Inquiry* 14 (1971):213–243.

13. The most convenient survey of this literature, which began with Robert Michels, is found in Lester W. Milbrath, *Political Participation* (Chicago: Rand McNally, 1965).

14. In turn, some one-party systems are vastly preferable to others: Some work to improve the living conditions of the downtrodden, while others work to perpetuate and deepen the exploitation of the poor. According to my criteria of legitimacy, Cuba's regime, for all its faults, is possibly the most legitimate regime in Latin America.

cratic make-believe, lest we keep congratulating our system on account of its procedural legitimacy, while taking in our stride all the miscarriages of substantive justice, even when they involve human lives or human rights.

Every regime tends to reduce individuals to mere objects, as does indeed every social organization of some magnitude and power. This is the most basic fact of political life. But this is precisely the point at which obfuscation starts: Democratic rhetoric is used to obscure and distort our perception of the realities of oligarchy and oppression.

There is in every liberal country an implicit notion of a social contract between the citizen and the government. For some citizens, this amounts to a Lockean type of understanding: his or her loyalty is to certain values, which the government is supposed to protect; to the extent that it fails to do this, the informed citizen is free to or feels compelled to withdraw his allegiance. To make such choices, of course, one needs knowledge; but first of all one needs to shed the myth of democratic legitimacy and to know that a government's policy can be profoundly illegitimate even if constitutionally enacted and apparently popular. Moreover, one must always suspect that the government will seek to withhold information that would put it in a bad light.

Most Americans, it would seem, normally see themselves (implicitly) as bound by a Hobbesian type of contract, which leaves them no options but to obey laws and directives. These Americans are "normatively integrated": They see their "relationship to the authorities as one governed by an implicit understanding, such that, while the individual abandons his freedom of choice, he is also liberated from a good deal of potential guilt."[15] And they take in good faith whatever information the government decides to share with them; it is not for them to be inquisitive or suspicious.

The Hobbesians are, from any regime's point of view, the ideal citizens: They comply and are easy to govern. Lockean citizens are those who may create discontent and opposition. And employers have much the same preference: The preferred employees are intelligent but uncritical; they ask questions about how best to perform their jobs, not about what kinds of life they personally would want to live, and much less about what kind of political or

15. Herbert C. Kelman and Lee H. Lawrence, "Assignment of Responsibility in the Case of Lt. Calley: Preliminary Report on a National Survey," *Journal of Social Issues* 28 (1972):177–212 and 206.

economic system they want to pass on to their children. Our schools and colleges, consequently, are geared to training and socialization, not to education in the sense of freeing the intellect and facilitating autonomous development and much less to humanization, in Paulo Freire's sense, discussed in the next section.

Yet individuals, if given a chance, badly want to become something more than mere pawns: *"Man's primary motivational propensity is to be effective in producing changes in his environment."*[16] One's success in becoming an origin rather than a mere pawn first of all depends, it would seem, on effective access to meaningful knowledge; but this access in turn depends, generally speaking, on one's position in the class structure.

Consider the Kelman-Lawrence data on public reactions to the trial of Lieutenant Calley. He was the archetypical Hobbesian citizen. He was taught to kill for his country, then went out to kill a lot of Vietnamese, only to be turned upon by his government and charged with war crimes early in 1971. Understandably, a ground swell of opinion in sympathy with Lieutenant Calley developed. According to the Kelman-Lawrence data collected in May–June 1971, from a national random sample, 51 percent declared that they themselves would have acted like Lieutenant Calley under similar circumstances and 67 percent expressed the view that most others would have done likewise. The attitudes for and against Lieutenant Calley had no apparent connection with pro- or antiwar attitudes; hawks and doves were about equally well represented on both sides. There was only one important difference between the pro- and the anti-Calley respondents: The former were disproportionately from strata with relatively low education, income, and social status. Why? Presumably because people who in their own lives feel they have few options but to do as they are told tend to empathize with Lieutenant Calley as a pawn and a scapegoat; as Hobbesians, they would attribute responsibility to the higher-ups only if indeed they saw anything wrong with killing defenseless Vietnamese.

Or consider Melvin L. Kohn's findings from three studies of class and parental orientations to child rearing, conducted, respectively, in Washington, D.C.; in Turin, Italy; and in a national survey in the United States. Kohn was particularly interested in how social class

---

16. Richard de Charms, *Personal Causation* (New York: Academic Press, 1968), p. 269. His italics.

position might affect self-direction or conformity as basic values to be taught to one's children, and here is what he concluded: "The essence of higher class position is the expectation that one's decisions and actions can be consequential; the essence of lower class position is the belief that one is at the mercy of forces and people beyond one's control, often, beyond one's understanding. . . . Self-direction, in short, requires opportunities and experiences that are much more available to people who are more favorably situated in the hierarchical order of society; conformity is the natural consequence of inadequate opportunity to be self-directed."[17]

Now compare these conclusions with Stanley Allen Renshon's findings about the actual impact of child-rearing practices on the development of personal control in the next generation, and the structure of psychological oppression becomes clear. Renshon finds that factors like a democratic family structure are important but that by far the most important single influence on the child's emerging sense of personal control, or lack of it, is the parent's own sense of personal control, or lack of it.[18] Hobbesian parents, then, tend to produce Hobbesian children, obedient to authorities and intolerant of nonconformity.

These are facts that should disturb us profoundly if we see ourselves as champions of either democracy or human rights. No other kinds of knowledge are quite as important as basic empirical premises, I believe, if we want to promote humanitarian values.

Yet these are precisely the kinds of facts that are obfuscated by the democratic make-believe; and this kind of political emasculation undercuts the roots of critical consciousness, not only the effectiveness of some of its applications, as fraud by way of selective governmental secrecy may do. Those who are being exploited in our social system are being pacified politically by being assured that they are all equal in the voting booth. Yet they lack not only the knowledge with which to assert themselves politically. They also lack the self-assurance it takes to acknowledge and declare that they are unjustly oppressed and to understand that it is possible, in solidarity with others, to attempt to resist and defeat oppression.

17. Melvin L. Kohn, *Class and Conformity: A Study in Values* (Homewood, Ill.: Dorsey Press, 1969), p. 189.

18. Stanley Allen Renshon, *Psychological Needs and Political Behavior* (New York: The Free Press, 1974).

PAULO FREIRE'S APPROACH TO EDUCATION:
LIBERATING POLITICAL KNOWLEDGE

Is it a lost cause, or can we within the framework of liberal society hope to develop and make generally available the kinds of knowledge that can liberate instead of pacify the disproportionally oppressed and deprived among us?

The most promising avenue toward eventual revolutionary change in our part of the world is, I believe, the one recommended by Freire's example and writings.[19] At the root of his approach to political education is his assumption that there are two kinds of social knowledge—positivistic knowledge and dialectical knowledge. The former accumulates facts and factual relationships and is ostensibly value neutral; it all adds up to something like a reservoir of processed human experience, which our teachers can tap according to the receiving capabilities of their pupils. The second kind of social knowledge is less tangible in substance, less neatly systematic, and more relative to time and place, more geared to the needs of people absorbed with problems; it is more a method of continuing learning through dialogue and praxis, less an assembly of tentative generalizations from accumulated empirical findings.

Man's vocation is to become more human, Freire assumes at the outset. This vocation "is constantly negated, yet it is affirmed by that very negation. It is thwarted by injustice, exploitation, oppression, and the violence of the oppressors; it is affirmed by the yearning of the oppressed for freedom and justice, and by their struggle to recover their lost humanity."[20]

The great humanistic and historical task of the oppressed is to liberate themselves *and* their oppressors. And this requires a conquest of the word by the oppressed; they must transcend their "culture of silence" and become able to name their world, instead of continuing to allow their oppressors to label their reality for them. What is required here in North America is a capacity to reject the conventional civics lessons about democracy achieved and about the moral obligation to obey the law and to substitute a more realistic picture of domination and oppression, of rights denied, and of thwarted

19. See especially Paulo Freire, *Pedagogy of the Oppressed* (1970; reprint ed., New York: Seabury Press, 1974 [Portuguese manuscript, 1968]) and *Education for Critical Consciousness* (New York: Seabury Press, 1973).

20. Freire, *Pedagogy of the Oppressed*, p. 28.

opportunities for human fulfillment at the lower rungs on the social ladder, or perhaps at most rungs.

"There is no such thing as a neutral educational process," writes Freire's friend Richard Shaull in his foreword to *Pedagogy of the Oppressed*. "Education either functions as an instrument which is used to facilitate the integration of the younger generation into the logic of the present system and bring about conformity to it, or it becomes 'the practice of freedom,' the means by which men and women deal critically and creatively with reality and discover how to participate in the transformation of their world."[21] Freire calls the former approach the "banking concept" of education and the latter, "problem-posing education." While the former entails active teachers and passive students, the latter entails a mutually reinforcing process of discovery, in which teacher and student jointly undertake to study, to comprehend if possible, and to *name* their own and one another's reality, with particular emphasis on illuminating the parameters of oppression they are up against, jointly and separately, in their joint and separate realities.

Every social order is oppressive in some respects; and in stable societies the habitual patterns of oppression tend to be taken for granted by those who benefit as well as by those who are exploited. Normal "banking education," along with the whole panoply of patriotic symbols, as well as the conventional definitions of key terms in everyday language,[22] tends to hide or gloss over or misrepresent the realities of oppression. Banking education is uncritical; it teaches how to find a place or how to make a career in the existing system; and to those who fail its tests it teaches the necessity of their finding their place among the oppressed.[23]

Freire's problem-posing education, on the contrary, aims at stimulating questions about reality, questions radical enough to penetrate conventional assumptions and labels. Through continuing dialogues between equals, attempts are made to transform habitual patterns of

21. Ibid., p. 15.

22. Christian Bay, " 'Freedom' as a Tool of Oppression," in *The Case for Participatory Democracy*, eds. C. George Benello and Dimitrios Roussopoulos (New York: Grossman, 1971), pp. 250–269, and "Violence as a Negation of Freedom," *American Scholar* 40 (1971):634–641.

23. See Ivan Illich, *Celebration of Awareness* (Garden City, N.Y.: Doubleday, 1970), chapters 8 and 9, and *Deschooling Society* (New York: Harper & Row, 1970); Alan Gartner, Colin Greer, and Frank Riessman, eds., *After Deschooling, What?* (New York: Harper & Row, 1973).

domination, or habitual acceptance of justifications of domination, into *problems* that can be discussed, named, and comprehended in terms that make it possible to devise realistic strategies in working for revolutionary changes.

Freire's task has been primarily to help to develop a liberating political consciousness among Latin America's impoverished millions, hitherto submerged in their defenseless "culture of silence." He has kept insisting that it is for them, and not for him as an educator, to reach the decisions about the directions in which to move once they have achieved the power to "name their world."

North America's population is oppressed, too, although one hesitates to use the same word applied to the destitute peasants in northeast Brazil. Yet we too are far from a realization of our potentialities of humanization, as is already evident in our collective lack of concern for the plight of the poorest even in our own part of the world. The poor are not invisible, not to TV viewers. What we are short of is not factual knowledge; nor are we barren of humanitarian instincts. The crucial shortage is, I believe, in our limited access to the kind of dialectical knowledge that can set us free to understand and to act; we must first of all become able to grasp and to label the realities of oppression and injustice, which we are being socialized not to see or to rationalize into insignificance. In this way we will become better able to understand and resist militarism and imperialism as well.

The most important front line in the struggle for liberating knowledge is, if we follow Freire, in the struggle for self-determination in our daily lives, that is, for an effective voice in deciding about the rules under which we live and work: in the family, in the office or factory, in the school or university, and of course, in our unions and political parties. As long as most citizens remain acquiescing Hobbesians in their daily lives, Politics II will continue to prosper: Political life will remain in a world of wheeling and dealing; efforts to establish knowledge about the public interest will be few and halfhearted, compared to the perfecting of the knowledge of how to manipulate and exploit people, in our own society and beyond.

As more people become responsible Lockeans *and* conscious of being oppressed as well as deceived, or of being oppressors and deceivers as well, on the other hand, support will build up for Politics I values, directed to human survival and the expansion of human rights. There are problems associated with Freire's approach, which must be left to one side here. All in all, though, I think his dialectical, problem-posing approach to political education offers the best hope in our time, probably in every society, for making liberating political knowledge more widely available.

3

The Information Revolution, Politics, and the Prospects for an Open Society

THEODORE J. LOWI

"That's very good, what you said about the Second Industrial Revolution," she said.

"Old, old stuff."

"It seemed very fresh to me—I mean that part where you say how the First Industrial Revolution devalued muscle work, then the second one devalued routine mental work. I was fascinated."

"Norbert Wiener said all that way back in the nineteen-forties. It's fresh to you because you're too young to know anything but the way things are now . . ."

"Do you suppose there will be a Third Industrial Revolution?"

He paused in his office doorway. "A third one? What would that be like?"

"I don't know exactly. The first and second ones must have been sort of inconceivable at one time."

"To the people who were going to be replaced by machines, maybe. A third one, eh? In a way, I guess the third one's been going on for some time, if you mean thinking machines. That would be the third revolution, I guess—machines that devaluate human thinking. Some of the big computers like EPICAC do that all right in specialized fields."

"Uh-huh," she said thoughtfully. She rattled a pencil between her teeth. "First, the muscle work, then the routine work, and then, maybe, the real brain work."

"I hope I'm not around long enough to see that final step . . . ."

KURT VONNEGUT, JR., *Player Piano**

* Published by Dell Publishing Co.

There can no longer be any question that the industrial nations of the world are producing another technological revolution of historic importance. It may well emerge as the single most important influence in the development of a postindustrial society. The trigger is the revolution in information technology. The changes are so sizable that they cannot fail to produce a discontinuous spurt in man's capacity to manipulate his environment. The question is whether the ramifications of this technological spurt will be comparable to those of the first and second industrial revolutions. Another question is whether we will be able to shape these ramifications to our own liking, or whether we will simply have to witness the changes and adapt to them.

This chapter seeks to assess the impact of the information revolution on political institutions. The governing proposition is that *as a result of information technology, man's power over his environment will increase greatly and his susceptibility to manipulation will rise proportionately*. These are coexisting tendencies to which societies adjust through cultural and institutional adaptation. The tension manifests itself at every level, from the single individual to the all-encompassing governmental structures. Information technology can contribute to the degree of openness in social and political processes. The top elites in governments and major corporations are making policies today that will cumulatively determine the outcome. No new invention or institution was ever more directly related to the prospects of an open or a secret society.

INFORMATION AS A RESOURCE: THE PROBLEM OF DEFINITION

Information can be most productively linked to the political process by defining it as a resource. Almost anything can be a political resource, as long as people value it highly. But resources differ in that some convert into effective political power more readily than others. The emergence of any new resource can significantly alter the political structure. Expansion of the suffrage, for instance, transformed people into political resources, whereas before they had been no more than economic resources.

The composition of the political elites, or top power groups, was altered still further with each successive influx of social or skill types, who were identified primarily by the new resources they commanded. In recent generations we have witnessed an influx of such new elite members as the *technical* personnel (whose resources are specialized knowledge or expertise), the *technological* personnel (whose resources are mechanisms), the *bureaucratic* personnel (whose resources are organizational), and the *technocratic* or *technetronic* personnel (whose resources are the information that passes through mechanisms and organizations).

As a resource, information bears a superficial similarity to energy. Fast, time-shared computers with universally distributed, small receiving sets bear some resemblance to large generators distributing energy to users, from big industries to small household appliances. Information also resembles electricity in that it probably works best when massed and distributed in large supply. Both are highly sensitive to economies of scale. This suggests the emergence of a number of large information utilities operating on community-franchised machines and delivery systems such as cable television (CATV).

If the resemblance to energy were close, this pattern suggests that information technology is but another industry, and that its impact would mean nothing more than expanded wealth, a change in the skills requirements, and a new group of influential corporate executives. If the resemblance were close, then the membership in decision-making elites might change, but not their character or function. But the resemblances between energy and information begin to weaken very quickly, and some interesting political implications emerge.

Information resources, unlike any other, *are not used up while being used*. This changes the very meaning of the words *resource* and *use*, because information resources do not follow the law of conservation of energy. Only symbols, not physical units or energies, are removed; and symbols are being fed in at the same time as they are being taken out. Even though it will cost money to use information, there will be far fewer constraints on the use of this resource than on any that we have used before. Problems such as cleaning and maintaining data, communicating it, and protecting proprietary interests and confidence are on their way to being solved. In short, with fewer constraints on use, the information revolution promises to expand human powers by a factor larger than electricity.

One other distinguishing characteristic of the information resource helps to mark how different the societal impact of a large-scale expansion of information is likely to be. Information is a heterogeneous resource; it has many forms. In contrast, energies are homogeneous resources. Many important differences follow from this fact. Since individuals with special needs can draw on information pools in different ways and for peculiar purposes, the power to the individual is enhanced far more significantly compared to what a sudden expansion of energy resources will do for him.

But this great selectivity can only be provided by development and constant maintenance of information storage and retrieval systems. Information must be kept up to date and credible; and currency and credibility require continual surveillance, occasional housecleaning, and regular validity checks. These are not technical matters to be dealt with by formulas. For example, uniform cost-of-living indicators affect wage and price scales, yet are themselves affected by changes in taste and consumer patterns. New devices and methods of sampling attitudes alter the very definition of what decision makers will accept as information for purposes of television programming, consumer production, or public policy making.

Ominously, one feature that information has in common with natural resources is that deliberate restriction—as in the recent case of the international oil producer cartel—greatly enhances prices and profits. But the information resource is still more sensitive. Not only can prices be manipulated by restriction, but restriction of information means secrecy, a deprivation of something more important, presumably, than physical comfort or efficiency. Information surpasses natural resources in another sense, too obvious, yet so easily overlooked: There is no objective way to distinguish the real McCoy from the bogus. Thus, the greater secrecy and the greater the value and price of information, the greater the likelihood of falsification, since in the short run, lies serve as well as the truth.[1]

INFORMATION, INTERDEPENDENCE, AND THE DISTRIBUTION OF POWER

All of these requirements for developing and maintaining the information resources suggest that the prospects for a decentralized system are not likely, even where the desire for decentralization is

1. On the concept of the "information marketplace," see Itzhak Galnoor, "Government Secrecy: Exchanges, Intermediaries, and Middlemen," *Public Administration Review* 35, 1(January–February 1975): 32–42.

strong. Moreover, the tendency toward centralization around these resources is joined by a propensity for stratification in our society. Perhaps we should call it *user stratification*, but its potential effects on our political and social structure are very broad. It is based on the prospect that while the cost of information is going to drop precipitously, the cost of *being informed* will not. As use of the new technology spreads from entertainment, home economics, and voting to planning, analysis, and decision making, the value to most users will change little, but the value to a few other users will increase; and the value to them will go up much faster than the cost. There is great potential here for stratification, yet it is only in small part related to ability to pay. It is related to intellectual preparation and functional responsibility. These will be the elements behind new forms of general social and political stratification.

But stratification is not the only tendency encouraged by the information resource. The same factors that produce a tendency toward stratification also produce interdependence. *Information enhances individual power through interaction rather than action.* When a farmer gets a tractor he gets a tool, and the tool gives him autonomy. He must depend on others to provide parts and fuel, but beyond that he has the tool and his use of it depends almost exclusively upon his decisions. Information in this sense is not a tool, nor is it fuel. Information is a process; it means little except in terms of regular interaction.

These two characteristics—stratification and interdependence (of users and their relationships to each other)—suggest the special significance of changes taking place in information technologies. The consequences for political power cannot be anything but enormous. Many will *know how*, yet few will *know*. Those who *know* will be setting—that is, programming—the agenda for those who only *know how*. This means a potentially extreme centralization of power to set the fact and value premises of all action. If a government or any other elite comes to monopolize this function, social control itself comes to be monopolized.

INFORMATION AND INDIVIDUAL POLITICAL BEHAVIOR

The earliest and most direct impact of the information revolution is probably on the individual's conceptual apparatus—his way of thinking. If these resources are to have any value at all to the individual, he must become adept at analysis and abstract thought. He must use this valuable commodity in special forms and through special kinds of procedures and technology. Already we see successive generations of school children brought up on thoughtways compatible with the computer.

Once the individual becomes adept in these matters, his power over his environment must increase. He can actually begin to plan rationally by systematically weighing alternatives, costs, and consequences. But he will relate to his environment largely through concepts, theories, and methods not of his own making and not examined by him for hidden premises before use.[2] This is why it was no paradox to propose at the outset that the power of the individual and his increased susceptibility to manipulation will go up proportionately. A homely but important example of this is the contemporary graduate student in any one of the social sciences whose analytic powers have increased but whose theoretical perspectives are largely the unquestioned commitments of the persons who designed the canned programs.

The impact of formalized approaches and conventionalized concepts goes beyond acceptance of unexamined premises. These factors also tend to remove the individual further away from direct experience with his environment. Information technology will be extremely flexible, but the experience gained through such processes will be indirect. Systematic use of experience requires that it be translated into indicators of experience. Indicators are measures of experience, that is, price of goods as a measure of "cost of living," or savings and investment as a measure of "prosperity." People must agree widely as to what are the proper and reliable indicators of experience. As a consequence, we shall be able to "tell about" nature and the "real world" far better than we can sense it. When knowledge is redefined as information, there is a gain in the power of analysis and a great risk of sensory deprivation. Among the problems to look for in this development is the susceptibility of the individual to mass mobilization. As we shall see, it has its good side as well as its bad and should not be looked upon as necessarily pathological.

At least since the birth of modern polling, mass attitudes seem to

2. See chapter 6, "The Generic Secrets of Government Decision Making," by David Curzon, especially the discussion of "premises."

distribute themselves around a central tendency. Some attitudes are polarized; some are dispersed into several different kinds of concentrations. But by and large, the distribution has a single bell-shaped mode based on consensus and moderation. This central tendency is in part natural. Mass communications media homogenize values. Mass programming and appeals tend to reduce extremes of feeling even as they raise expectations. But part of the phenomenon is artificial. Sample surveys structure responses to questions in such a manner that some intensities of feeling are eliminated or averaged out, and many intense but peculiarly individual responses go unclassified. In either event, the central tendency has been important in shaping the strategies of business and government decision makers. It is rational for them to assume the central tendency, and their strategies make it a reality and reinforce it.

The revolution in information technology could change this quite considerably. An explosion in the number of media of all types is inevitable, and this explosion is going to have some broader effects. For example, the multiplication and specialization of television channels will ease the pressure to maximize single Nielsen ratings, and this alone will introduce some degree of heterogeneity. Cable TV will use a lot of canned material in visual and data transmission, but it also makes possible a much larger variety of specialized services to particular audiences.

This is a move from broadcasting to "narrow casting," and it involves a massive diversification of cues: There will be a multiplication, even an explosion, in ideas, values, images. Almost nothing is more likely to fragment real attitudes; and improvement in two-way communication is likely to facilitate the expression and the counting of these attitudes, thereby producing entirely different data to decision makers. It will become increasingly rational for merchandisers and politicians to differentiate their products and to appeal to differences rather than only similarities.

All of these factors promise significant changes in the politically relevant aspects of behavior. Political sophistication and participation will expand. Specialized appeals are more informative, and the technology will make further inquiries so easy and inexpensive that the average citizen will be able to do a little research on issues and candidates for himself. Introduction of electronic voting apparatus in every household could revolutionize the size of the active electorate. The reduced cost of access to communications media is likely to increase the amount of political communication and could significantly reduce economic differences among candidates and parties. The contribution of CATV in large cities will be immediate and significant merely in making television available on a strictly neighborhood basis, whereas today it is uneconomical even for congressional candidates to use metropolitan television or newspapers.

All of this will contribute to a far looser political situation than any we have known in the twentieth century. Traditional party loyalties are likely to weaken. Given the referendum potential of the new media, politics for the average citizen is likely to be a good deal more issue oriented. Still more significantly, the lag between the emergence of new interests and their recognition as public issues will be drastically reduced. Distance will no longer limit discovery of common interests.

FROM FRAGMENTATION TO MOBILIZATION

But even if these potentialities are realized to the fullest, it is entirely possible that the political system at the level of institutions might remain unchanged. Here we begin to face quite concretely the discontinuity between microscopic and macroscopic reality. The loosening and spreading of politically relevant mass attitudes will produce two distinct tendencies at the macro level, interacting but quite contradictory: (1) The heterogeneity of attitudes, coupled with increasing participation, will tend to reaffirm and strengthen the party system along more or less traditional lines; (2) with access to political institutions still limited, however, ease of communication and heightening of expectations will intensify the tendency toward direct political action through social movements and special interest groups. These tendencies will manifest themselves in changing power relations, institutional patterns, and governmental policies.

1. Paradoxical as it may sound, history backs the first contention. Prior to the advent of efficient national communications, attitude distributions in the United States were decentralized and complex. They made fertile soil for political parties, and party politics became essential to well-functioning state and local government. Between 1832 and 1896, a period of great attitudinal diversity in this country, the party system was vigorous in every state and at the national level. Except for the 1860s it held true even for the South (and in the

South it was the very uniformity of salient attitudes that hampered parties during the Confederate period). After 1896, beginning in New England and the South, opinions began to grow closer toward national norms, and party structures seemed to loosen as a direct consequence.

Even when greater diversity of attitudes is accompanied by increased participation and weaker party loyalties, party institutions do not necessarily weaken. As elections come to be based on clearer policy alternatives, greater efforts have to be made to establish agenda on which meaningful ayes and nays can be expressed. Parties set agenda. And although parties may continue to avoid taking clear positions on some of the issues, the party role in setting the agenda—the simple agreements on what to disagree about—could become more important. And as long as there are presidents to elect and congresses and bureaucracies to control, some localized factions will continue to coalesce into larger aggregates with a regional and national focus.

2. Persistence of this older structure does not, however, close off emergence of other, newer forms of mass organization. The trend is likely to be toward increased direct action through social movements. Ease of communication and rising expectations, as well as an easing of access to political institutions, will on the whole increase the "movement-forming capacity" of the country. People will find it easier to discover and to communicate with others who share their irritations and aspirations. Physical proximity—in the past essential for the creation of social movements—will count for little. Men of like mind will be able to organize without ever coming together under one roof. The new information base will help directly: The availability of seventy or eighty local television channels could eliminate a good deal of bias in information. It could in fact reach viewers with a wide variety of information in "odd lots," no longer filtered through a city editor or a national news network producer.

United States history shows ample precedents for the notion that a change in information technology will help spawn new social movements. The Populist movement of the late nineteenth century would have been impossible without the mass newspapers of the time. And what the press did for geographically dispersed social classes then, television seems to be doing for (or to) races and classes in concentrated areas today, as a producer of images that strengthen weak identifications and create aspirations where there were none before.

The two major tendencies, then—reemergence of party and multiplication of social movements—could combine to instill in the United States, and perhaps also in other industrialized countries, a new political vigor.

A third side development, an increase of withdrawal movements, is also likely. They may arise out of a felt inability to pierce established institutions or a genuine distrust of the available information flow. Easy access to information resources facilitates permanent withdrawal into tribes and communities and conventional new towns. These withdrawal movements, almost by definition, are not necessarily of any significance to the political order.[3] They become politically significant mainly when withdrawls are so numerous that they raise serious questions about the legitimacy of society and government.

These three trends are already in evidence. But the development and availability of new communications systems will multiply their potential political impacts and the speed with which any one of them may shape events in the future. These trends can produce a healthy and reinvigorated society, but only if the various possibilities are allowed to take place. The most serious problem lies with whether the regime will be able to accept the social movements that arise and appear to challenge the system. Social movements will always be seen as producers of social disorder, and the tendency is for elites to declare disorder unlawful. If movements are defined as a threat to the social fabric, then the tendency will be to foster or allow only those political parties and communications media that can be used as instruments of social control. This was true even when governmental capacity to manipulate the news was still inefficient. In the future the potential for peaceful control through manipulation of information will go up at a rate even faster than the potential for individuals and movements to use the media for their own purposes.

Social control operates through consensus, in fact through privately organized consensus. But social control is also a deliberate function of public policy through the coercion of military, police, and other regulatory agencies. The new technology offers still newer and more potent means of social control through "manipulated consensus."

3. See chapter 4, "The Symbolic Uses of Information," by Rozann Rothman.

There was always some capacity for manipulated consensus: Witness the effectiveness of anti-Japanese propaganda movies in the United States during World War II. The new integrated information system presents new potentials in the extent to which it can provide the individual with an altered set of fact premises on which to base his opinions; or it can provide him with new and well-developed sets of value premises that could alter his opinions as well as his treatment of the facts. Bipolar worlds, containment, or, before that, Manifest Destiny and Yellow Peril made for tremendously effective propaganda because they are literally systems of analysis. Once such generalized views are internalized in a people, the influence is *within* rather than *on* the individual.

Opportunities for distributing such canned programs most certainly will increase in the next twenty years, and with them will grow the capacity of decision centers to manipulate the fact and value environment of the individual. This is the means by which the healthy interplay between parties and mass movements could be weakened, resulting in a very tightly knit society indeed.

IMPACT ON INTEREST GROUPS

Social scientists generally believe that the problem of mass mobilization is in part, if not altogether, solved by the presence of an intermediate stratum, that is, by private groups that intervene between the isolated, "atomized" person and the central authorities. It is taken as a fact as well as a necessity that to be free a society must be plural.

It seems quite clear that the information revolution will spectacularly expand the resources available to groups and that it will make possible much more effective control of the environment by smaller and smaller groups. Groups may ultimately come to mean a large aggregate of persons coordinated by a tiny number of brilliant people. Groups have, of course, always been shaped most fundamentally by problems of communication. The development of small computing and communications apparatus, and access on a shared-time basis to immense computer systems, will virtually obviate the difficulty of communicating in groups of all sizes.

This is bound to have some important political meaning. A large number of more efficiently operating groups will lead to sharper distinctions in society, thus greater potential for constructive conflict. However, the changes will not be distributed evenly. Computerized access to vast information pools is far more likely to enhance the capacity of old groups to persist than of new groups to form. We already know in the field of professional societies the extent to which medical and legal associations control both the number of practitioners and a great deal of their behavior. Generalizing this pattern, the result could be a kind of functional feudalism, rather than a vigorous system of group competition. Because of the severe statistical limits on the number of persons who can create new trade associations and pressure groups, one of the probable and fearful consequences of a revolutionary spread of information technology is tighter, rather than looser, organizational structure among all groups large or small, old or new.

This presents a certain and severe dilemma to the individual and to decision makers. The choice is not a simple one between centralization and decentralization of power. The emergence of a computer-based group system is a very important third scenario: It involves a great deal of pluralism—and that means decentralization in a certain sense—but it also involves a great deal of mobilization, that is, centralization inside groups rather than inside movements (as in mass society) or within a tightly bureaucratized governmental system (as in totalitarian regimes). Given a sufficient amount of technology, private groups can in effect become "private governments."

In short, there are three possible extremes, all of which are unacceptable: (1) a so-called decentralized system with minimal structure, which runs the danger of anarchy followed by mass mobilization; (2) a centralized system; and (3) a system some might call a combination of centralization and decentralization, but that can itself be tyrannical if public policy is nothing more than a policy of sponsoring group government of its own members, for example, state professional societies, trade associations, labor unions.

The third tendency already seems the most pronounced. This means tighter rather than looser social structure, despite greater pluralism. In such a context social movements may eventually appear to be the only means for loosening up. The primary sources of politics in such a society could be conflicts between old and new groups, rather than orderly competition between political parties or between established groups on opposite sides of the market. This kind of process, where new groups must fight for a place, is almost certain to be defined as disorder, and this gives established elites additional incentive to use information as a means of social control.

INFORMATION, POWER, AND SOCIETY—EMERGENCE OF THE SEPARATE MANAGEMENT COMPONENT

What in sum is the most likely set of outcomes for the political structure at the macro level? There is ample basis in history to expect broad changes in power structures and policies following changes in technology and resources. There is, in fact, no reason to expect otherwise from changes as significant as those centering on the information revolution. Indeed, these political changes seem already well under way and may already be too far advanced to be shaped by public policy. The following is a very tentative sketch.

Large governments as well as corporate organizations have begun to move away from hierarchical control. External supervision through span of control, formal hierarchies of authority, and narrow definitions of jobs are being supplemented and may in the long run be replaced by other principles of organization, including professionalization, lower-level decision making, and network patterns rather than simple vertical patterns of communication. Narrow job classification is already being defended more by unions than by management. Much bureaucracy will still be left, but there are definite signs of broadening the notion of jobs and of ensuring uniform behavior by setting "decision rules" rather than by direction, inspection, and review.

All of these trends seem to point toward one central development —the emergence of a *separate management component*, where management will in fact be an information process. Control and coordination in virtually all organizations will be carried on through the self-conscious manipulation of the information environment. This is what is most likely to replace hierarchy.

Modern management works through what we have already called "the fact and value premises." To put it in the extreme, lower-line administrators need have no contact at all with the outside world. Decision making can be handled on the basis of careful modeling of real-world situations and proper manipulation of the model, depending upon a person's responsibilities.

Management, then, becomes a process that can be factored out and placed in a separate control unit, as budgeting, personnel, and finance were once separated out to auxiliary units. But management is more: It means control over those other auxiliary units.

Management also becomes a function that is interchangeable among organizations. The subject matter may change, but many of the functional requirements do not. As a direct consequence, interchange among large organizations becomes a way of life. C. Wright Mills recognized this interchange already in the 1940s. The universalizing of some organizational principles and the development of a profession of management is making the interchange possible, and it is affecting power relations in the society.

One can disagree with Mills in his contention that the regular interchanges among corporate, military, and civil government elites proved the existence of a single, national "power elite." But it would be difficult, perhaps unwise, to deny that such interchanges could come to constitute such an elite. Management is a political phenomenon at the macro level; *it is merely a name for the effective use of information as a power source.*

Such a development would no doubt bring great gains to society. It would inevitably lead to more rationality and efficiency, insofar as leadership was based upon knowledge and command of the machinery of rational calculation and control. Even the loosening of old hierarchies could be considered again.

But there are also likely to be some fundamental costs, and while the gains might be immediate, the costs are cumulative and difficult to assess for the purpose of formulating public policies designed to control costs. By *costs* we mean power developments that could be contrary to basic democratic values.

One of the most profound costs of this change in the distribution of power is its very subtlety. When conduct is influenced by manipulating the *environment* of conduct rather than conduct itself, it is most difficult to judge the manipulation, to criticize it, to oppose it, to plug different values into it. The use of management methods of decision making in the Vietnam War may very well explain why there was a slow but unstoppable escalation despite the fact that, as a number of people reported after leaving office, they and others opposed the expansion of the war. Once a process is set in train, it is very difficult to step back and criticize it. Small steps based on a priori analysis can literally demoralize the opposition and never be perceived, until too late, as a large commitment.

That, in turn, many lead to magnification of error. Large computers will be able to check against error if it occurs to someone that the model of the outside world devised by management might be in error. But, as in Vietnam, or with the introduction of a new product that fails, unexpected events might not be perceived as shortcomings in the model.

Another likely political development that can be treated as a cost is loss of the legitimacy of elected political people in relation to management in the competition for responsible control of the upper echelons of decision making. There has always been a tendency for the elected amateur to lose out to the professional in any direct confrontation. The legitimacy of management, based as it is on talent as well as higher education, may prove to be the most effective adversary ever to face electoral and party-based power.

But perhaps the most fundamental and insidious cost of the rise of management could be the blurring of the distinction between public and private spheres. Interchange among top management personnel is both a measure and a cause of this obfuscation. That is to say, the notion of a public could be blurred by the simple continuity of management once it is established as a separate function with its own highly legitimate access to all decision centers. Government authority, whether directed by political personnel, capitalists, or managers, has very traditional roots. Management, in public agencies and the military, is an essential part of effective government. But the emerging power holders and the emerging structures of authority depend little for their claim to control on traditional roots that are grounded in sovereignty, citizenship, and loyalty. This transformation could easily reduce government to a position of mere power based on superior resources and more elaborate management techniques.

We begin to appreciate the costs of this kind of transformation when we ponder the social choices we may have to make in order to cope with the information revolution. A 1984-type scenario will be the most likely outcome if things are let go at the present rate and no attention is paid to the information revolution. Yet it is also widely assumed that a redirection of these trends toward more decentralized and individualized patterns requires some significant types of governmental intervention in the near future.

This means that "freedom scenarios" are demanding independent government at a time when it may be losing its independence. There was never any reason to expect that politics and government would be immune to change. Indeed, the information revolution could alter the very process of governing. Politics and government could turn into one continuous process of management, and if that came to pass, there would be little capacity left for planning actions outside the process itself. Democratic theory in the West is predicated upon some type of "mixed regime," that is, government made up of institutions whose powers are based upon different constituencies. A society integrated around a system of information and controlled by even the most responsible of managers could eliminate the mixed regime, making all institutions, public and private, responsive in the same way to the same challenges.

GOVERNMENT AND SOCIAL CHOICE

Within this immense and diffuse context it does not seem highly probable that the individual will improve his own life tremendously. The new technologies do make incremental improvement possible, but improvement is based upon three related assumptions: (1) that the revolution itself will and should go on relatively unabated; (2) that society can and should be left to cope with the costs if it is to enjoy the benefits; and (3) that society has a government and a well-organized political process capable of maximizing gains over costs and of equitably distributing the costs.

It is the third assumption that is so questionable. The blurring of the distinction between public-private spheres may be the single most important political development during the next generation. Governments show little sign of developing greater capacity for acting as an independent force, a counterpoise to private forces.

The National Aeronautics and Space Administration and the Communications Satellite Corporation are good examples. In both instances government proved itself capable of acting forcefully only in consonance with and in support of existing private interests. Neither program brought into question the monopolistic tendencies of any cooperating company or carrier. Both programs have been effective insofar as they were efforts to work with the grain of history. In NASA, change amounted to acceleration but no appreciable change of direction. COMSAT has essentially been an effort to ensure that no disruptive change will take place at all. It is hard in either case to know where public ends and private begins.

Where government is still clearly independent there is serious doubt about its capacity. In antitrust, government lawyers tend to be outnumbered and outclassed. In the drug and cosmetic field and in the ecology areas, government agencies have usually been one step behind in protecting the public. Yet in almost all areas, the most important social choices depend upon government's being *ahead* of the private sector. This would be particularly true in the esoteric skills. Extensive government use of contracting powers with universities and corporations, plus government programs of subsidizing research and training centers, will continue to put government in arrears.

Added to this is the fact that governments have been increasingly organized along lines parallel to and indistinguishable from private organization. There is thus no basis for expecting that governments will act in any way contrary to tendencies already in train in the economy at large. Current ideology actually supports the parallels. In the United States, Republicans talk about "partnership," Democrats about "creative federalism," old liberals about pluralism and responsibility through bargaining. The New Left intellectuals talk about decentralization, power to the people, and so on. In all these instances the sum total is government indistinguishable from, and indeed collaborative with, private interests. Effective regulation of monopolies by government requires an independence we have no basis for expecting.

These are some of the reasons why the blurring and weakening of the public-private dichotomy could be the most important political development in the coming decades. Society may never become totally mobilized. Upward mobility and even outward mobility will probably be tolerated. What is really more likely is the building of a Hell of Administrative Boredom. That is already the current of industrial organization. Unless appropriate initiatives are taken now, the information revolution may simply turn the current into a rapids.

CONCLUSION

The most agonizing problem about this is that all information is proprietary. Open access to lower members and nonmembers too readily deranges the authority structure and the delicate balance of interdependence of all the parts in a well-run organization. Secrecy as a policy is forced upon people not otherwise so inclined. Executive privilege claimed against demands for information did not begin with President Nixon.[4] Moreover, every claim to executive privilege, except where allegations of a crime are involved, will be upheld. The Supreme Court in *U.S.* v. *Nixon* has affirmed this position for the chief executive, and the chief executive can affirm it for every subordinate whose files, computers, or sound equipment need protection from the public. Under present law, the chief executive does not have to claim national security.

Government by a separate management component is almost inevitably and by definition a politics of secrecy—until such point that no one is aware of any secrets to demand.

Education would be the one system capable of resolving the various tendencies in favor of open society, open politics, and the autonomous individual. But the educational institutions are also uniquely capable of programming the individual for a full life of comfort within the Hell of Administrative Boredom. Here indeed is an area where deliberate policy choices are going to determine the actual shape of the future.

The most important dimension of impact here will be on social stratification—in a new and more severe form: While many will learn to use the new apparatus, only a few will understand it. As observed earlier, many will *know how*; some will *know*. This may be the new version of "Many are called, few are chosen."

Those who know how will use the technology to their own benefit and to that of mankind. Who could ever oppose greater productivity? But those who know the new technology become the inventors, the innovators, the critics. This will be the basis for elites in a restratified society. How many will know? Will it be 1 percent? Or 10 percent? Whatever the figure, we can be certain it will be limited— a pyramid of intelligence, but of what kind and with what values?

Institutions of higher education are already becoming technocra-

4. See chapter 8, "The United States: The Doctrine of Executive Privilege," by Bernard Schwartz.

tized. More and more frequently do we find university curricula being judged by criteria of "relevance." Regents, educators, and students disagree with each other on the definition of relevance, but their disagreements may be settled when it becomes clear that technocratic training provides access to a neutral or value-free apparatus rather than merely to a specific position in a specific organization. Such an education would not be free of dependence on some kind of regime. It might not be a regime of present governmental and corporate power holders, but it would be a regime just the same. The education process could be universalized and totally egalitarian, but that would not prevent it from serving as a channel through which regime-supporting talent would be recruited. In fact, use of the general education process as a universal pool from which to recruit elites would be a strong legitimizing force for the whole regime of the information revolution.

For the elite, education would be continuous and cumulative; for all others it would probably concentrate on the practical arts and problem solving. Problem solving would, of course, involve analysis at a level more advanced than today's, but it would be advanced only in terms of programs made available by elites. This means that the whole present middle class of professions and skills could be converted into a mere middle-income proletariat.

The outcome could, of course, be otherwise, since education could shape as well as be shaped by the information revolution. The following is a list of questions that must be asked if present elites, fearful of the future, are to head it off in accord with democratic-liberal values:

1. Can the new mass education be tailored to fit more closely the peculiarities of each individual? Could the new apparatus provide an antidote to bureaucratized teaching by reducing the fund of human knowledge to human scale? Individuality is the only ultimate defense against *any* large establishment. Can education of self be combined with education about the outside world?

2. Can we instruct for real literacy in the new information process, or are we doomed to teaching utilization, cookbook-style? Public schools never succeeded in any vast expansion of foreign language literacy. Is information technology, because of its more immediate utility, going to be easier to convey to the casual student?

3. Can education be combined with training? That is, can data banks be coupled with a rich historical and cultural context independent of but always associated with the specific items of data to be retrieved? Such a soft, or humane, overlay to hard data would be another check against tacit submission to someone else's conceptual framework.

4. Can *political* education be combined with training? Will the citizen be able to make rational and effective use of the new levels of participation available to him? Will he have superior means of obtaining relevant information and cutting through political propaganda, or will the citizen be free only to withdraw or to support the regime more vigorously than today?

5. Will the education system in fact equip the individual to withdraw if he wishes, or will his increased power be conditional upon use within prescribed technical boundaries and procedures?

6. The questions above had to do with intellectual and psychological self-reliance. Here is a question of sheer physical self-reliance: Will new educational systems militate against or facilitate formation of tribes and communal groups?

HEADING OFF THE FUTURE

The chances of getting attention, let alone answers, to these questions are extremely slight, precisely because education serves the information revolution so well and education is so responsive to where the money is. But the chances of heading off the future are not entirely gone until the questions cannot be asked at all. The chances have disappeared only when no demands for autonomy and no complaints against secrecy are voiced.

The two "information crises" in the U.S. actually offer solid basis for modest optimism. These were the Pentagon Papers and Watergate. Both indicate the enormous political value of information and information technology. Both indicate the immense degree to which government controls all information of concern to itself and the tremendous power of government to keep secrets and to manipulate in its own favor what does leak out. But both indicate also that when the public becomes aware of existing information, especially in relation to criminal activity, there is almost no way to prevent revelation. The copier and magnetic tape explosions have worked both ways, and as long as information (as news) is a very valuable commercial item, the decline toward a secret society can be slowed.

But can it be stopped? Not unless present governments take action to ensure the capacity of private citizens and groups. Here are a few policy choices that could become some sort of agenda:

1. Head off the centralization of production capacity of information technology. Unlike the automobile or electrical utilities industries, the computer and related industries could involve centralized use as well as centralized production. Once information retrieval and analysis capacity is centralized, it will be extremely difficult to decentralize it. All talk of heterogeneity and checks and balances would be useless. However, once this capacity were widely distributed, it would in fact be impossible for later regimes, desirous of concentrated power and secrecy, to centralize the information process. *Antitrust in this area is more important than in any other industry.*

2. Head off government legal rights to secrecy regarding its policy plans or activities. The Supreme Court decision on executive privilege helps some, but not nearly enough. In one respect, the cause of government secrecy was strengthened by the holding, inasmuch as a demand for secret information can only be sustained where a criminal indictment against some government official has first been secured. Of far greater value would be establishment of the legal right of citizens to bring civil suits against any government agency where there is reasonable ground for believing that the agency is exceeding its statutory power. Then a court order could obtain otherwise secret data.

3. Head off government legal rights to secrecy in regard to information it holds on individuals. This has rightly been described as the development of *habeas data* law, and it should, of course, apply to private (for example, credit bureaus) as well as public data archives. The citizen cannot have the right to deprive government or many private agencies of information on himself; social control would be rendered impossible. But now that information on all citizens can be acquired, stored, retrieved, and used at relatively low cost, each citizen must have access to his own files to contest what exists in it and at least to add more to, if not subtract from, the fund of information.

These make only a beginning. And indeed they would not work at all unless the culture and the institutions of education produced a true citizen, a person who demands knowledge of the world around him.

4

The Symbolic Uses
of Public Information

ROZANN ROTHMAN

Democratic citizens are socialized to accept and respond to the values of liberty and individualism and to expect a free marketplace of ideas, a marketplace that allows truth or at least the most useful idea to prevail. In the liberal schema, the function of the media is the presentation of a neutral summary of the facts to be used as the common ground for a rational discussion of alternatives.

This schema is contradicted by the symbolic uses of public information, for such uses are generated by the ambiguities and inconsistencies of behavior and by the strong proclivity of the public to respond to the messages of government. The citizens of democratic nations typically find themselves in the position of ratifying decisions made by others rather than choosing between alternative governmental policies.

This chapter explores the conditions under which this development takes place by showing that democratic values provide the people with an ideal paradigm of government that shapes public expectations in systematic ways. The decisions of modern government affect every individual, evoking such conflicting emotions as fear, hope, rage, and frustration, yet expectations color perceptions of government, its purpose, and mode of operation. Government has become a focus of interest and a primary dispenser of data in modern society, and one prerogative of the position is the ability to shape the implications of data for policy. Power accrues to government from this position because democratic expectations predispose the public to accept the government's premises of reality as authoritative.[1] Expectations therefore constitute a major obstacle to realization of the people's right to know in that they provide the preconditions for the exercise of governmental discretion and control over information.

The uneasy coexistence of conflicting values in the democratic mind augments governmental discretion and control. Disparities between the liberal schema and the operation of democratic government are rationalized and their import is not perceived by the public. For example, Americans equivocally accept a sacred liberal value, the free marketplace of ideas. In the historical and contemporary proclamations of devotion to the free marketplace of ideas, a small proviso appears: The marketplace of ideas must be subject to the constraints imposed by authority, order, and the need for security. American statesmen, jurists, and theorists have over time sought a balance between these conflicting imperatives. Oliver Wendell Holmes, in his famous dissent in *Abrams* v. *U.S.*, paid homage to the ambiguities that cluster around the free marketplace of ideas even as he defended the marketplace. Men must learn to seek the ultimate good by free trade in ideas as

> the best test of truth is the power of the thought to get itself accepted in the competition of the market. . . . That at any rate is the theory of our Constitution. It is an experiment. . . . While that experiment is part of the system I think that we should be eternally vigilant against attempts to check the expression of opinions that we loathe, . . . unless they so imminently threaten immediate interference with the lawful and pressing purposes of the law that an immediate check is required to save the country.[2]

The most eloquent defense of the free marketplace of ideas contains ambivalent nuances, which function to reinforce public ambivalence as to which imperative ought to be served, the degree to which it should be served, and the consequences of unambiguous choice.

The pervasiveness of ambivalence and the government's ability to use the symbols of democracy allows an incumbent government the

1. See chapter 6, "The Generic Secrets of Government Decision Making," by David Curzon.
2. Abrams v. U.S., 250 U.S. 616(1919).

latitude in which to present its policy as optimum. Modern societies are

> characterized by the selective release and publication of information and the dilution of public communication through the mass media.[3]

The public neither objects to this diminution nor appears to notice it, perhaps because a major expectation about democratic government—that it serves the people—is rarely questioned. Criticism is not directed at the ideal but at the present incumbent and whether he is in fact serving the people. The separateness of the ideal, even as the immediate manifestation of the ideal is criticized, reassures the public about the meaning of political activity.

Elections focus public interest on a choice between candidates and parties and divert attention from substantive issues such as whether significant changes are needed in institutions and policies. Because the candidate needs a majority to win, he typically adopts a moderate political position to gain votes. A moderate position has wide appeal because it augments customary understandings of the nature and operation of the political order while criticism is channeled into questions of equitable distribution. The symbolism of elections provides a reservoir of legitimacy, which incumbents draw on to add weight to official definitions of conflict situations and official explanations of current crises. The presentations of an elected official, his explanations, and especially his plea for public ratification of policy generate a chain of connections that is able to withstand the shock of traumatic events.

MEANING AND INFORMATION

An explanation of why official presentations are more compelling than other interpretations rests on the distinction Murray Edelman has drawn between meaning and information and their respective effects on political cognition:

> Meaning is basically different from information and incompatible with it. Meaning is associated with order—with a patterned, cogni-

3. Claus Mueller, *The Politics of Communication: A Study in the Political Sociology of Language, Socialization, and Legitimization* (New York: Oxford University Press, 1973), p. 6.

tive structure that permits anticipation of future developments, so that perceptions are expected and not surprising. . . . Information involves complexity or lack of order, inability to foresee. Unlike meaning it is transmitted; and what is transmitted is complicating premises.[4]

Information offers complexity and the contingencies of facts. It diminishes the capacity to plan or anticipate future events and is therefore a threat to meaning. Information offers neither easy clichés nor a firm base from which to contemplate reality, and it is predictable that the implications of information will be resisted by elites and much of the public. Meaning, a pattern into which the random bits and pieces of behavior can be fitted, is further strengthened by the formal actions of a democratic government.

The people's right to know is symbolized by the First Amendment, and Supreme Court decisions that protect the individual exercise of these rights reinforce public acceptance of the performance of government and the resistance to information. We periodically reaffirm the belief that government is limited and its power extends so far and only so far. Government's ability to withhold information was allegedly reduced by the Freedom of Information Act of 1966. The need for legislation was supported by the press, the American Civil Liberties Union, the American Bar Association, and some legal scholars. They argued that executive agencies often used existing laws as an excuse to withhold information from the public. Administration representatives opposed the substitution of a stringent rule for flexible executive branch judgments.

The bill that was designed to expand the public's right to know codified the ambiguities of balancing conflicting imperatives. Lyndon Johnson signed the bill and praised it as a product of free society, which "provided for Government confidentiality when necessary, while at the same time protecting the public's right to information."[5] The public was assured that, despite the expansion and bureaucratization of government, traditional values were still in effect, and the Freedom of Information Act became an additional symbol of these values.

After attempts were made to obtain information, it became ap-

4. Murray Edelman, *Politics as Symbolic Action: Mass Arousal and Quiescence* (Chicago: Markham, 1971), p. 31.
5. *Congressional Quarterly Almanac*, 1966 (Washington, D.C.: Congressional Quarterly, Inc., 1966), p. 556.

parent that even with a new law, executive agencies retained sufficient discretion to control the extent of disclosure. But the act fitted into a schema of meaning, and the critics who contended that the Freedom of Information Act did not restrict government's ability to selectively release information focused their suggestions for reform on stricter implementation. Ralph Nader attacked the discretion left to government agencies and accused the news media of "shirking its responsibility as 'prime public guardians' of freedom of information." He concluded that the Freedom of Information Act "will remain putty in the hands of narrow-minded government personnel unless its provisions are given authoritative and concrete interpretation by the courts."[6]

Although there is evidence of governmental reluctance to implement full disclosure, the information that is generated by government agencies is often overlooked or dismissed by the public because the legal structure meets expectations, symbolizes the ideal, and monopolizes the attention of critics and supporters alike. When a critic like Ralph Nader labels information as deviant behavior and assumes that it is correctable if only the press and the courts live up to the norms of their respective roles, it is probable that the public will also concur in this assessment.

The House Government Operations Subcommittee on Foreign Operations and Government Information held hearings in 1972 on the need to amend the act and proposed reforms. Advocates of reform contended that the law had not worked as anticipated; the act was full of loopholes, it did not specify precise guidelines, and agencies had opportunities to delay their response to requests for information.[7] A bill to amend the act was passed by Congress, vetoed by President Ford, and the veto overridden in November 1974. The amendment provided for judicial review of governmental classification decisions, set deadlines for agency response to requests for information, and in general tried to set a standard of governmental responsiveness to citizen inquiries.

---

6. David Roe, "U.S. Agencies Violate Information Act," *The Los Angeles Times,* August 27, 1969, part I, p. 8, reprinted in Theodore L. Becker and Vernon G. Murray, *Government Lawlessness in America* (New York: Oxford University Press, 1971), pp. 244–45.

7. *Congressional Quarterly Weekly Reports* (Washington, D.C.: Congressional Quarterly, Inc., 1972), pp. 423–25, 619, 686, 807–808, 1092–1093, and 1214.

Although these amendments impose more stringent constraints on agency behavior, they do not dispose of the problem of governmental discretion and control over information. Additional constraints do not reduce the tension between the democratic objective of a fully informed public and what government defines as the need to protect confidentiality. The most probable effect of additional constraints is to reinforce widely held assumptions: The public will continue to perceive specific examples of agency reluctance to release information as deviant behavior, not as the manifestation of a more fundamental problem. The rhetoric of supporters and critics conceals the basic dimensions of the problem of government discretion and control over information because the conditions that create the problem cannot be remedied by exhortation or tightening regulations.

As long as government is in a position to shape the implications of data for policy, it will continue to exercise control over information. To obtain some insight into the dynamics of this type of control, Erving Goffman's analysis of communication contingencies will be used. According to Goffman, the audience misreads the meaning of a cue or reads embarrassing meanings into gestures or events that are accidental, inadvertent, or incidental. Also, performers must attempt to make sure that every event in a performance is under control, that it occurs in such a way as to convey an impression compatible and consistent with the official definition of the situation. Such a strategy is necessary; a performer cannot tolerate an unmeant gesture, for such gestures differ from his official presentation and call his definition into question.

> This difference forces an acutely embarrassing wedge between the official presentation and reality, for it is part of the official projection that it is the only one possible under the circumstances.[8]

To maintain its credibility and authority, government is compelled to adopt a similar strategy. In order for the public to perceive governmental decisions as legitimate, government has to convince the people that the particular decision is the only one possible under the circumstances.

Modern government possesses the power to control communication contingencies and routinely utilizes this power. It is not a matter of

---

8. Erving Goffman, *The Presentation of Self in Everyday Life* (Garden City, N.Y.: Doubleday Anchor Books, 1959), pp. 51–52.

manipulation or the evil machinations of a power elite; it is rather the postulates of democratic theory transformed into the justification for modern mass government that generate this control. Democratic government is supposed to serve and be responsible to its citizens, yet it retains discretionary power as to whom it serves and to what extent. Before government can serve any segment of its citizenry, the symbols and rhetoric of democracy compel government officials to justify their decisions. Objective and factual grounds for action are established, which appear as the official authoritative definition of reality. Officials may use shortages, crises, national emergencies, or the good of the whole as their leitmotiv, but the case must be made fully and in accord with accepted procedures if the credibility of government is to be sustained.

Facts are offered to citizens as the justification for policy decisions. The facts are routinely collected and produced and may be gathered by the Bureau of Labor Statistics, collected during congressional hearings or by the statisticians, economists, and clerks of the departments of health, education and welfare; housing and urban development; or agriculture. Wherever the facts are accumulated and assembled, the public is socialized to see them as objective because the collection of information is a routine function, a practical concern, and an everyday accomplishment of government.

Government exercises its most significant control of information by shaping beliefs about which data are relevant and the implications of data for policy formation. The Vietnam War went badly for years before the American public realized that official body counts had no relevance to the progress of the war. Every American citizen has felt the pinch of inflation, but administration officials assure the consumer that the rate of inflation has leveled off and promise that if administration policies are followed, this year will be better than last year. If this year is not better than last year, the administration will assure the public that the result is due to the failure to implement the administration's program, and it will have the facts to support this position.

As long as public expectations are not disturbed by the actions of government, the notion that data derive their meaning from particular values is not recognized and the contingencies of facts are not likely to be perceived. A public that believes that merit, work, and the American system provide opportunities for every individual is unlikely to be interested in a revolutionary solution to the problems of poverty. Governmental programs such as Head Start and the manpower training programs compensate for the handicaps of the disadvantaged and fulfill society's obligations to the poor. The solution neatly fits the requirements of meaning; those who want more are labeled as agitators. The public possesses an authoritative, objective account of reality and can discount the information presented by agitators.

GOVERNMENT AS THE HUB OF COMMUNICATIONS

Once these connections are established, government is in a position to use facts to justify particular policies, even though the logical connection between facts and policy is dubious, problematic, or nonexistent. The ploy is supported by an irony that offers strategic advantages to the government.

The official, authoritative account of reality defines the problem and subsequent redefinitions or criticism cluster around the original account. The government's claim to need 500 ballistic missiles in order to have a sufficiently strong bargaining position to successfully conduct disarmament negotiations might excite ridicule in some quarters, but criticism will center on the number of missiles needed and not on the proposition itself. The potency of routinely collected facts, marshaled into a justification of policy and presented as a plea for public approval, cannot be underestimated, for the routine operation of government is the base of recognition of authority.

Because government occupies the center of the configuration and is the source of the authoritative, official account of reality, it has options as to which strategy it will pursue; whether it will withhold information, stress specifics, or release a torrent of data. There is usually little need for government officials to consciously plan to release or withhold information because the government's central position in the communications process assures its control over the flow and the impact of information.

Thus the optimum strategy for democratic government is a policy of full disclosure because information will go undetected amidst the data that are routinely released. The quantity of data will obscure the significance of specific items that could be perceived as information.

The most complete and comprehensive data about American government and the priorities of an incumbent administration are contained in a public document—the budget. The data are presented in terms of what the government intends to purchase and not in terms of programs or potential beneficiaries compounding the difficulty of assessing the impact of budget allocations. Few citizens are in a position to understand, interpret, or draw comprehensive conclusions from the data, and few make the effort because a conspicuous characteristic of budgets is dullness. Neither the worker, the educated middle class, nor the average congressman has the time, the specialized knowledge, or the inclination to comprehend this authoritative statement of the intentions of the American government. Those who benefit from the publication of the budget—middle-level administrators, defense contractors, savings-and-loan-association officials, and Office of Economic Opportunity employees—possess the expert knowledge to learn what the budget portends for them and the capacity to take appropriate political action.

For the public, the presentation of the budget is a ritual of meticulous public disclosure and accountability that satisfies expectations about the operation of government and contributes to the maintenance of meaning. The ritual strengthens public willingness to leave the budget to experts and minimizes awareness of the benefits that flow from this allocation of values. In this way, democratization of knowledge, which was intended to benefit the people, in fact strengthens the few who are in a position to possess and use specialized knowledge.

The politics of budget allocation are obscure to all but interested clienteles because the public assumes that the official authoritative account of reality is legitimate. Claus Mueller, in his analysis of language codes and socialization patterns in advanced industrial society, discussed the relationship between class position and willingness to accept the actions of government as legitimate. The restricted speech code of the lower classes narrows the ability to conceptualize, to analyze, to discriminate, and to perceive alternatives and functions to obscure perception of needs and societal problems.[9] The lower class becomes the principal supporter of existing institutions in advanced industrial society.[10]

The language code and socialization patterns of the middle class enable them to perceive alternatives, and they as a class are more

9. Claus Mueller, *Politics of Communication*, p. 23.
10. Ibid., p. 85.

likely to be alienated by the specific actions of government.[11] However, their alienation is often due to an incumbent government's failure to conform to expectations, and the extent of alienation is constrained by middle-class acceptance of the norms of democratic government. If the public accepts the system as the best possible, it can discount the information it receives about incumbents. If an incumbent regime can persuasively present its difficulties as a crisis, the middle class is as likely as the lower class to support existing institutions. To label difficulties as a crisis implies that the reasons for the difficulties lie outside the control of political and economic leaders and that special sacrifices are required to surmount them.[12] This is a configuration into which the bits and pieces of random data can easily be fitted and allows information about the unequal sacrifices exacted by a crisis to be attributed to the deviant behavior of a corporation seeking windfall profits or a corrupt politician.

The demand for meaning is linked to expectations about the purpose and conduct of government and is a crucial variable in public response to the presentations of government. Meaning serves deep-rooted public needs, and it takes events of great magnitude—the demonstrations of the 1960s, the credibility gap of Lyndon Johnson's presidency, the Vietnam War, the Pentagon Papers, and the corruption of Watergate—to shake the public's customary acceptance of presidential leadership. Carl J. Friedrich in his discussion of the functions of secrecy and propaganda suggested that both tamper with communication and that the "crucial function, then, of both political propaganda and secrecy is to manipulate men in relation to the political order to make them support it or at least not to oppose it. . . . "[13] Our analysis suggests that democratic government does not need to resort to the techniques of secrecy and propaganda until the attractions of meaning have been weakened. Democratic government routinely, and without conscious tampering with communications, uses widely accepted symbols to justify its allocations of value and to win support for the political order. In other words, as long as the routine performances of freely elected leaders satisfy expectations about the operation of government, the result will be public quiescence. The most consequential forms of govern-

11. Ibid., chapter 4.
12. Murray Edelman, "The Uses of National Crises," (in press).
13. Carl J. Friedrich, *The Pathology of Politics: Violence, Betrayal, Corruption, Secrecy and Propaganda* (New York: Harper & Row, 1972), p. 176.

mental control are derived not from the simple suppression of information, but from the subtle control of the implications of information for policy.

Elected officials are likely to be perceived as legitimate until conflicts of interest are transformed into political issues and criticism of government policy and operations reaches a specific threshold. When incumbents feel threatened by criticism (the level at which threats are recognized depends upon the incumbent), they are motivated to secure their flanks and to deliberately control the flow of information.

However, when a leader consciously adopts the strategies of secrecy and propaganda, he has recognized that the attractions of meaning have weakened. An explicit policy of control of information because it conflicts with democratic symbols defeats the official purpose. No strategy is as likely to become visible to the public or to facilitate the discovery of "information" in the most routine acts of government. It may take years to build the momentum to cross the threshold, but once it is crossed, an incumbent regime is unable to reverse or stop the destruction of meaning.

The present time is a transitional period, and official positions on the Vietnam War and Watergate hasten the destruction of previously accepted meaning. The sacred words *national security* no longer function to cordon off selected issues from critical scrutiny. National security considerations prevented *The New York Times* from publishing the plans for the Bay of Pigs invasion in the 1960s but did not prevent the *Times* from publishing the Pentagon Papers. Richard Nixon invoked "national security" as a defense of the "plumbers," but the words did not ward off criticism: The burglary of Ellsberg's psychiatrist's office was investigated, and Congress proceeded to investigate the CIA's role in assassinations and illegal tampering with mail and the cables of foreign governments. Blatant infringements on sanctioned rights increases public disaffection, and dissatisfaction typically centers on an incumbent's use of power.

GOVERNMENT AND THE PERFORMANCE OF THE MEDIA

The liberal schema gives the press the task of overseeing the operation of democratic institutions. The press becomes the eyes and ears of the people; it gathers the facts and presents them to the public in order that an informed public may rationally discuss alternatives.

The tradition of investigative journalism and the norms of professional journalism stress the reporters' duty to gather facts regardless of their implications, to expose wrongdoings, and to insure that the public learns of the activities of governmental officials.

This paradigm of performance is socially reinforced and monopolizes public attention. It gives apparent proof of the health of the free marketplace of ideas and masks the extent to which journalists are dependent upon public officials and pronouncements for news and the reciprocal relationships that develop from this dependence.

The endurance of the *Washington Post* in pursuing the Watergate story is the material of legend and reaffirms socially accepted meaning. The government attempted to dissuade the *Post* from pursuing the story. The Post Newsweek Company was threatened with the loss of profitable TV licenses in Florida, it watched the stock of the *Post* drop sharply, and it suffered a White House counterattack led by the president's press secretary; but the publisher, editors, and reporters stayed with the story.[14] The resignations of Haldeman and Ehrlichman vindicated the newspaper, and the reporters Carl Bernstein and Bob Woodward received the Pulitzer Prize for their steadfastness and ingenuity in uncovering the story.

It is no denigration of the *Post*'s achievement to underscore the quality of legendary devotion to professional norms or to argue that it is the exception which proves the rule. No newspaper or TV news organization has the money, time, or resources to independently investigate every important story, and these shortcomings create the conditions under which journalists rely on government handouts.[15] While the *Post* investigated, the rest of the Washington press corps, behaving in more typical fashion, attended Ronald Ziegler's briefings and reported official statements, announcements, and press conferences.

The achievement of Bernstein and Woodward reaffirmed liberal perceptions of the role of the press and obscured the extent to which the reporters were dependent on government for the Watergate story. Their search for material resembled typical behavior in that their story was pieced together from records compiled by government and tips from sources in government.

14. James McCartney, "The Washington Post and Watergate: How Two Davids Slew Goliath," *Columbia Journalism Review* (July/August 1973):18–19.
15. Leon V. Sigal, *Reporters and Officials: The Organization and Politics of News Making* (Lexington: D. C. Heath, 1973).

Don't Blame the People has 311 pages of examples of the mediocrity and timidity of the media of communication. If reporters do investigate, their stories are often squelched because publishers prefer to avoid controversy, are biased ideologically, or fear the economic repercussions of a story.[16] If controversial stories are newsworthy, their placement in relation to other stories, or the headlines that attract reader attention, serves to reassure the public, allay disquiet about contemporary problems, or create or destroy the images of politicians.[17]

The contrast between exemplary behavior and routine behavior is great, but exemplary behavior attracts the more important response from elites and much of the public. Exemplary behavior gives credence to extant beliefs about the capability of a free press to limit an incumbent regime's ability to tamper with communications and serves to allay misgivings about the quality of press coverage. These beliefs are shaped by societal norms which assume that the press provides a neutral summary of facts to serve as the base for rational discussions of the alternatives. When the press fails to perform this task, criticism overlooks institutional dependencies and focuses on individual shortcomings and lack of resources.

For example, a recent critique of media coverage of Congress claimed that Congress and the media were partners in propaganda. Too many newsmen did not investigate congressional news releases and simply passed them to the public as fact, and too many local TV stations present public relations shots of congressmen as news. These conditions are correctable: the remedy is an independent, professional news service, such as the Capitol Hill News Service, which would eliminate propaganda by providing the intensive coverage of congressmen that voters need to make intelligent decisions.[18]

The obvious remedy for inadequate performance seriously underestimates the government's central position in the channels of communication and the control afforded by this position. The media of communication are closely bound to the institutions of government. Newsmen are not only dependent on an incumbent regime for the

---

16. Robert Cirino, *Don't Blame the People: How the News Media Use Bias Distortion and Censorship to Manipulate Public Opinion* (New York: Vintage Books, 1972), pp. 63–102.

17. Ibid., pp. 134–79.

18. Ben H. Bagdikian, "Congress and the Media: Partners in Propaganda," *Columbia Journalism Review* (January/February 1974):3–10.

official version of what is happening, they are even dependent on government officials for critical evaluations. Douglas Cater noted that

> the primary cause for the almost constant revelation of behind-the-scenes episodes of government is the power struggle that goes on within the government itself or among the governments doing business in Washington.[19]

Journalistic norms mandate that newsmen be scrupulous about the facts. But facts contain contingencies and can be ignored or dismissed unless they are supported by authority. Even to reveal the secrets of government, an official imprimatur is necessary before an allegation of fact has the power to move the public. Government officials are the source of news, and the resulting dependence permeates critical as well as laudatory stories. The position of the press places constraints on behavior and limits their ability to perform as guardians of the people's right to know.

CONCLUSION

Public expectations affect the credibility of facts and their interpretation. The symbolism of democratic government predisposes the public to accept government's part in gathering, shaping, and presenting the facts. As long as the actions of government conform to expectations, there is little likelihood that government's role in the formation of communications will be perceived, let alone criticized. Even when elites and much of the public become disenchanted with an incumbent regime, their skepticism about the performance of incumbents is accompanied by their proclamation of need for real leaders, especially for a president who can transform the confusions of politics into a coherent and meaningful configuration.

A Harris survey showed that 76 percent of a national cross section of 1,503 households felt that too many government leaders were in politics for personal and financial gain and did not share the idealism of the people.[20] The survey was taken during a period of

19. Douglas Cater, "Secrets, Scoops and Leaks," in *The Politics of The Federal Bureaucracy*, ed. Alan A. Altshuler (New York: Dodd, Mead & Company, 1973), p. 395.

20. Louis Harris, "Discontent with U.S. Leadership," printed in *The Chicago Tribune*, May 16, 1974, section 1, p. 19.

intensive media coverage of the misdeeds of the Nixon administration and daily revelations about the corruptions of Watergate. The administration was unable to use its position to conceal its misdeeds, and public dissatisfaction with the Nixon presidency was pervasive. Nevertheless, the survey reported that 60 percent of the people who were queried believed that "most people are too quick to condemn most things government leaders do," and 44 percent felt that "the way the media treat government leaders, they have little chance of succeeding in the public's eye."[21]

The reservoir of public support for real leadership suggested by this survey is one example of the relationship between public expectations and perceptions of the operation of government and the behavior of leaders. Public expectations are the foundation on which the framework of meaning is built, and herein lies their potency. The strength of democratic symbols, their ability to survive the misdeeds of an incumbent regime, and the capacity of symbols to predispose the public to perceive the world of politics in predictable configurations affect assessments of government officials and the performance of the media and preclude an easy transformation of the system. The public has an investment in meaning because the costs of rejection are uncertainty, incoherence, and perhaps chaos.

Elites and the public have been urged so often to conform to the ideas of democratic government that the exhortations appear banal and of no significance. But this rhetoric reassures the public about the routine performance of government and generates a climate of acceptance for governmental policies, making it possible to label "information" as deviant behavior. When criticism focuses on deviant behavior, deviants are expected to reform, complicating premises are dismissed, and the perception of alternatives is reduced. The momentum of the continuing operation of government serves as background and reinforcement for this interpretation of data. Government by routine operation shapes beliefs about which data are revelant and the implications of data. The control afforded by this ability is more powerful and less susceptible to checks than the techniques of secrecy and progaganda.

21. Ibid.

5

The Information Marketplace

ITZHAK GALNOOR

Secrecy in public affairs is said to be needed in order to protect a public interest, which is judged to be, on balance, more important than other public interests. In external affairs the public interest to be protected is usually national security and the effective conduct of diplomatic relations with other countries. In the context of government activities related to domestic affairs—which is the subject of this chapter—the important public interests to be protected are usually the efficiency of the governing process and the privacy of individuals, groups, and organizations.

A functional way to look at this issue is to regard information as a commodity in the political and administrative marketplace where various suppliers and customers operate.[1] Government, albeit a major supplier of information, is also a customer of the information required for policymaking, feedback, and support. Demand for public information is therefore based on the need to know, and the "price" paid for it is determined by the benefits the receiver expects to derive.

Group pluralism as a supplement to democratic representation is

This is a modified version of my article "Government Secrecy: Exchanges, Intermediaries, and Middlemen," in *Public Administration Review* 35, 1 (January–February 1975):32–42. I would like to thank the American Society for Public Administration for permission to use this article.

1. For a discussion of information as a political resource, see Warren F. Ilchman and Norman T. Uphoff, *The Political Economy of Change* (Berkeley: University of California Press, 1971), p. 67.

the theoretical basis of this approach: the interplay of interests in which everyone has an equal opportunity to form a pressure group and try to influence government. Contacts between government and groups and the trading of information is a necessity because of the complexity of modern life and the intensity of government involvement in social services. Groups and organizations need intelligence about government operations, not to satisfy curiosity, but in order to survive. Government, on the other hand, cannot survive without close cooperation from private groups. The task of governing has become too complex, and public officials have a critical need to exchange information and maintain alliances with nongovernmental groups. In short, the exchange marketplace is functional, and it makes government more responsive.

This approach to government secrecy obviously comes close to describing reality. As a normative paradigm, however, it ignores well-known "imperfections" in the information marketplace and does not provide solutions to the problem posed by government's propensity to withhold information and to engage in propaganda.

In more general terms, this approach ignores the fact that secrecy is the *added value* of the information commodity in the exchange marketplace. Value fluctuates according to circulation and the number of knowers. Access, rather than being an absolute right or a legally defined property, is a process whereby data becomes a means of influence and power.

PRACTICAL ARRANGEMENTS FOR EXCHANGES

It can be argued that there is no such thing as total government secrecy. Only a small amount of information pertaining to military plans or diplomatic negotiations is totally monopolized by a few authorized officials. Even in sacred areas of security and foreign affairs, most of the classified information is known to "outsiders" such as foreign adversaries or trusted confidants.[2] The clandestine

2. Attempts to really do something secretly in government require extraordinary precautions. In the July 1963 negotiations with the Soviet Union over a nuclear test ban treaty, a special cable system had to be installed in order to keep it secret within the State Department secrecy apparatus. See David Wise, *The Politics of Lying* (New York: Random House, 1973), p. 77.

bombing of Cambodia by the United States up to May 1970 was no secret to the people in the area when the bombs started to fall; French officials knew about the secret preparations in Great Britain for the Suez campaign in 1956; the International Telephone and Telegraph Company (ITT) seems to have had access to classified government information when it became involved in the election in Chile in 1970. All of these transactions are reciprocal, and access to information is gained on an exchange basis. Officials are prevented from disclosing information by organizational loyalty and secrecy oaths, but they have numerous opportunities to circumvent these restrictions by leaks, the cultivation of clientele groups, or—as a last resort—thunderous resignations.

In domestic affairs the need for officials to share information is even more acute, and few things can be kept secret for very long. Information as such is not secret. The context of a certain piece of information in the policy-making process and the additional pieces that can solve the jigsaw puzzle are the commodities that administrators can bring to the marketplace. We can also witness a tendency toward secrecy within secrecy in the executive itself. Not only are "second opinions" not sought by one department from another, but also vital information is mutually concealed or used for manipulations. The ability to withhold information from the other governing bodies and to determine with whom to share it is one of the strongest manipulative powers of the executive in modern democratic states.

At the same time, an important phenomenon has been observed by students of pressure groups: The really significant public will consists, as far as government departments are concerned, of opinions articulated by recognized groups.[3] Consequently, a new kind of government machinery not yet fully explored by students of public administration has emerged. It consists of complex systems of private and public organizations, of providers and consumers of public services in areas such as defense, transportation, education, housing, and health. Neither libertarian democratic theory nor constitutional and legal provisions can reveal much about the functioning of these modern systems. The new democratic Leviathan, according to Robert Dahl, is based on a consensus of professional leaders in highly

3. Graeme C. Moddie and Gerald Studdert-Kennedy, *Opinions, Publics and Pressure Groups* (London: Allen & Unwin, 1970), pp. 95–96; Lester W. Milbrath, *The Washington Lobbyists* (Chicago: Rand McNally, 1963).

organized elites who constitute a small part of the citizen body, as well as on compromises ironed out by a process of technical bargains.[4]

The very basis of justifying some measure of administrative discretion has been eroded when preliminary consultations are carried out within inner circles that include selected outsiders. Government cannot claim executive privilege for information that it is willing to disclose to co-opted or self-appointed guardians of particular interests. If this system worked perfectly, each legitimate interest would have found its place within the overlapping networks. But the very basis of these communications is the *selectivity* of organizations, groups, and members of the mass media. The ability to exclude establishes these networks as formidable gatekeepers armed with the political power that goes with it.

In pluralistic terms, lobbying entails an ever-present conflict between adversary and cooperative relationships with governments. But there are some groups that have "made it" and become established. A group becomes established when the option of open conflict has been replaced by some form of mutual accommodation with government decision makers. The first commandment of the lobby, wrote S. Finer, is "get advance intelligence."[5] The established groups can afford to be concerned with the second commandment of lobbying—direct influence. Exclusiveness (and the secrecy that makes it possible) is the chief concern of the established lobby.

The less-established lobby operates in an environment where there are still no dominating arrangements with government, no prescribed channels of communication, and no fixed commitments on either side. In some cases the groups will offer information, money, prestige, or votes in exchange for information (and influence) secretly provided. In other cases, a cooperative relationship is rejected, and access is attempted through pressure tactics and public campaigns.

However, there are also organizations, groups, and individuals that are out of the information exchange marketplace altogether. They cannot or do not want to have discreet relationships with government. The reason for a group's position at this end of the lobbying continuum vary. Some groups, such as the various nuclear disarmament societies, simply refuse to "discuss" their position with gov-

4. Robert A. Dahl, ed., *Political Oppositions in Western Democracies* (New Haven: Yale University Press, 1966), pp. 399–400.

5. S. E. Finer, *Anonymous Empire*, 2d ed. (London: Pall Mall Press, 1966), p. 56.

ernment because of their uncompromising demands.[6] Others, such as the environmental groups in the United States up to the mid-1960s, could not even begin to influence policymaking because they had nothing important to offer in exchange for governmental information.

The boundaries between these clusters are blurred, and the shape of these networks changes frequently. Moreover, one can hardly separate the process of *obtaining* information from the process of *using* it for political and administrative leverage. Nevertheless, some practical insights can be gained by focusing on the dynamics of secrecy arrangements in government-lobby relationships.

THE ESTABLISHED LOBBY

Within the established lobby there are certain groups that have opted for a formal role in government decision making and have become in fact part of the administrative machinery. The Ministry of Agriculture in Great Britain is controlled by the farmers mainly through their National Farmers Union. The same can be said of the labor and commerce departments and the veterans administration in the United States. In these cases, interest groups share not only information but also responsibility for government policies and secrecy procedures. They are ready to trade independence for direct influence and are willing to forgo the option of exerting public pressure for greater control of their special interests. They sometimes find it extremely difficult to switch back to conventional lobbying and pressure campaigns because of their public image as an accessory of government.[7]

In Great Britain there seems to be more tolerance of political lobbying and of MPs representing special interests in Parliament.[8] At the same time, a certain aura of conspiracy surrounds the functioning of the lobby within the administrative machinery. The exchange relationships in Great Britain are more institutionalized, and those groups that have made it can be regarded almost as H. M. Loyal Lobby. But the essence of these exchanges are quite similar

6. For an account of such a group encounter with the British Official Secrets Act, see David Williams, *Not in the Public Interest: The Problem of Security in Democracy* (London: Hutchinson, 1965), pp. 106–112.

7. David Truman, *The Governmental Process* (New York: Alfred A. Knopf, 1964), p. 461.

8. Samuel H. Beer, "Pressure Groups and Parties in Britain," *The American Political Science Review* 40, 1(March 1956):5.

to those in the United States and equally secretive. There are "continual day-to-day contacts between public bureaucrats in government departments and private bureaucrats in the offices of the great pressure groups."[9] In Great Britain this is quite surprising in view of the draconian prohibitions of the Official Secrets Act on passing official information to outsiders.

Closely aligned with the established lobby is the machinery of advisory bodies. These organizations are formally outside of government but for all practical purposes serve as a meeting ground for government and special interests. "What the government basically wants from advisory committees," observed Harold Seidman "is not 'expert' advice, although occasionally this is a factor, but support."[10] In the same vein, what the constituencies want from advisory bodies is access to rule-making information and direct influence. A special study prepared for a House subcommittee conducting hearings on access to public information lists 1,940 advisory commissions within the federal executive branch alone.[11] They include presidential advisory committees such as the National Aeronautics and Space Council and the President's Commission on School Finance as well as department committees such as the prestigious Defense Department Science Board, the powerful Business Advisory Board to the Commerce Department, and the State Department Committee on Art in Embassies. A British study reports the same phenomenon in scope and substance.[12]

The expansion of the administrative machinery represents an institutionalization of the symbiotic relationship between groups and government whereby the exchange relationships become legal, fluid channels of communication become prescribed, and confrontations are removed from the public arena into closed chambers. The American study found out that many meetings held by advisory committees were not announced, only 51 percent of them were open to the public, 68 percent of the committees failed to transcribe their proceedings,

9. Ibid., p. 7.

10. Harold Seidman, *Politics, Position and Power* (New York: Oxford University Press, 1970), p. 239.

11. U.S. Congress, House, Committee on Government Operations, *Public Access to Information From Executive Branch Advisory Groups*, 92d Cong., 2d sess., part 9, (June 6, 8, and 19, 1972), p. 3424.

12. PEP, *Advisory Committees in British Government* (London: Allen & Unwin, 1961).

and not all committees that had transcripts made them available to the public.[13]

Modern democracies are also characterized by a great number of professional mediators who interact between the citizen and the government. They are the middlemen who have become familiar faces in the corridors of power. They sell accessibility to public officials to those who can afford the costs involved.

In developing countries these exchanges are well documented.[14] Government officials are accessible and provide information if they are approached by recognized arbitrators. This is done as a favor, especially if nepotism exists, or on a give-and-take basis. If corruption prevails, the fee paid by the interested party is shared by the officials and the middleman. The same phenomena, only on a much more sophisticated level, can be observed also in developed countries. There are fewer studies of the role of the middleman in the United States and British governments. The private detective who exchanges information with the police officer or the scientist discussing research funds with the head of the grant institution in a private club appear mainly in fiction and popular movies, perhaps because they know how to conceal their secrets.

Some professional middlemen tend to become generalists, establish themselves as Whitehall or White House liaisons, and deal only with matters of high importance; while others utilize the whole array of their contacts as former government employees. Middlemen may also restrict their services to functional areas, such as health, education, energy, and even poverty.

The best preparation for this kind of career is apparently legal training. It has been estimated that the majority of professional lobbyists in the United States are lawyers.[15] Watergate has revealed the extent of their involvement as secret emissaries between government and outside groups. When it became necessary, another group of lawyers stepped forward to do the cleaning up. In addition to lawyers, we can find a host of other middlemen with professional

13. House, Committee on Government Operations, *Public Access to Information*, p. 3424.

14. See, for example, Lucian W. Pye, "Administrators, Agitators, and Brokers," *Public Opinion Quarterly* 22 (Fall 1958):342–348.

15. *The Washington Lobby* (Washington, D.C.: Congressional Quarterly, Inc., 1971), p. 3.

training in public relations and marketing; finance, accounting, banking, and taxation; journalism and communication; labor relations and other forms of arbitration.

Independent intermediaries willing to sell their services to whoever requires it are less common in Great Britain. It goes against the highly structured nature of contacts between public administrators and pressure groups and the disciplinary restraint imposed by political parties and ideologies. The British liaison experts have to work within the established networks in which government departments, political parties, and pressure groups operate.[16] Their success is measured by their ability to ring up their "opposite numbers" in Whitehall and exchange information on a first-name basis.[17] Government officials tend to respond favorably to this development because it facilitates their dealing with the public and confines communication to a few knowledgeable people. Instead of an anonymous and annoying citizen, they deal with a reliable expert in the same way they deal with other interest groups. This arrangement also creates ample opportunities for information exchanges and the manipulation of outsiders. Favorable reaction by public officials is by no means universal. In some cases the middlemen are felt to be too strong, while in others the department cherishes its direct contact with the public. The department may then decide to employ its own spokesmen who serve as information brokers for middlemen and for the public.

We cannot conclude this section on the established lobby without noting the direct and unheralded access that certain interests have to the centers of power. John A. McCone, former head of the CIA and later a director of the ITT Corporation, did not need formal representation in either government departments or advisory groups, or for that matter the services of middlemen, to gain access to information pertaining to his corporation's interests.[18] Needless to say, being discreet is the absolute rule of such direct access.

This function is performed in many Western democracies by political parties when political affiliations are the most important credentials for administrators, legislators, interest groups, and influential individuals. In Great Britain the cabinet system makes room

16. Committee on Intermediaries, Report (London: HMSO, Cmnd. 7904, March 1950), para. 6.

17. Beer, "Pressure Groups and Parties in Britain," p. 8.

18. See his testimony before a special subcommittee of the Senate Foreign Relations Committee as reported in *The New York Times*, March 21–22, 1973.

for strong influence by the parties on the executive, but there is some evidence that the role of parties as information channels is declining. Even MPs may get better access to government in their capacity as members of pressure groups.[19] Furthermore, interest groups prefer to direct their lobbying efforts to government and not to Parliament.[20]

In the United States the institutionalized role of political parties is overshadowed by their function as a clearinghouse for campaign contributions. Between elections the established lobby, notably private business and multinational corporations, can bypass the parties and enjoy direct contacts with the centers of power. Their lobbying activities are not covered by the Legislative Reorganization Act of 1946. Organizations such as General Motors, Ford, the American Banking Association, and the National Rifle Association are not registered as lobbying associations in Washington.[21] The fact that there are fewer studies of their "liaison offices" in Washington is quite indicative of their more secretive deliberations with the executive.

THE LESS-ESTABLISHED LOBBY

Groups and organizations are less established when a choice between symbiotic and independent relationships with government is still possible. "Pure" lobbying needs a free democratic process where interests can obtain information and exert influence openly and in accordance with their moral, social, and political merits. It is this role of outside groups in a pluralistic society that so impressed Tocqueville: "Intermediary bodies stand between the isolated individual and the tyrannical potential of the majority or the state."[22]

But the political price of independence may be intolerably high. Some groups are not "established" simply because they have not been recognized as responsible or respectable enough to share government confidence. They may encounter great difficulties in merely finding

19. R. T. McKenzie, "Parties, Pressure Groups & British Political Process," *Political Quarterly* 24 (1958); S. H. Beer, *Modern British Politics* (London: Faber, 1965).

20. Anthony Barker and Michael Rush, *The Member of Parliament and His Information* (London: Allen & Unwin, 1970), pp. 119–121.

21. Lawrence Gilson, *Money and Secrecy* (New York: Praeger, 1972), p. 9.

22. Alexis de Tocqueville, *Democracy in America* (New York: Alfred A. Knopf, 1945), p. 191.

out what is going on. The various small groups supporting some form of national health insurance in the United States are a good example of this case.[23] Government may be willing to share relevant information if a group agrees to join the inner circle, and the group may be willing to do so. The trouble with this perfectly normal political process is that at a certain point the balance may tip overwhelmingly in the direction of the executive and its satellites. At this point, more information (and influence) will be denied to outsiders and higher prices will have to be paid in order to become established. Another example is the process whereby scientific and research groups gain exclusive access to governmental information sources (and their financial resources). Thus a majority of the consultants to the National Institutes of Health were also members of organizations that received most NIH grants.[24] The transcripts and minutes of these bodies were regularly withheld from the public.[25] We should note in passing that government dominance is not necessarily the outcome of symbiotic relations. Collaboration between the executive and interest groups may turn into colonization of the former by the latter. In this case, it is government that loses the option of choosing between symbiotic and independent relationships with established groups.

The real stuff of government-groups interaction is usually not exposed. The prevailing rule of confidentiality is observed as long as it serves both sides. As noted by Francis Rourke, "secrecy is not exclusively advantageous to bureaucratic organizations themselves. It serves the interests of a wide variety of groups outside the government, and its continuation is in no small measure sustained by their support."[26]

The mass media also belong to this cluster through their role as brokers of information between the government and the attentive publics. The mass media and every individual newsman face the dilemma of cooperative versus adversary relationship with the executive. To the degree that the first is chosen, we find more informed

23. For a general survey, see Alice M. Rivlin, "Agreed: Here Comes National Health Insurance," *The New York Times Magazine*, July 21, 1974.

24. U.S. Congress, House, Committee on Government Operations, *The Administration of Research Grants in the Public Service H.R. 800*, 90th Cong., 1st sess., pp. 61–62.

25. Gilson, *Money and Secrecy*, p. 24.

26. Francis E. Rourke, "Bureaucratic Secrecy and Its Constituents," *The Bureaucrat* 1, 2 (Summer 1972):119.

newsmen and more confidential information passed on to them "off the record" or as "backgrounders." If the adversary relationship predominates, the mass media encounter greater difficulties in securing access and tend to use publicity as their main pressure device. The phenomenon is well known and has recently received some documentation.[27]

The mass media profit professionally and economically from access to public officials. They can use information to sell advertisements and to make a profit. They also have a vested interest in secrecy because it raises the value of published information. Secrecy is sometimes the process whereby trivial information becomes valuable news. The same piece of concealed information that serves as a source of bureaucratic power can serve as a source of media power when published as inside information, leaks, and scoops. Media can become fully "established" if fully controlled by government. By contrast, a free press retains the ability to use the weapon of publicity to prevent government domination. The Nixon administration was not known for its close friendship with the media, but one remarkable aspect of the discussions revealed in the White House transcripts is the repetitive reference to "cultivation of the press." Mutual cultivation is a good description of the two-sided relationship between the media and public officials. Mass media organizations, like other pressure groups, can exchange independence for private knowledge as well as publicity for the prestige and other benefits that go with belonging to the inner circle. Another danger not entirely unimaginable in a modern society is the formation of an interest amalgamation, with the media as part of it. In such cases reporting concentrates on "purely" governmental affairs (usually foreign relations) or on crime and sex, thus providing little information on the real happenings of governmental activities through and with other interest groups.

In the same way, the mass media's crusade on behalf of the people's right to know can take place in either type of relationship with government. As an outsider, the mass media crusade may aim at establishing an alternative route for opening up the mouths and files of government officials. As an insider, it may only pay lip service to professional values.

27. For instance, Ben H. Bagdikian, *The Effete Conspiracy and Other Crimes by the Press* (New York: Harper & Row, 1972).

The media's position is also influenced by the general political and administrative culture in a country. For instance, newsmen covering Whitehall are usually deprived of the excitement that their colleagues in Washington enjoy—being used as tools in fights between officials and departments of the same government. Moreover, "the automatic instinct of the British citizen is to identify not with the Press, but rather with the victims of its curiosity—be they public figures or (much more understandably) private individuals."[28] In contrast, the mass media in the United States have revealed both the negative and the positive potential of the cooperative-advisory nexus.[29] On the one hand, established relationships may turn the media into an instrument of propaganda.[30] It makes little difference, in this respect, whether the propaganda originates in the government, other pressure groups, or the mass media themselves. Dependence is disguised and very little is known about the mass media's policies and campaign decisions.[31] On the other hand, the position of the mass media as a powerful mediator between government and the public enables the mass media to become extremely useful watchdogs of democratic processes in general and of administrators' behavior in particular. Mass media, like the other groups and organizations in this cluster, become fully "established" when the possibility of *open* conflict with government is no longer an option.

THE NONESTABLISHED LOBBY

This cluster includes groups and individuals that are not engaged in exchange relationships with the guardians of public information. A distinction should be made between those who are too ignorant to

28. Anthony Howard, "Behind the Bureaucratic Curtain," *The New York Times Magazine*, October 23, 1966, p. 94.

29. Edward A. Shils, *The Torment of Secrecy* (Glencoe, Ill.: The Free Press, 1956), p. 52.

30. See Carl Friedrich, *The Pathology of Politics* (New York: Harper & Row, 1972), pp. 196, 206–207.

31. Wilbur L. River and Wilbur Schram, *Responsibility in Mass Communication*, rev. ed. (New York: Harper & Row, 1969), p. 54. See also Jerome A. Baron, "Access to the Press—A New First Amendment Right," *Harvard Law Review* 80 (June 1967):1644–1678.

know the exchange game or too weak to play it and those who decided to use publicity instead of secret cooperation.

The first category includes groups and individual citizens whose interests are not organized, whose awareness of political and administrative procedures is uncertain, and whose demands for information are inexact. They are the new "politically illiterate" masses whom the right to know is supposed to protect.[32] In a different context these groups have been identified by Murray Edelman as those who are more interested in the symbolic values of politics and administration.[33] Deprived of access to operational information and the tangible benefits that come with it, their quiescence is secured by the appearance and images of democratic processes. Thus dramatic moves such as the enactment of a new freedom of information act substitute symbolic reassurances for real change. By adjusting to symbolic values, these groups become defenders of a system that favors the more organized groups.[34]

Studies of public opinion, mass communications, and participation have refuted time and again the notion that citizens in democracies are capable of indicating "where the shoe pinches." It takes access, advance intelligence, and familiarity with bureaucratic networks to turn citizen complaints into public policy.

These requirements raise the question about the effectiveness of the other types of groups in this cluster—promotional groups, civic associations, and public interest groups. By definition these groups have no definite clientele. They try to articulate the public interest by promoting policies that are not of exclusive benefit to their members. They also try to make governments more open by using the whip of publicity. Citizens can write letters to newspapers, send complaints to their representatives, or use formal procedures such as the ombudsman or the courts. Sometimes the mere threat of publicity is enough to start a cycle of disclosure. In many cases, however, government is immune to these pressures, based as they are on partial information that can easily be ignored.

What the British call "cause groups" is not a new phenomenon.

32. Stein Rokkan, *Citizens, Elections, Parties* (New York: McKay, 1970), pp. 31–32.
33. Murray Edelman, *The Symbolic Uses of Politics* (Urbana: University of Illinois Press, 1964), pp. 35–36.
34. Ibid., p. 40.

The National Council for Civil Liberties was established in the 1930s to articulate demands of the disadvantaged or aggrieved.[35] The British groups are more promotional in nature and less involved in direct confrontations with government. A British Ralph Nader will probably not go as far as advocating that civil servants should "blow the whistle" and reveal government secrets whenever they think it is morally right to do so.[36]

In the United States the emergence of the "citizens lobby" is aimed at counterbalancing the dominant influence of the established private-interest groups. The purpose of Public Citizen, Inc., an organization established by Ralph Nader, is to help citizens acquire the know-how to protect themselves against private industry and government bureaucracies.[37] The targets of Common Cause's activities are "politicians who ignore the people, unresponsive bureaucracies, and behind-the-scenes betrayals of the public interest."[38] The following two are among the lines of citizen's actions that are suggested:

1. Enact laws prohibiting secret meetings of all public bodies and enabling public access to legislatures, committees, advisory boards, commissions, and so on.

2. Enact lobbying disclosure laws requiring registration of any lobbyist and middleman who communicates with legislators or public officials with the purpose of influencing their actions.

New laws such as these can be circumvented as easily as the old ones. They may also have their strongest impact on the symbolic rather than the pragmatic level. But in addition to using legal remedies, groups like Common Cause try to exert direct pressure on government operations. They are also engaged in specific projects aimed at spreading information that a problem exists. The main difference between these efforts and traditional lobbying is the attempt to conduct them publicly. It is a serious effort to change the mode of government interaction with groups and therefore goes to the heart of the matter. An organization that can effectively use the publicity weapon to call

35. Robert Benewick, "British Pressure Group Politics: The National Council for Civil Liberties," *The Annals of the American Academy of Political and Social Sciences* 413 (May 1974):145–157; Peggy Crane, *Participation in Democracy* (London: The Fabian Society, December 1962).

36. Ralph Nader et al., eds., *Whistle Blowing* (New York: Bantam, 1972).

37. See, for instance, Donald K. Ross, *A Public Citizen's Action Manual* (New York: Grossman, 1973).

38. John W. Gardner, "Introduction," in Gilson, *Money and Secrecy*, p. xiii.

attention to latent interests of various neglected groups is operating in the political and administrative marketplace. The initial success of the environmental coalition that supported the discontinuance of federal funding for the supersonic transport (SST) in 1971 indicates the possibilities in this area. More important, perhaps, is the fact that this coalition defeated an intensive campaign by SST supporters led by the AFL-CIO, the Aerospace Industries Association, the United Steel Workers of America, and the Air Lines Pilots Association.[39] So far, most of the efforts of public interest groups have been aimed at reforming the law and changing the behavior of legislators. Changing the secretive mode of operations of the executive and the established lobbyists might prove to be much more difficult.

THE UNWRITTEN RULES OF GOVERNMENT SECRECY

Imagine the reaction of a public official when approached by a citizen who demands to know what is going on in his department and cites the right to know as a justification for this request. What is the startled official most likely to do? We may assume that he would not use the occasion to lecture the citizen about the right of the public to exercise control through publicity not being an absolute right or about the need for discreet and confidential deliberation. More likely, the official would choose one or more of the following options.

Being practical, he would try to find out why and what specific information is requested ("Who sent you? What is bothering you? Are you a journalist?"). For him the general democratic stipulation about the right to know has to be translated into pragmatic "need to know" reasons. Hence the first unwritten rule of government secrecy reads:

> Information requests will be denied on the threshold unless accompanied by specific need-to-know justifications.

Being cautious or uninterested, the official may refuse to answer, quoting the civil service code or other regulations and laws. He will then probably refer the concerned citizen to an official spokesman, the information bureau or the complaint department ("They handle public relations; besides, I am too busy"). In this case, the citizen's

39. For a full report, see *The Washington Lobby*, pp. 108–112.

legal right, if any, can be easily countered with government legal provisions for withholding information or with practical arrangements prohibiting free access. The second unwritten rule thus reads:

> Legal provisions and practical obstacles aimed at preventing disclosure of official information are used whenever an exchange process does not take place.

Being interested, the official may try to find out what he, his group, or his organization can get in exchange for divulging information ("I will tell you, but don't forget to mention . . . ; I will tell you, but off the record," and so on). Thus the encounter turns into a barter, and the citizen, although he is an outsider according to the official definition of "authorized personnel," may gain access by virtue of his ability to reciprocate. Excluding the illegal cases in which official information is traded for money and other tangible goods, the exchanges we are referring to are functional and aimed at facilitating the governing process. This unwritten rule reads:

> Regardless of the legal provisions, official information is divulged to selected confidants in return for some equivalent and on the basis of mutual interests.

Finally, a great deal of information about government activities gets published. But this is not necessarily a result of democratic principles or constitutional and legal provisions aimed at securing freedom of information. Government can supply information *independently* of demand, for purposes of educating the people, public relations, propaganda, or brainwashing. At the same time, the effectiveness of citizens' demands is usually a function of their ability to mobilize attractive political resources and exchange them for otherwise undisclosed information. This tends to discriminate against those citizens whose interests are diffused, more intangible and less organized.

Hence government secrecy is not an isolated process. Focusing on the information marketplace reveals the practical and rather neglected dimensions, but the broader context of secrecy is the political and administrative culture of the governing process. As the laws we have described operate, there is a high probability that the aggregation of information which circulates as a result of demand and supply will not add up to the desirable equilibrium between secrecy and publicity in democracies.

The Generic Secrets of Government Decision Making

DAVID CURZON

When we speak of the public's "right to know," what is it that we refer to? What is it that we wish disclosed? What is hidden by government secrecy?

Since secrecy in government is virtually coextensive with it and therefore as complex as government itself, there must be a variety of approaches to the study of secrecy. One could, for example, examine secrecy in relation to the individual citizen's privacy, or the symbolic uses of public information, or the doctrine of executive privilege, as is done in other chapters in this book. But secrecy also functions to hide the deliberations preceding decisions, and it is this aspect of secrecy that I wish to examine here. In order to do this it is first necessary to describe this deliberative process in general terms, and the first half of this chapter will be taken up with this task. The vocabulary introduced there will then be used to show the problems that keeping the deliberative process secret can hide and exacerbate.

For illustration I will make use of the memoranda, reports, and transcripts and summaries of conversations that comprise the Pentagon Papers, since this is the type of material in which the secrets of government decisions are embodied and in which they have been and will be disclosed.[1] The use of excerpts from the Pentagon Papers, however, is open to several misunderstandings, so that it seems necessary to anticipate these reactions in the reader.

First, this paper is not primarily concerned with the Vietnam War but rather with the way in which high-level decisions are made and the generic problems of the process.

Second, while taking the Pentagon Papers at face value, I am aware that the face is often a mask. All bureaucratic documents are part of bureaucratic politics and usually do not accurately or fully reflect the views of their authors.

Third, a great many of the significant determinants of decisions are not written down by the participants and are perhaps not even consciously understood by them.

There is, however, no case study or historical interpretation intended in my quotation from the Pentagon Papers; I draw on them for purely illustrative purposes in the first part of this paper. The unspoken, unconscious, and implicit aspects of policy formulation are considered in the second part.

POLICY-LEVEL DECISIONS: A VOCABULARY

An examination of the documents of the Pentagon Papers reveals a world of exploratory discussion in which issues of fact, value, and action are mixed together. None of these elements is given; all are subject to query and disagreement within an unspecified, but narrowly circumscribed, range of deliberation. Although the deliberations have a logical tone, it is a verbal, and not a mathematical or quantitative logic, and in order to describe it we must use a vocabulary that will accurately convey its essence. For this purpose, I wish to introduce the following terms taken, with modifications, from the early writings of Herbert Simon:[2]

1. premise of reality
2. premise of value
3. concept of action

1. The quotations and the page citations in the text are from *The Pentagon Papers* (New York: Bantam Books, 1971). While this edition is a drastic abridgment, it is adequate as a source of illustration and widely available.
2. Herbert Simon, *Administrative Behavior*, 2d ed. (New York: The Free Press, 1957).

4. rationality
5. bounded deliberation

A premise of reality is an assumption about the world outside the decision-making circle, and since it is a proposition about fact, it may be wrong. The images of reality that guide decisions are made up of many premises. For example, General Maxwell Taylor, in a cabled report to President John F. Kennedy in 1961, stated that "North Vietnam is extremely vulnerable to conventional bombing. . . . There is no case for fearing a mass onslaught of Communist manpower into SVN (South Vietnam) and its neighboring states, particularly if our airpower is allowed a free hand against logistic targets" (*The Pentagon Papers*, p. 143). Taylor's report was an important one, and the premises he formulated conditioned many years of official U.S. thinking on the war. McGeorge Bundy, presidential assistant for national security affairs, used additional premises of reality in advocating a policy of reprisal bombing of North Vietnam some years later. He predicted that the bombing "would have a substantial depressing effect on the morale of Viet Cong cadres in South Vietnam" (p. 426). In these two examples, the premises of reality are expectations, assumptions about the future. But premises of reality can also be about the present and the past. Many of the memos of the Pentagon Papers have a section entitled something like "the present situation," and these sections contain dozens of reality premises. The importance of obtaining images of current reality is heightened in a crisis, but even in the absence of crisis a great deal of organizational effort goes into perceiving and reporting simplified images of the changing world to decision makers. This simplification is necessary, since it is impossible to know reality in its full complexity.

There are two types of "premises of value": objectives and constraints—a distinction now common in modern decision theory. In its mathematical form this theory provides models of maximization in which an objective function is to be maximized subject to constraints, but our subject matter requires a more literary interpretation of these terms, since the objectives and constraints of high-level government decisions are qualitative rather than quantitative and couched in sentences rather than in number and symbol. For example, Robert F. McNamara, former U.S. secretary of defense, formulated U.S. objectives in Vietnam as "preventing the fall of South Vietnam to Communism" (p. 148). Later, in a draft memo of November 6, 1964, McNamara's deputy, John T. McNaughton, formulated the objectives at greater length, giving prominence to the "protection of U.S. reputation as a counter-subversive guarantor." The main political question to ask about objectives, once identified, is: Whose interests and what interests are embodied in them?[3] In the McNaughton example, this question involves seeking an entity such as a class or group whose interests were furthered by the protection of the U.S. reputation as a "counter-subversive guarantor."

Constraints derive from budgetary, legal, moral, electoral, or other considerations. When Bundy, in a memo advocating a policy of "sustained reprisal" bombing of North Vietnam, argues that "the international pressures for negotiation should be quite manageable" (p. 427), he is referring to a potential constraint. Similarly McNamara is alluding to the potential constraints of domestic politics in the U.S. when he says in the 1961 memo quoted above that "it is our feeling that the country will respond better to a firm initial position than to courses of action that lead us in only gradually and that in the meantime are sure to involve casualties" (p. 149).

I have used the term *concepts of action* instead of the more usual term *alternatives* because the latter conveys the sense of already-existing options from which a selection is made. The concepts of action in policy-level decisions, however, do not in general exist prior to images of the future that are developed as deliberations proceed. For example, in a cable of August 29, 1963, to Dean Rusk, former U.S. secretary of state, Henry Cabot Lodge, the former U.S. ambassador to South Vietnam, presented the following concept of action: "We are launched on a course from which there is no respectable turning back: the overthrow of the Diem government" (p. 197). But Rusk, in response, took issue with this concept of action. In a cable of the same date he replied:

> You appear to treat Diem and the Nhus[4] as a single package whereas we had indicated earlier to the Generals that if the Nhus were removed the question of retaining Diem would be up to them. . . . In

3. Bertram Gross, *Organizations and Their Managing* (New York: The Free Press of Glencoe, 1968), p. 298. See also "Political Process," in *International Encyclopedia of the Social Sciences* (New York: Macmillan, 1968).
4. Ngo Dinh Diem was premier of South Vietnam from 1954 to 1963. Ngo Dinh Nhu, his brother and head of the Diem government's secret police, and Nhu's wife were prominent public figures. Diem and Nhu were killed on

any event, I would appreciate your comment on whether any distinction can or should be drawn as between Diem and Counselor and Madame Nhu.

Just as the decision makers' view of reality is made up of many premises, each of which could be challenged in the course of deliberations, so a strategy is made up of many concepts of action, each of which may be debated, bargained over, and modified. Most formal bargaining and negotiation is done in this manner: Words, phrases, and sections of strategic plans and agreements are discussed and modified in a manner that assumes that they are separable.

In practice, these three components of reality—premises of reality, premises of value, and concepts of action—interact strongly. For example, McNamara, in a report of a fact-finding mission to South Vietnam dated December 21, 1963, stated: "The situation is very disturbing. Current trends, unless reversed in the next 2–3 months, will lead to neutralization at best and more likely to a Communist-controlled state" (p. 271). This could be treated purely as a premise of reality and be challenged like any assertion of fact. But this would ignore the implicit value judgment that orients McNamara's entire view of the facts and makes them "disturbing" to him. As Sir Geoffrey Vickers says: "The relation between judgements of fact and of value is close and mutual; for facts are relevant only in relation to some judgement of value and judgements of value are operative only in relation to some configuration of fact."[5] Any two components of decision could be substituted in Vickers's remark and it would remain equally applicable—the relation between premises of reality and concepts of action, and between concepts of action and premises of value is also very "close and mutual." When Taylor says that "North Vietnam is extremely vulnerable to conventional bombing" (p. 143), he is stating a premise of reality about North Vietnam that focuses on an aspect of reality that would have remained unexamined, and indeed could never have been formulated, had not the concept of action *conventional bombing* been in his mind. This strong interaction of the components of decision means that the mixture of reality premises, value premises, and action concepts cohere—they form a

November 1, 1963, in a coup carried out by generals of his own army. The U.S. embassy was in contact with the generals while the coup was being planned, as is indicated in the quotation.

5. Sir Geoffrey Vickers, *The Art of Judgement* (London: University Paperbacks, 1968), p. 40.

viewpoint. When McNamara went on a "fact-finding mission" to South Vietnam, the facts he examined were circumscribed by the current U.S. objectives and strategy. The National Liberation Front of South Vietnam (NLF), in learning what was ostensibly the same reality, may well have agreed on those facts that overlapped, but they would in the main have examined different facts.

This brings us to the important but misleading term *rationality*. Its usage in economic theory, which we will follow here, is that a decision is rational if it is internally consistent. In other words, if, in the minds of the decision makers, the action selected is compatible with the given objectives and constraints and premises of reality, then it is "rational." Rationality in this sense has nothing to do with morality, for the decision makers may ignore moral constraints in formulating their premises of value. Nor does it imply sanity in the sense of acting under accurate premises of reality. It implies only the coherence associated with a consistent viewpoint. For example, if it is a U.S. objective to prevent the "fall" of South Vietnam to the National Liberation Front and if U.S. premises of reality are that North Vietnam controls the National Liberation Front of South Vietnam, that North Vietnam is vulnerable to conventional bombing, and that such bombing would force North Vietnam to use its control to stop the insurgency in the south, then advocating the bombing of North Vietnam would, under this definition, be considered rational since it would be consistent with the premises of reality and value used in the deliberations on policy. Suppose, however, that the objective remained the same but the premises of reality were different: If it was believed that North Vietnam was not vulnerable to conventional bombing, that the National Liberation Front was independent of North Vietnam, and that the causes of the insurgency lay in the conditions of the peasantry or other groups in South Vietnam, and that it would continue unless these conditions were changed, then advocating the conventional bombing of North Vietnam would be irrational in the sense of being inconsistent with these premises of reality.[6]

This concept of rationality as internal consistency is important for

6. Here I have reversed several of the premises of reality simultaneously. If only one is reversed, then a change in the concept of action advocated may not follow.

an understanding of the dynamics of decision processes since it provides the criterion for terminating deliberations. In order to understand this termination it is useful to divide the decision process into three phases—the first being the perception of a problem, the second deliberative search, and the third termination in decision. Sometimes the search is terminated by an act of choice among formulated alternatives. But perhaps more often what happens is that a commitment to a single course of action has developed gradually through the process of deliberation and the search is terminated when a sense of consistency is reached, within the decision-making group, between this concept of action and the premises of reality and value that were adopted implicitly or explicitly by the group. The deliberative process will then have achieved one of its major purposes, which is to arrive at agreement among the participants in the form of a shared rationalization for action. It may be, of course, that events intervene during the deliberations and the discretion on which the search was predicated evaporates, or else circumstances change, presenting a new problem so that the process of search continues or, at any rate, is not terminated by a decision.

The search process is conducted within implicit limits that restrict the deliberations. An example of this restriction is provided by the search for a solution to the problem posed to U.S. decision makers by an impending coup against Diem. The debate in these circles was over whether or not to support the generals planning the coup. There is no evidence in the Pentagon Papers or elsewhere to suggest that the U.S. decision makers considered conducting negotiations with the NLF. Such an action was outside the range of the deliberations, which, in comparison with the range of conceivable debate, or even the range of opinion in the U.S. electorate, was narrowly circumscribed. Borrowing from Simon, we can label this the "bounded nature" of the decision process. This bounding is necessary. It is impossible to exercise choice by first considering all conceivable actions and their implications. However, while the principle of bounded deliberation is common to all human choice, the characteristics of the viewpoint that determines the range of acceptable and unacceptable debate in a particular government decision will vary with the ideology of the participants and the idiosyncracies of the leaders.

THE SECRETS OF GOVERNMENT DECISION MAKING

Now that we have a vocabulary we can make use of it to answer our introductory question: What is hidden by governmental secrecy? Secrecy hides the content of the decision-making process that consists of the premises of reality, the concepts of action, and the objectives and constraints that operate within this bounded deliberative process, and the character of the viewpoint that constrains debate. This answer leads to the real question: What problems might be hidden and exacerbated by keeping this content secret?

1. Secrecy can hide the fact that the premises of reality on which decisions are based can be wrong, or be such gross simplifications that they distort reality, or be deliberately biased in order to protect subordinates from the adverse judgments of a superior, or be based on prejudice and ideology. The advisors surrounding the president, as can be seen in the disclosures available, often formulate premises of reality that display remarkable ignorance. For example, in 1961, speaking as the top U.S. expert on counterinsurgency, General Maxwell Taylor argued that "the North Vietnamese will face severe logistical difficulties in trying to maintain strong forces in the field in South East Asia" (p. 143). But 1961 was just seven years after the same forces in the same area defeated the French in a protracted war in which the logistical capacities of the Viet Minh were a significant element in their victory. These capacities were subsequently demonstrated again by the continuous flow of supplies down the Ho Chi Minh trail from North to South Vietnam under heavy U.S. bombardment. Events have also disproved another of Taylor's premises in the same memorandum, namely that "North Vietnam is extremely vulnerable to conventional bombing" (p. 143). The falsity of this premise could have been predicted at the time for reasons that are similar to the conclusions drawn from the extensive analyses of the effects of bombing during World War II.[7] Yet Taylor's premises, and others equally ignorant and equally important, far from being challenged in the policy deliberations, formed the view of reality that was accepted by the inner circle. The general level of background knowledge operating in the deliberations on the Vietnam War is indicated by Daniel Ellsberg when he says that "there has never been an official of Deputy Assistant Secretary rank or higher (including myself) who

7. See the "Vietnam Bombing Evaluation by the Institute for Defense Analyses," *The Pentagon Papers*, pp. 502–509.

could have passed in office a midterm freshman exam in modern Vietnamese history."[8]

Secrecy not only permits such ignorance to continue unchallenged but creates the climate that makes it inevitable.

The problem of deliberate bias can be illustrated by McNamara's firsthand fact-finding missions to South Vietnam, which were the source of important reports. L. Fletcher Prouty remarks that "McNamara would be taken on an itinerary planned in Washington, he would see 'close-in combat' designed in Washington, and he would receive field data and statistics prepared for him in Washington. All during his visit he would be in the custody of skilled briefers who knew what he should see, whom he should see, and whom he should not see."[9]

The understanding of reality that is most significant in deliberations, however, may be grounded less in facts, even of these kinds, than in ideology, prejudice, and idiosyncrasy. The reality premises contained in reports, briefings, and memos have to enter minds in order to have any effect on actions. The limitations of these minds to receive and comprehend the strange and unknown, and the biases and opinions of formed and egotistical men, compete with the facts generated by embassies, intelligence agencies, and expert analysis. What gets through? What images strike a response in the receiving mind of a Lyndon Johnson, a Richard Nixon, or a McGeorge Bundy? In 1964, for example, Lyndon Johnson told some reporters that he "grew up with Mexicans. They'll come right into your yard and take it over if you let them. And the next day they'll be on your porch. . . . But if you say to 'em right at the start, 'Hold on, just wait a minute,' they'll know they're dealing with somebody who'll stand up. And after that you can get along fine."[10] This may be regarded as mere prejudice, but it is more important for our purposes to see that it is a premise of reality and one that Lyndon Johnson presumably felt had been supported by his experiences. Few around him would have wished to contradict these convictions, and many pandered to them. But even if someone had tried to argue him out of his convic-

8. Daniel Ellsberg, *Papers on the War* (New York: Simon & Schuster, 1972), p. 28.

9. L. Fletcher Prouty, *The Secret Team* (New York: Ballantine Books, 1974), p. 14.

10. Richard J. Barnet, *Roots of War* (Baltimore: Penguin Books, 1973), p. 87.

tions, he is unlikely to have succeeded. These convictions form part of the world view that appeared in the confidential report on Vietnam that Johnson, as vice-president, submitted to President Kennedy in May 1961 after his trip to Southeast Asia:

> The battle against Communism must be joined in Southeast Asia with strength and determination to achieve success there—or the United States, inevitably, must surrender the Pacific and take our defenses on our own shores (p. 128).

The premise of reality in this sentence, an exaggerated version of the domino theory in which the U.S. must "inevitably surrender the Pacific," surely played a significant role in determining the form of the continuation of Kennedy's policies on Vietnam. As Johnson says earlier in the same report, "I took to Southeast Asia some basic convictions about the problems faced there . . ." (p. 128).

The Nixon Watergate tapes offer us a direct glimpse of the ignorance operating at the highest levels of government. President Nixon and H. R. Haldeman, his Chief of Staff, are talking about a major international economic crisis.[11]

HALDEMAN: Did you get the report that the British floated the pound?
NIXON: No, I don't think so.
HALDEMAN: They did.
NIXON: That's devaluation?
HALDEMAN: Yeah. Flanagan's got a report on it here.
NIXON: I don't care about it. Nothing we can do about it.
HALDEMAN: You don't want a rundown?
NIXON: No, I don't.
HALDEMAN: He argues it shows the wisdom of our refusal to consider convertibility until we get a new monetary system.
NIXON: Good. I think he's right. It's too complicated for me to get into. (Unintelligible)
HALDEMAN: Burns expects a 5-day [sic] percent devaluation against the dollar.
NIXON: Yeah. O.K. Fine.
HALDEMAN: Burns is concerned about speculation about the lire.
NIXON: Well, I don't give a (expletive deleted) about the lire. (Unintelligible)
HALDEMAN: That's the substance of that.

11. *The New York Times,* August 6, 1974, p. 14.

Presumably the concurrence of the chief executive in many technical decisions is a matter of formality. But in those deliberations where the president must be an arbiter, the knowledge that he brings to bear may be minimal. Under these conditions, prejudice and ideology must provide the premises of reality and value that are needed in order to make a decision.

2. Secrecy can hide the fact that the objectives orienting a decision may represent the interests of a small group, or of one class, or of the personal interests of elected or appointed officials. For example, hearings before a subcommittee of the Senate Foreign Relations Committee disclose that high officials of ITT Corporation, which owned a subsidiary in Chile, had met in 1970 with officials of the CIA and the State Department and the White House in a "prolonged and extensive pattern of consultation." These consultations concerned plans contained in ITT memoranda suggesting an attempt by agencies of the U.S. government to "prevent the election of Salvador Allende Gossens, a Marxist, as president of Chile" by such actions as "fomenting violence that might bring about a military takeover of the country." President Nixon, according to ITT memoranda before the committee, gave the U.S. ambassador to Chile a "green light" to "do all possible short of military action to keep Allende from power."[12]

Domestically also the protection or enhancement of the interests of a small group is often a dominant objective of policy, even when this conflicts unambiguously with the interests of the rest of the population. This was the case when the Nixon administration raised the support price of milk in exchange for contributions to the Committee to Re-elect the President from milk-producer groups. The fact that private interests influence both domestic and foreign policy is hardly a revelation, but the methods by which it is done and the extent to which it is done are secret, so that the public has little direct knowledge of what the real objectives of government policy are and how they are formed.

Secrecy can also hide the fact that there may be few legal or moral or electoral constraints operating in the deliberations. For example, the Pentagon Papers present no evidence that questions of

12. *The New York Times,* March 22, 1974, p. 1, and March 23, 1974, p. 1. As I was finishing this paper, corroboration of the U.S. role in the overthrow of the Allende government was given in an article in *The New York Times,* September 8, 1974, p. 1, reporting on testimony to Congress by the head of the CIA.

international law or of morality were even formally discussed by those who approved general policies involving reprisal against civilian populations. Yet Telford Taylor, the chief counsel for the prosecution in the Nuremberg trials, in a discussion of the legal issues associated with the approval of these U.S. policies in Vietnam concludes:

> [I]t is clear that such reprisal attacks are a flagrant violation of the Geneva Convention on Civilian Protection, which prohibits "collective penalties" and "reprisals against protected persons," and equally in violation of the Rules of Land Warfare.[13]

In the case of electoral constraints, disclosures such as the Pentagon Papers provide excellent examples of how secrecy permits the electorate to be manipulated by selective information on government actions. During 1964, prior to the first U.S. bombing of North Vietnam and during the presidential election campaign, the U.S. was supporting raids by boat from South Vietnam for such activities as the "destruction of section of Hanoi-Vinh railroad" (p. 302). These activities were kept secret from the U.S. electorate and Congress. A major purpose of these activities appears to have been to provoke North Vietnam into actions that could be used as an excuse to obtain public and congressional support for bombing. A "Plan of Action for South Vietnam," drafted in September 1964, listed five "desiderata" for U.S. actions, including "they should be likely at some point to provoke a military DRV (Democratic Republic of [North] Vietnam) response" and "the provoked response should provide good grounds for us to escalate if we wished" (p. 356).

3. Secrecy can hide the concepts of action that were considered and rejected. The use of tactical atomic weapons or the threat of mass murder, for example, might have been seriously considered and rejected narrowly or on grounds that show that such action could be used in the future. For example, the Pentagon Papers show that the threat of mass starvation was considered by senior U.S. officials. McNaughton, in a memorandum of January 8, 1966, suggested that the destruction of locks and dams in North Vietnam might "offer promise":

> It should be studied. Such destruction does not kill or drown people. By shallow flooding the rice it leads after time to widespread starva-

---

13. Telford Taylor, *Nuremberg and Vietnam* (New York: Quadrangle Books, 1970), p. 145.

tion (more than a million?) unless food is provided—which we could offer to do "at the conference table."[14]

In the opposite vein, secrecy can hide the fact that the concepts of action considered will be only a few of the actions that are conceivable under the circumstances. Those not considered or rejected may be superior to the action taken. But it is not possible for an outsider to make this judgment, since secrecy also hides the premises that underlie the adoption or rejection of a particular action. By doing so, secrecy can also hide the fact that the actions taken may be "irrational," even in the narrow sense defined above. For example, President Johnson's half-formulated doubts were apparently crystallized by Dean Acheson, a former U.S. secretary of state whom Johnson respected, who told him in a private meeting that "the Joint Chiefs of Staff don't know what they are talking about."[15] Acheson's conclusion was that the actions advocated by the Joint Chiefs of Staff were inconsistent with his perception of the reality in Vietnam.

4. Secrecy hides the fact that the deliberations are circumscribed by an ideology. This could only be illustrated by an extended case study, but the point itself is simple enough. There are two complementary ways of examining the debate and conflict in deliberations. The first is to recapitulate the conflicts of judgment of the debate. But, as Gabriel Kolko points out, that debate and conflict occur is often of less significance than that the debate is circumscribed, perhaps unconsciously, by the shared ideology of the participants.[16] An example of the effects of shared ideology is pointed out by the fact that no one in the U.S. executive branch during the entire period covered by the Pentagon Papers ever presented the case of supporting the NLF. The ideology of the participants determined this absence, and any conflicts of judgment occurred within a perspective in which the NLF view of events in South Vietnam could not be presented. But this perspective should not be taken for granted in an analysis. Any attempt to comprehend the U.S. policy deliberations on the Vietnam War, in which premises of reality and objectives and concepts of

14. Mike Gravel, ed., *The Senator Gravel Edition: The Pentagon Papers* (Boston: Beacon Press, 1971), 4:43, cited in Ellsberg, *Papers on the War*, p. 295.

15. Townsend Hoopes, *The Limits of Intervention* (New York: McKay, 1969), pp. 204–5.

16. Gabriel Kolko, *The Roots of American Foreign Policy* (Boston: Beacon Press, 1969), p. 7.

action were heatedly debated, must begin with some characterization of, and explanation for, the limits within which this debate occurred. The second way of examining the conflicts of judgment in a policy debate, then, is to characterize the ideology shared by those who were disagreeing. This is usually implicit in the debate, and the participants themselves will usually not be aware of it; they may even deny having an ideology. Nonetheless, the word *ideology* is appropriate to designate this bounding of deliberation. In the case of U.S. policy toward the Allende government in Chile, for example, if the ITT memoranda were representative of the deliberations, the implicit ideology can be most easily characterized as the protection of the common (or "class") interests of the owners of U.S. property in Chile and (if a domino theory was also one of the premises of reality) in the rest of Latin America.

5. Finally, secrecy can hide the fact that those exercising power may be persons inadequate to the moral and intellectual complexity of the problems that they face in the roles that give them so much power over others' lives. Individuals act differently in different situations, and the character and capacities of officials in the job of deliberation under pressure may be surprisingly different from their characters and capacities in more static circumstances, such as public meetings or private interviews and dinners.

The tapes of President Nixon and his aides discussing Watergate illustrate this point voluminously. Often newspaper stories provide glimpses of the psychological climate and quality of deliberations on momentous decisions. Some former aides to Henry Kissinger, for example, report that he told his staff on the afternoon of the 1970 U.S. invasion of Cambodia, that "our leader has flipped his lid. But you're all expected to rally round. If you can't, get out. We can't have any carping in the back room."[17] This is hearsay, but it is terrifying hearsay, for it indicates that it may be possible that democracies, like totalitarian regimes, are modes of government that permit sufficient discretion to leaders for them to launch an invasion of another country for idiosyncratic, as distinct from ideological, reasons.

17. *New York Post*, June 13, 1974, p. 33.

CONCLUSION

What exactly is discussed and what is taken for granted at high levels of government when decisions are made? What is the implicit ideology? In what ways do the democratic institutions of election, legislative activity, a free press, and the rule of law actually influence executive decisions? The Pentagon Papers, the Watergate transcripts, and the other disclosures of the early 1970s have made us realize the importance of the truism that political power, in democracies as in other forms of government, is exercised by identifiable persons of limited intellectual and moral capacities who act in an environment of influences that determine some, but not all, of their thoughts and actions. But until we know what the determinants of these actions are and the scope of the discretion exercised by leaders, we will not have any direct empirical knowledge about the way in which we are governed. Nor is there any reason to suppose that high officials would be capable of giving an objective account of the decision processes that they have engaged in. They are certainly acting within institutions and under the influence of ideological and psychological forces that they do not fully comprehend or control. It should be recalled that the original purpose of collecting the Pentagon Papers was to permit the study of governmental decision-making processes within the Pentagon, in secret. The generic secrets of government decision making are, to a large extent, a secret from everyone.

The problems indicated in this chapter will remain problems under any form of government. The members of all governments always have made and will make decisions within an ideological viewpoint that excludes, without rational scrutiny, the bulk of the alternatives and objectives that constitute the full range of political opinion on some given issue. And this exclusion of alternatives and values drastically narrows the range of facts and the type of facts that will be taken into account in policy deliberations. The only way to make a fundamental change in the orientation of policy is to alter the ideology of those holding power through electoral or revolutionary means. Factual arguments conditioned by a perspective different from that governing policy deliberations will almost invariably prove fruitless since they are likely to refer to aspects of reality that are never discussed by the policymakers. To those who were involved with detailed factual assessments of the "vulnerability of North Vietnam to conventional bombing," the facts of the peasants' situation under the land tenure system in South Vietnam were, at best, peripheral. Accurate assessments of the situation of the peasants were written by the CIA, as well as opponents of the war, but these assessments were ignored in policy-level discussions, not because they were disbelieved, but because they had no place in deliberations narrowed by the necessities of choice through the mechanism of implicit agreement on fundamentals.

An ideology of some sort is a necessary prerequisite of the exercise of the will to choose, and this limits the possible scope of the influence of factual and rational analysis on policy deliberations. But within the severe limits set by the governing ideology there is still room for incompetence, illegality, and idiosyncratic craziness. Can reforms be conceived that would reduce these defects of political-decision processes?

No single person is responsible for a major political decision. But identifiable persons can be assigned responsibility for formulating certain premises of reality (such as those of Maxwell Taylor or McGeorge Bundy quoted in this chapter) or advocating certain concepts of action. The evidence is available in material that could be subpoenaed since all governments are now bureaucracies, with all the minutes of meetings, memoranda, and reports that must be written in order to formulate policy, discuss positions, resolve differences, and coordinate and communicate among large numbers of specialized persons. Furthermore, the technical means now exist for invading the privacy of policy deliberations and recording them on tape. Within the U.S. political system, at any rate, it is conceivable that a law requiring the videotaping of all deliberations in the committee rooms and offices of designated senior officials, and the preservation of all memoranda, could be passed. If passed, this law, like all others, would be evaded, but the evasion would be illegal, and it could hardly be claimed that a decision to commit one nation to bomb another, for example, was taken without a meeting or without position papers. Even if fitfully policed, this would be Orwell's *1984* in reverse: the people's eye watching them.

The evidence required and secured by this law would show, to any duly constituted body investigating a debacle or conducting a routine review of a major decision, who was responsible for advocating illegal action, or for formulating or concurring in delusions during deliberations. There is no reason why precedent and due process could not establish here, as it has elsewhere, expected levels of competence and moral action under various contingencies of information and pressure, and personal liability if behavior falls below these levels. The private citizen is liable, under an elaborate system of law, for harm caused by his negligence. Why should the negligence or stupidity or viciousness of those holding high office be outside the scope of systematic judicial review?

PART II

Government Secrecy in Ten Democracies

7

The United States

FRANCIS E. ROURKE

INTRODUCTION: SECRECY AND THE "ISSUE ATTENTION CYCLE"

Public interest in issues involving the reform of governmental operation or procedure has traditionally had a very short life span in
American politics. As a general rule the public is not greatly interested in such questions and is aroused from its indifference only when
scandalous misconduct by an officeholder is suddenly revealed.
Dramatic exposure of wrongdoing usually does excite widespread
public interest and, while it persists, the prospect for reform of the
political process brightens if the wrongdoing can be linked to some
basic defect in the system. But this support for change commonly
recedes as the impact of the scandal wears off, and members of the
public return to their customary private concerns. Relevant here is
the model of an "issue attention cycle," which Anthony Downs uses
to suggest that reform is generally a transient phenomenon in a
political system ordinarily quite resistant to change.[1]

The issue of secrecy, however, has proven extraordinarily durable
in recent American politics. This may be because the media of communications themselves have a vested interest in the question of
secrecy in government, and they are unwilling to allow it to recede
from public attention. Moreover, public interest organizations like

1. Anthony Downs, "Up and Down with Ecology—The 'Issue Attention'
Cycle," *The Public Interest* 28 (Summer 1972):38–50.

Common Cause have also taken a keen interest in the problem of secrecy in government. In this respect their behavior has been entirely consistent with that of reform groups which preceded them. It has long been characteristic of American reformers to put the cause of exposure at the top of their agenda.

With the events of Watergate providing dramatic proof of the reform belief that official secrecy can be used to conceal criminal misconduct, the movement against secrecy in American government, already strong, has acquired extraordinary vitality. In this chapter we will look at some of the recent changes that have taken place in information policies and practices in the United States as a result of legislative and executive action. While these changes reflect the impact that traumatic events like Vietnam and Watergate have had upon the political consciousness of Americans, they stem also from underlying characteristics of political culture in the United States that were firmly established long before these contemporary developments occurred.

THE POLITICAL CULTURE

While it is a very broad generalization that increasingly requires qualification, it is still true to say that the fundamental American political style is one of openness. Shils's description of the American political system as being based on "luxuriating publicity" remains close to the mark.[2] This is particularly true when the American system is viewed in comparison with other political systems around the world, where conventions of secrecy or privacy in governmental affairs are little questioned and where strong legal penalties may be attached to the disclosure of information that executive officials wish to conceal.

However, the image of the United States as an open political system tends to change considerably if we look at it, not from the vantage point of other societies with which it might be compared, but from the perspective of its own internal development in the last three decades. Clearly, the evolution of American politics since

2. Edward A. Shils, *The Torment of Secrecy* (Glencoe, Ill.: The Free Press, 1956), pp. 37–44.

World War II has been in the direction of secrecy. It began most notably perhaps with the atom bomb—a development with awesome implications for modern life. Born in secrecy, the bomb was developed behind tight security precautions until suddenly sprung on the world in August 1945.

For the generation that came to political power after World War II, the atom bomb thus became a symbol of success through secrecy. The bomb was looked upon as an extraordinary technological achievement by many Americans, insofar as the United States was able actually to build such a weapon. It was also regarded as a success because the United States was able to end World War II by using it. (So at least it seemed in the eyes of the public, although historians were later to dispute the point.) Out of that beginning there grew a conviction that secrecy was an essential prerequisite for national security, and this view was to become firmly fixed as part of the dominant political consensus of the cold war. The opposite viewpoint—that secrecy can sometimes be damaging to national security— was hard-pressed to make itself heard.

No institution has contributed more to the shift in the American perspective on secrecy than the presidency—the office chiefly responsible for the conduct of foreign affairs in the United States. Presidential ascendancy in American politics since World War II is linked in many ways to the growth of secrecy, and the defense of secrecy has thus become essential for American presidents as a means of defending the power and prerogatives of their own office. Among the advantages the White House derives from secrecy is the fact that it enables a president to conceal disagreements within his official family and thus present the public with an impressive even if spurious display of unity behind White House policies. Secrecy also adds to the mystery of the presidential office, helping to give it the air of authority on which it so often trades in American politics. Having secrets of state in their possession is another means by which presidents can exact awe and deference from their subjects.

So to the traditional American belief that openness on the part of government was essential to the successful functioning of democracy there came to be added the idea that secrecy was indispensable for both the success of the nation's foreign policy and the effective operation of the central office of the political system—the presidency. As a result there exist in the United States today two cultures that exert sharply conflicting pressures on the development of political life. One is rooted in the tradition of openness, so dominant in the progressive era in the early part of this century and so well expressed by Woodrow Wilson:

> I, for one, have the conviction that government ought to be all outside and no inside. I, for my part, believe that there ought to be no place where anything can be done that everybody does not know about. . . . Everybody knows that corruption thrives in secret places, and avoids public places, and we believe it a fair presumption that secrecy means impropriety. . . . Government must, if it is to be pure and correct in its processes, be absolutely public in everything that affects it.[3]

This tradition of disclosure is sustained by a variety of powerful institutions in American society, especially Congress, the media of communication, and on occasion, the courts.

The other culture, which took form in the period immediately following World War II, defends and seeks to magnify the value of secrecy. Presiding over this culture of secrecy is the presidency, and it is buttressed by a variety of resourceful national security organizations from the Pentagon to the CIA. These institutions generate and exploit fears of the dire consequences that may ensue if the secrets of the United States are exposed to its enemies abroad, and they enjoy no small measure of public support in this endeavor.

Vietnam and Watergate have given new life to the traditional Wilsonian faith in publicity as the best remedy for the ills that may plague a democratic society. As a result there has been a reinvigoration of the instruments and institutions of disclosure. But the culture of secrecy also remains intact—weak at the periphery, but strong at the core. Growing strain between these two divergent cultures of publicity and secrecy has generated recurrent crises in recent American politics over such matters as the Pentagon Papers, the Vietnam War, Watergate, and most recently, the operations of the CIA. Neither culture seems to be weakening appreciably, and conflict between them seems likely to be no less intense in the future than it has been in the past.

---

3. Woodrow Wilson, *The New Freedom*, edited with an introduction by William E. Leuchtenburg (New York: Prentice-Hall, 1961), pp. 76, 84.

THE CONSTITUTIONAL AND LEGAL BACKGROUND

Secrecy in the United States today is sustained by a wide and deeply rooted network of laws and constitutional practices. Perhaps the best known of the legal underpinnings on which it currently rests is the executive privilege that presidents have invoked in recent times to justify withholding information when its release would, in their view, jeopardize national security or the ability of the White House to function effectively. The scope and constitutionality of the doctrine of executive privilege have often been challenged—most clearly and most notably by the Watergate special prosecutor's office during its effort in 1973 and 1974 to gain access to tapes and documents withheld by the Nixon White House. But the decision of the Supreme Court in the Watergate case did seem to sustain the president's privilege to withhold information when he considers that its release would jeopardize national security, hamper him in his efforts to obtain candid advice, or have an otherwise damaging effect upon his ability to carry out his executive responsibilities.[4]

But while executive privilege has been at the forefront of public attention as a result of the frequent and sometimes searing confrontations it has triggered between Congress and the president since World War II, much of the secrecy that administrative officials practice in the United States rests on legal grounds other than executive privilege. This is necessarily so, since the courts have ruled that executive privilege belongs only to the president and cannot be claimed by any of his subordinates as a prerogative of their office.[5]

There are, for example, more than 100 statutes enacted by Congress that either allow or require executive agencies to withhold information from the public. Much of this legislation is designed to protect what the legislature regards as rights of privacy on the part of either individuals or organizations. The material thus given statutory protection includes data in the personnel records of government employees, information submitted by citizens on their tax returns, and what business firms regard as trade secrets that would be eco-

4. United States v. Nixon, 94 S. Ct. 3090 (1974). However, the Court held that the privilege did not apply if the information requested was needed by the courts for the administration of justice.

5. For fuller discussion of executive privilege, see chapter 8 in this volume, "The United States: The Doctrine of Executive Privilege," by Bernard Schwartz.

nomically damaging to them if disclosed. In enacting these statutes, Congress commonly seeks to protect not the secrets of bureaucracy but the privacy of nongovernmental groups and individuals.

Another major source of secrecy in the United States is the classification system under which information is given a security stamp and withheld from disclosure. The legal basis for this system is a series of executive orders issued by modern presidents, as, for example, executive order no. 11652 put into effect by President Nixon in 1972. These orders empower a variety of executive agencies and officials to put a secrecy stamp on documents that they believe would embarrass the United States or damage its security if exposed to public view.

Inevitably, bureaucratic caution and self-interest lead executive agencies to classify many more documents as secret than security interests actually require since the penalties attached to unauthorized disclosure may be severe, while overclassification is not likely to be punished. In view of this skewed system of incentives, it is hardly surprising that executive agencies should choose to conceal so much of the information placed under their jurisdiction.

Efforts to reform the classification system center on reducing the number of officials authorized to classify documents. The Interagency Classification Review Committee reported in 1975 that the number of persons holding classification authority had declined from 59,316 in June 1972 to 15,466 at the end of 1974. But the pace at which documents continue to be classified is phenomenal. In 1974 alone officials in the Defense Department classified 14,275 documents as top secret, 800,600 as secret, and 2.4 million as confidential. The Pentagon's way of declassifying many documents is to destroy them. The shredder has thus taken its place along with the classification stamp as a major instrument of concealment within the executive branch.

Perhaps the most ironic twist in the development of legislative protection for secrecy in the United States is the extent to which the Freedom of Information Act as enacted in 1966 and amended in 1974 has been used to reinforce practices of secrecy in the United States. The act was designed to require executive agencies to furnish citizens and other interested parties outside of government with information they requested from the executive branch. If an agency proved unwilling to cooperate, these outside parties could obtain the assistance of the courts in getting access to the information they wanted. No legislation ever enacted in the United States represents a more comprehensive charter for disclosure than the Freedom of Information Act. The 1974 amendments even included provisions for penalizing officials who wrongfully withheld information.

As it turned out, however, the act also specified nine different categories of information that agencies could legitimately withhold from the public. These exemptions from the act's preferred policy of disclosure represent a formidable legal basis for the practice of secrecy by executive officials. For example, the first exemption permits agencies to keep information secret "in the interest of national defense and foreign policy." The third exemption allows them to withhold information that is "specifically exempted from disclosure by statute," thus reinforcing the statutory basis for secrecy already described. The fifth exemption sanctions the withholding of interagency memoranda, while the seventh exempts "investigatory files compiled for law enforcement purposes." In total effect, these exemption clauses tend to strengthen patterns and powers of secrecy that already prevail within the executive branch in the United States.

THE POLITICS OF INFORMATION AND SECRECY

Democracy assumes that citizens can hold government officials accountable for what they do and can expel them from office when their policies do not meet with public approval. By shielding official action from public knowledge and review, secrecy makes such accountability impossible. Citizens can scarcely influence decisions they know nothing about. Where secrecy reigns, government officials are in a position to rule at virtually their own discretion.

Clearly, a practice that flies so directly in the face of democratic ideology and yet survives must have a very high degree of utility for the political system, or at least for major institutional clusters within the larger system. However incompatible secrecy may be with the norms of democracy, its prevalence and durability as a governmental practice suggest that it has become extremely functional for the operation of a wide range of institutions in American society.

The Executive

A large number of the major presidential decisions by which American political life has been shaped since World War II were made by presidents operating in almost total secrecy. Witness, for example, the development of atomic weapons under Roosevelt, the conduct of U-2 flights over the Soviet Union during the Eisenhower years, the Cuban missile crisis in the Kennedy era, the planning for the escalation of American involvement in Vietnam under Johnson, and the Nixon rapprochement with Communist China in 1972. The withholding of information on these and many more such events testifies to the powerful role that secrecy has come to play in the conduct of the presidency in modern American politics.

In the past all American presidents, beginning with George Washington, have had occasion to resort to secrecy. Every chief executive has been convinced of the necessity of maintaining his prerogative to withhold information, and each has been able to rely upon precedents set by his predecessors in doing so. This was true of presidents like Thomas Jefferson, celebrated for their association with the ideals of liberal democracy, and of conservatives like William Howard Taft and Calvin Coolidge. However much they may have disagreed in other respects, presidents have been united in this conviction that some measure of secrecy is essential for the conduct of White House business.

But even in the context of this historic tradition of presidential attachment to secrecy, Richard Nixon stands out in terms of the extraordinary salience the question of secrecy acquired during his years in office. In one way or another, the secrecy issue played a role in each of the major events of his administration: the conduct of the war in Vietnam; the negotiations with Hanoi, Peking, Moscow, and in the Middle East; the release of the Pentagon Papers; and then, ultimately, Watergate and the president's resignation. Never before in American history had more continuous public attention been drawn to the issue of executive secrecy than during Nixon's five and a half years in office.

Nixon was also distinctive with respect to the very great importance he placed upon secrecy as a prerequisite to effective governance. The Watergate scandal triggered multiple demands for disclosure by the White House, and the president's inability to gratify these requests without incriminating himself led inevitably to a wide-ranging defense of confidentiality in the conduct of public affairs. In justifying its refusal to release Watergate-related materials, the White House resurrected all of the traditional arguments in favor of executive secrecy, including the need to guarantee candor in executive deliberations and to insure protection against the intelligence-gathering activities of potential adversaries abroad.

However much he was motivated by self-interest in this defense of secrecy, Nixon appears to have genuinely convinced himself of the linkage between secrecy and effective presidential performance. In speaking before the American prisoners-of-war who had returned from Vietnam in 1973, the president was quite explicit in linking what he felt were the great successes of his administration—including the return of the prisoners themselves—to the use of secrecy in diplomatic negotiations. "Had we not had secrecy," Nixon argued, "there would have been no China initiative, there would have been no limitation of arms for the Soviet Union and no summit, and had we not had that kind of security and that kind of secrecy that allowed for the kind of exchange that is essential, you men would still be in Hanoi rather than Washington today."

Unfortunately for Nixon, however, a preoccupation with secrecy could also be said to have played an equally large part in his administration's failures. The decision to establish the "plumbers" organization in the White House to ferret out the secrets of Daniel Ellsberg, the man who had leaked the Pentagon Papers to the press, led ultimately to the ill-fated burglary of Ellsberg's psychiatrist's office. Consider also the Watergate burglary itself—the surreptitious entry into the headquarters of the Democratic National Committee for the purpose of installing or removing eavesdropping equipment.

The costs of all these secretive ventures to the Nixon administration proved to be enormous and ultimately fatal. Moreover, these costs rose sharply as each stage of the Watergate drama unfolded—beginning with the original burglaries and culminating in White House claims of executive privilege in refusing to release evidence bearing on the affair—especially the celebrated tapes. The suspicion bred by each successive step in this continuing strategy of secrecy brought a precipitous decline in the president's standing in the eyes of both Congress and the public and led to his eventual departure from office.

The irony of the Nixon years may well be the fact that a president so devoutly committed to the value of secrecy in the conduct of governmental affairs actually brought about a major swing toward disclosure on the part of presidents. Future occupants of the White House are not likely to be favorably impressed by the results Nixon achieved through his use of secrecy. On the contrary, the Nixon precedent may actually serve to underline the advantages of openness as a presidential strategy in dealing with the public, Congress, and the media. One of the first steps taken by Nixon's successor, President Gerald Ford, was to announce a "policy of candor" as the keynote of his administration. While this policy was not adhered to religiously, its immediate proclamation reflected a widely shared perception that it was Nixon's strategy of secrecy that led to his political demise.

Citizen Organizations and the Mass Media

Because of the creation of citizen organizations like John Gardner's Common Cause and the network of public interest groups under the direction of Ralph Nader, it is now possible to say that reform has become a permanent force in American politics. The establishment of these new public interest organizations means that the cause of governmental reform now has a continuing presence in Washington in the form of both an office and a staff of representatives who can buttonhole congressmen or quickly organize an avalanche of phone calls to their offices.

The power of such organizations has been greatly reinforced by the advent of the new media of communication, especially television, which make it possible for official misconduct to be given wide and instantaneous publicity throughout the country. In this way public indignation of great intensity can be quickly aroused, and through a communications device like the telephone network of Common Cause, it can find rapid and effective political expression. As a result of these developments, governmental reform now has a staying power it never before enjoyed in American politics, and when some governmental malfunction appears, the political system is subject to pressures for change it did not previously experience.

Linked together, as they often are, citizen organizations and the mass media represent major elements in what might be called the "antisecrecy" lobby in Washington—a lobby that has been working assiduously during the past decade to open up the processes of government to greater public scrutiny. The strategy of secrecy pursued by President Nixon during the Watergate affair greatly added to the strength of this antisecrecy lobby. Because of the success of its investigative reporting, the press emerged from Watergate with greatly enhanced authority as a fourth branch of government in the American political system, charged with the task of exposing wrongdoing on the part of public officials, while at the same time public interest organizations have become much more aggressive in pushing for legislation that would require greater publicity for executive deliberations and decisions.

But while the news media correctly regard themselves as being in the vanguard of the "freedom of information" movement in the United States—deeply hostile to all efforts on the part of government to interfere with the people's "right to know"—there are significant ways in which individual reporters benefit from executive secrecy and have on occasion been very supportive of it. Such secrecy gives some reporters an opportunity to publish information obtained from inside sources that would be of little value if it were freely available to the public at large. By sharing the fruits of their monopoly of information with selected reporters, government agencies can put themselves in a strong position to reward friends and punish their enemies in the news media.

Newspaper columnists are particularly likely to acquire a stake in executive secrecy and become defenders of it.[6] The practice of their craft requires the preservation of privileged accesses to official sources. Disclosures that threaten the value of this access impair their ability to obtain inside information that is essential to maintain their reputation as pundits. A close relationship between secretive agencies like the CIA and friendly newspaper columnists is not uncommon in the United States. An agency that has secrecy as one of its distinguishing characteristics is in a very advantageous position to give a columnist preferred access to a story.[7] Thus, while executive secrecy often seems to create divergent interests on the part of government and the media, it is also a means through which segments of the press

6. For illustrations of such news media support for executive secrecy, see Francis E. Rourke, "Bureaucratic Secrecy and Its Constituents," *The Bureaucrat* (Summer 1972):119–20.

7. For an analysis of the role of such leaks in the relationship between executive agencies and the media, see Leon V. Sigal, *Reporters and Officials: The Organization and Politics of Newsmaking* (New York: D. C. Heath, 1973), pp. 143–48.

are linked to the government in a mutually advantageous exchange relationship.

Secrecy and the Private Sector

In their expanding assault upon secrecy in recent years, reformers have increasingly had private as well as public organizations as their target. The energy crisis of winter 1974 highlighted the power of private corporations over the development of public policy in the United States, since it quickly became clear that private oil companies controlled most of the information available to the public on fuel supplies and the ability of the Federal Energy Office to handle the crisis heavily depended upon the willingness of these companies to share their data with the government. For years reformers had been highly critical of secrecy when it was practiced by public agencies because of the danger it posed to the basic assumption of a democracy that the people control the government. The energy crisis made it abundantly clear that secrecy by private corporations could be no less threatening to the public's ability to exercise sovereignty over major policy decisions.

Sometimes secrecy can be linked together in the public and private spheres in ways that are mutually advantageous to organizations in both sectors of society but highly detrimental to the rest of the country.[8] In 1972 a Federal Advisory Committee Act was passed in order to provide full publicity regarding the deliberations and decisions of outside advisory committees to the federal government on which representatives from many powerful private corporations sit. The major purpose of this legislation was to prevent private organizations from wielding in secret an influence they would never be allowed to exercise in public or from joining together with government agencies in the development of policies harmful to the country. However, the new law did not succeed in opening up advisory committee meetings nearly as much as its sponsors had originally hoped, since executive agencies were quick to use certain of its provisions as a mandate for secrecy rather than publicity.

8. See Mark V. Nadel, "Corporate Secrecy and Political Accountability," *Public Administration Review* 35 (January–February 1975):14–23.

In any case, there are a host of groups in American society that have transactions with the government that they prefer remain unpublicized, and a variety of statutes has been enacted to insure that their wishes in this regard are respected. Many of these transactions involve citizens reporting information to the government that they wish kept confidential, such as the personal history of an applicant for government employment or the economic status of a taxpayer. Some, of course, are much less innocent, such as the efforts of a private corporation like ITT to obtain a favorable settlement of an antitrust suit by the government or to influence American foreign policy in parts of the world like Chile where the company has a major financial stake. But whether the claim to privacy for any such transaction would receive general public sanction or not, the fact of the matter is that the secrecy which results springs in no small measure from the pressures of groups outside the governmental apparatus itself. An outside party supplies information to the government that he does not wish to have revealed to his business competitor or seeks a favor that might not look very well in the cold light of public scrutiny.

The Congressional Role

On the surface, congressmen in the United States are opposed to all executive efforts to withhold information from the public. Attacks on secrecy are a common feature of legislative life, and there have been major initiatives in Congress, including the Freedom of Information Act enacted in 1966 and amended in 1974 to curb excessive secrecy on the part of executive agencies.

And yet, while the corporate attitude of Congress toward secrecy is one of hostility, individual congressmen stand to gain a great deal from having privileged access to official information. Witness, for example, how much legislators may benefit from the opportunity afforded them by executive agencies to make public announcements about the establishment of new government programs or facilities in their districts. In disclosing such information, congressmen can do a great deal to promote their visibility and stature in their own constituencies. They depend upon these information opportunities offered by the executive in much the same way as they once leaned upon executive patronage to nurse support in their own home districts.[9] As was true in the case of patronage, legislators are expected to return political support for these exclusive opportunities to disclose newsworthy items to the public.

Thus, while Congress has done a great deal to open up the affairs of the executive to greater outside scrutiny—through the passage of legislation, the conduct of investigations, and relentless pressure for greater disclosure—individual legislators have also been willing to participate in the process of withholding information from the public when they are allowed to share in the secrets of the executive. The Pentagon and other national security agencies have recognized this legislative tendency to become more tolerant of executive secrecy when they are allowed to share in its benefits, and they have used it to build support among strategic groups like the armed services committees in both the House and Senate.

REFORMING GOVERNMENT SECRECY

As the preceding discussion has shown, it is necessary to look at the entire political system in which executive agencies are linked in order to understand the strength and durability of secrecy in American government. Viewed from this systemic perspective, secrecy can be seen in its true colors—as a practice that serves a wealth of interests both inside and outside of government, besides those of executive officials themselves. It is not only because of bureaucratic tenacity but also because a diverse range of institutions and groups in American society finds secrecy useful that it has become so difficult to uproot through reform legislation.

Nonetheless, efforts to reform information policy and practices can be expected to continue in the United States. For while bureaucratic secrecy does serve the needs of a broad constellation of groups and organizations in the American political system, recent history clearly demonstrates that it is subject to sharper attack in the United States than it encounters in other parts of the world.

For one thing, secrecy has less legitimacy as a governmental prac-

9. See Stanley Kelley, Jr., "Patronage and Presidential Legislative Leadership," in *The Presidency*, ed. Aaron Wildavsky (Boston: Little, Brown, 1969), p. 275.

tice in the United States than in any other advanced industrial society, with the possible exception of Sweden. This became very clear during the Watergate affair, when President Nixon met with little success when he tried to justify his withholding of tapes and other information by claiming that such secrecy was essential to the effective functioning of the White House. His defense of secrecy on this ground seemed only to weaken Nixon's credibility at home and to further erode his standing in the public eye. In Great Britain, by way of contrast, a prime minister might very well have been able to persuade the public that such secrecy was necessary for the effective conduct of official business.[10]

A second distinctive attribute of American political culture is the fact that the network of organizations opposed to executive secrecy is so much stronger in the United States than in other parts of the world. Congress has infinitely more leverage in ferreting out information from executive officials than legislative bodies elsewhere, the media enjoy a privileged position they do not generally occupy in other political systems, and finally, the extraordinarily tenacious and highly influential cluster of public interest groups opposed to secrecy finds no counterpart in countries other than the United States.

So, while it may never be possible or desirable in the modern world to attain the "government in a goldfish bowl" toward which reformers often seem to be striving in the United States, it seems safe to say that secrecy will always be on the defensive in American politics and that the events in the early seventies will make it even more vulnerable to attack in the future than it has been in the past.

However, what the American experience with secrecy also suggests is the wide gap that exists between what reformers intend and what they achieve. Officeholders in political institutions whose information policies reform organizations are seeking to change have defenses in depth against altering procedural arrangements in which they have acquired a vested interest, and they are very adept at transforming a mandate for change into a license to continue or even expand the secretive practices that are under attack. Thus the Freedom of Information Act was the crowning achievement of reform energy in the United States during the 1960s. By the 1970s, it had become a

---

10. For a discussion of the role of secrecy in British culture, see James B. Christoph, "A Comparative View: Administrative Secrecy in Britain," *Public Administration Review* 35 (January–February 1975):23–32.

prime target of the reform movement, as agencies proceeded to use certain provisions of the act that permitted withholding of information under certain very limited conditions as a broad charter for the preservation and even the expansion of secrecy.

The United States:
The Doctrine of Executive Privilege

BERNARD SCHWARTZ

In his April 29, 1974, speech announcing the public release of transcripts of the Watergate tapes, President Nixon asserted that his efforts to guard the privacy of the tapes had been based upon recognized constitutional principle: "This principle is recognized in the constitutional doctrine of executive privilege, which has been defended and maintained by every President since Washington and which has been recognized by the courts whenever tested as inherent in the Presidency."[1] This assertion is remarkably inexact, supported neither by governmental practice nor law. The doctrine of executive privilege is, in the characterization of a recent book, "a constitutional myth."[2] The very term *executive privilege* itself is of recent origin.[3] The notion that executive officers had a "privilege" to withhold evidence from Congress and the courts and that they

1. *The New York Times*, April 30, 1974, p. 32.
2. Raoul Berger, *Executive Privilege: A Constitutional Myth* (Cambridge: Harvard University Press, 1974).
3. Berger asserts that it was not used before 1958. Ibid., p. 1. The present writer, however, used the term in a 1957 congressional committee memorandum. Memorandum of Law, *Right of Access by Special Subcommittee on Legislative Oversight to Civil Aeronautics Board Files and Records*, 85th Cong., 1st sess., 1957, p. 4.

themselves had the "uncontrolled discretion"[4] to define the limits of the privilege and hence to determine what evidence they might refuse to divulge would, until our own day, have been rejected as constitutional heresy. Yet it is precisely that notion that has been put forward in all seriousness in recent years.

Executive privilege itself is the American counterpart of the British doctrine of crown privilege. This is the name given in Great Britain to the government's power to claim that the disclosure of evidence being given in court will be against the public interest. In the leading case until recently, the House of Lords had held that a ministerial claim of privilege was unquestionable in law.[5] This was, in effect, to recognize in the British executive an uncontrolled discretion to suppress evidence of the type put forward in the United States in recent years. But the House of Lords has now unanimously repudiated its extreme position and asserted judicial control. Under *Conway v. Rimmer*[6] the courts will not allow claims of crown privilege unless the public interest in secrecy really outweighs the public interest in doing justice to the litigant; and this is to be determined by the courts, not by the executive.[7]

The problem of executive privilege gains an added perspective when placed in the context of the recent movement to eliminate secrecy in government. This movement culminated in the enactment in 1966 of the Freedom of Information Act, under which the citizen is, for the first time, given a legally enforceable right of access to government files and documents. In addition, the courts in the United States have increasingly refused to allow executive suppression of information. The judicial attitude received striking confirmation in the Pentagon Papers case,[8] where the Supreme Court refused an injunction against publication by a newspaper, even though the material published had been classified top secret by the Defense Department. These developments in the law on government secrecy emphasize the anomalous nature of the recent extreme claims of executive privilege.

4. Attorney general's memorandum in support of president's May 17, 1954, letter to secretary of defense, *Right of Access by Special Subcommittee on Legislative Oversight* . . . 85th Cong., 1st sess., 1957, 68.
5. Duncan v. Cammell Laird & Co., A.C. 624 (1942).
6. Conway v. Rimmer, A.C. 910 (1968).
7. See Bernard Schwartz and H. W. R. Wade, *Legal Control of Government* (Oxford: Clarendon Press, 1972), p. 193.
8. New York Times Co. v. United States, 403 U.S. 713 (1971).

HISTORICAL PRACTICE

"A page of history is worth a volume of logic," according to the celebrated statement of Justice Holmes.[9] This is particularly true where the history is contradicted only by self-serving executive ipse dixits, which either ignore or distort the mass of historical experience.

The doctrine of executive privilege is usually said to start with the refusal of President Washington to furnish correspondence relating to negotiation of the Jay Treaty in 1796 to the House of Representatives. But that refusal was based upon the view that the House lacked the power under the Constitution to inquire into the treaty-making power, not upon an executive privilege to withhold documents absolutely from Congress. Indeed, Washington had laid before the Senate all the papers affecting the negotiations.[10] Washington's refusal is not really a precedent to support executive power to withhold information from Congress, but only one to limit congressional investigatory authority to the legislative power of the House concerned.

Other early presidential refusals to furnish information to Congress also turn out, on closer analysis, to be far from assertions of an unlimited sphere for executive privilege. Andrew Jackson refused to supply information to the Senate during a confirmation proceeding;[11] the Senate then refused to confirm Jackson's nominee—scarcely a victory for the president. During the pre–Civil War period, there were also refusals by Tyler and Polk to furnish information to the House,[12] as well as an assertion by Tyler of the president's "discretionary authority in reference to the information called for by either House"[13] in a case in which virtually all the information requested by the House was actually furnished.

Against the handful of assertions of the power to refuse information must be placed the plethora of cases in which requested papers were sent without demur to the House concerned. The general picture during the nineteenth century was one of all-but-unquestioned

9. New York Trust Co. v. Eisner, 256 U.S. 345, 349 (1921).
10. Berger, *Executive Privilege*, p. 132.
11. See Bernard Schwartz, *From Confederation to Nation: The American Constitution 1835–1877* (Baltimore: Johns Hopkins, 1973), p. 72.
12. See ibid.
13. Quoted ibid. This 1843 Tyler message contained the first elaborate and reasoned justification for executive privilege; but it was far from the recent extreme assertions of the doctrine. See Berger, *Executive Privilege*, pp. 184–185.

presidential compliance with congressional requests for information. In 1886, a leading member of the Senate, Senator Edmunds, was able to state that in the past forty years neither House had "failed on its call to get the information that it has asked for from the public Departments of the Government."[14] After Polk's referred-to refusal, the practice was one of unfailing assent to such requests. The Edmunds speech contains a list of instances from the 1840s to the 1880s, in which senatorial requests for papers were complied with without question.

The general pre–Civil War practice may be exemplified by what happened under Polk. Our picture here extends beyond what is normally available to the historian in public documents because of the detailed information given in the diary that Polk kept while he was president. From it we can see that most congressional requests to see papers were worked out by agreement between Capitol Hill and the White House. Sometimes the legislators concerned were persuaded that the disclosure would indeed be against the national interest. In July 1846, the Senate passed a resolution calling for certain papers. Polk called the mover, Senator Reverdy Johnson, to the White House and showed him that the papers contained military plans for the invasion of California, which should not be made public. On Johnson's advice, Polk left the Senate call unanswered.[15]

In other cases, Polk acceded to congressional calls for papers, even against the advice of his cabinet. In one instance, in 1846, the House called for information on the military governments set up in territory conquered from Mexico. Polk decided to "send in all the information called for," despite the strong opposition of Secretary of State Buchanan.[16] Earlier the same year, Polk had sent to Congress the correspondence with Louis McLane, then minister in London, relating to English military and naval preparations,[17] after having originally decided not to communicate it.[18]

14. 17 Congressional Record 2215.
15. James K. Polk, *The Diary of James K. Polk during His Presidency*, ed. M. M. Quaife, 4 volumes (Chicago: A. C. McClurg & Co., 1910), 2:13–14.
16. Ibid., p. 281.
17. J. D. Richardson, *A Compilation of the Messages and Papers of the Presidents* (Washington, D.C.: Government Printing Office, 1896), p. 422; Polk, *Diary*, 2:212.
18. Polk, *Diary*, 2:209.

A particularly difficult case arose in 1848, when the House called for the instructions of John Slidell, who had been engaged, before the war with Mexico broke out, as a presidential envoy who was to attempt to negotiate with that country.[19] Polk was most reluctant to communicate the instructions "because I deemed their publication, pending the war with Mexico, and until a Treaty of peace was concluded . . . , prejudicial to the public interests."[20] In accordance with this view, he sent a message declining to comply.[21] But he did communicate the instructions confidentially to the Senate in executive session,[22] and a few months later, he sent the Slidell instructions to both houses, among the documents included with the transmission of the ratified peace treaty with Mexico: "Upon the conclusion of a definitive Treaty of peace with Mexico, the reasons for withholding them at that time no longer exist."[23]

The pre–Civil War practice culminated in appearances by John Tyler and Abraham Lincoln before congressional committees. In 1846 an investigation was made by a House committee into a charge that Secretary of State Webster had misappropriated a secret State Department fund. Among those questioned was ex-President Tyler, on the subject of the expenditure of secret funds during his presidency. The committee concluded that there was no proof "to impeach Mr. Webster's integrity, or the purity of his motive in the discharge of the duties of his office."[24]

Even more striking were two appearances before congressional committees by Lincoln during the Civil War. The first was in 1862, when (according to a contemporary newspaper) "President Lincoln today voluntarily appeared before the House Judiciary Committee and gave testimony on the matter of the premature publication in the Herald of a portion of his last annual message."[25] Then, in 1863, Lincoln made a dramatic appearance before the Joint Committee on the Conduct of the War to declare: "It is untrue that any of my family hold treasonable communication with the enemy." The com-

19. Ibid., 1:289.
20. Ibid., 3:398.
21. Richardson, *Compilation of the Messages and Papers of the Presidents*, p. 565; Polk, *Diary*, 4:27–28.
22. Polk, *Diary*, 3:399.
23. Ibid., 4:4.
24. U.S. Congress, *Congressional Globe*, 29th Cong., 1st sess., 1846, p. 1946.
25. Quoted in *The New York Times*, June 30, 1973, p. 15.

mittee members "were so greatly affected that the committee adjourned for the day."[26]

During the Civil War itself, Lincoln gave in to virtually all demands for information made by Congress, particularly by the Committee on the Conduct of the War.[27] Military secrets, conduct of operations, diplomatic matters, and the like were all provided without question by the president. When Senator Edmunds, in his already-referred-to 1886 speech, declared that during the previous forty years Congress had not failed to get the information it had asked for from the executive, he was including the Civil War period.

There were, it is true, executive refusals in addition to those already mentioned.[28] But they were strikingly few by comparison with the whole mass of instances in which congressional demands for information were complied with. If executive and legislative practice is to be considered, the grants as well as the refusals of information should be considered if a true picture is to be obtained. The readiness displayed by the president and executive agencies in innumerable cases in furnishing information is at least as strong a precedent as the comparatively rare instances of refusals.

This point was well made by a congressman during the questioning of the present writer in a 1956 hearing:

> MR. MEADER: Let me ask you if there is not just as respectable a history of precedents where the executive branch of the government has given information to Congress on request of congressional committees?
>
> PROFESSOR SCHWARTZ: Yes.
>
> MR. MEADER: Would that not argue just as strongly that because the executive time after time had obeyed the order of the Congress and had furnished information upon request, that therefore the right existed in the Congress to have that information and it

26. Carl Sandburg, *Abraham Lincoln* (New York: Harcourt, Brace & World, 1954), p. 385.

27. There were only two minor exceptions (see Schwartz and Wade, *Legal Control of Government*, p. 158) as well as a refusal to turn over the dispatches of Major Anderson to the War Department concerning the defense of Fort Sumter, which clearly involved war secrets (Richardson, *Compilation of the Messages and Papers of the Presidents*, 6:12).

28. According to a memorandum prepared for President Truman, there were fewer than ten such refusals during the last century, all on minor matters that were not pursued by Congress. See Nixon v. Sirica, 487 F2d 700, 732–733 (D.C. Cir. 1973).

had the power to have that information and it had consistently been recognized by the executive branch?

PROFESSOR SCHWARTZ: Yes, except, of course, the executive answer is that the accessions to congressional demands are matters of grace. We have the power to refuse but we are going to be good about it and not do it.

MR. MEADER: Could not the argument be made, on the other hand, that the Congress in not pressing and exercising its power was using its discretion to acquiesce and as a matter of grace in the specific instance did not press the point?

PROFESSOR SCHWARTZ: Yes, I think certainly.[29]

RECENT PRIVILEGE ASSERTIONS

"Herman Wolkinson has a lot to answer for."[30] In 1949, this obscure Justice Department functionary wrote an article in the *Federal Bar Journal* upholding executive power to withhold information from Congress.[31] In 1954, President Eisenhower directed the secretary of defense to instruct employees of his department to refuse to testify or produce documents during the Army McCarthy hearings.[32] The president's directive was supported by a memorandum of the attorney general, which asserted that the president and the heads of departments and agencies have the absolute privilege and discretion to withhold from Congress any papers and information that they deem to be required to be kept secret in the public interest.[33]

This was an assertion of executive privilege far beyond any previously made. It was based almost entirely upon the Wolkinson article, for the attorney general's memorandum was lifted virtually word for word from that article.[34] For the attorney general's real source of

29. U.S. Congress, House, Committee on Governmental Operations, *Hearings on Availability of Information from Federal Departments and Agencies*, 84th Cong., 2d sess. (1956), pt. 3, p. 501.

30. Garry Wills, *The New York Times Book Review*, May 5, 1974, p. 1.

31. Herman Wolkinson, *Demands of Congressional Committees for Congressional Papers*, 10 *Federal Bar Journal* 103, 223, 319 (1949).

32. Reprinted in *Right of Access by Special Subcommittee on Legislative Oversight . . .* , 85th Cong., 1st sess., 1957, p. 67.

33. Reprinted ibid.

34. See Bishop, *The Executive's Right of Privacy: An Unresolved Constitutional Question*, 66 *Yale Law Journal* 477, 478 (1957). The same was true of a 1958 memorandum by Attorney General Rogers. See Berger, *Executive Privilege*, p. 163.

authority to be an obscure law-review writer (himself a Justice Department employee) is most disturbing. Once upon a time legislative power was sought to be restricted by the authority of the crown. But here we have a case where an essential function of the people's representatives is emasculated, not by royal proclamation, but by the prerogative of one Herman Wolkinson.

Raoul Berger has just demonstrated the amazingly weak scholarship of both the Wolkinson article and the attorney general's memorandum:[35] They are based upon an incredible melange of bad history, bad logic, and bad law.[36] Thus, to give an example mentioned by Berger[37] (but not sufficiently stressed by him on its main point), the memorandum (parroting Wolkinson) asserts that "one of the best reasoned precedents" of presidential refusal to permit the disclosure of confidential information was President Tyler's refusal to communicate to the House certain reports relative to the affairs of the Cherokee Indians and to the frauds practiced upon them.[38] The memorandum refers to Tyler's January 31, 1843, message, in which he asserted an executive power to withhold information. But it neglects to state that in that message Tyler did furnish to the House virtually all the information it had requested.[39]

The recent development of executive privilege well illustrates the legal saw that hard cases make bad law. The president's 1954 directive to the defense secretary and the attorney general's supporting memorandum were called forth by the Army McCarthy hearings. Those who might have opposed the assertion of executive privilege remained silent rather than appear to lend support to McCarthyism and all that it represented.[40] But the doctrine used to deny informa-

---

35. Berger, *Executive Privilege*, chapter 6. Berger deals with the 1958 memorandum referred to in note 33, but his devastating criticism applies equally to the 1954 memorandum, which is also taken almost verbatim from the Wolkinson article.

36. U.S. Congress, House, Committee on Governmental Operations, Hearings, p. 501.

37. Berger does discuss the Tyler refusal (*Executive Privilege,* p. 183), but he does not emphasize (though he mentions it in a footnote) what is the key fact: that Tyler did give the House almost all the information it asked for.

38. Quoted in *Right of Access by Special Subcommittee on Legislative Oversight . . . ,* 85th Cong., 1st sess., 1957, p. 70.

39. See Richardson, *Compilation of the Messages and Papers of the Presidents,* 4:220.

40. Thus a *Washington Post* editorial of May 20, 1954, emphasized the president's rebuff to "government-by-McCarthy."

tion to Senator McCarthy could also be used twenty years later to deny information to the Senate Select Committee investigating Watergate. People who approved refusals to protect the executive from McCarthyism might deplore refusals designed to "stonewall" penetrations of Watergate. But both refusals rested upon the same uncontrolled executive-privilege doctrine, with its core the assertions contained in the attorney general's memorandum.

Legal rules, unlike those in the physical sciences, do not have fixed areas of strains and stresses. Instead, they tend to be pushed ever further, to the very verge of the breaking point permitted by expediency. "You cannot blame the Minister for trying it on," declared a British civil servant over a generation ago on the executive tendency to seek to go beyond the letter permitted by the law.[41] Similarly, it would be naive not to expect the doctrine asserted in 1954 to be extended by later presidents. Executive privilege has proved to be peculiarly of an encroaching nature, particularly in its assertions by President Nixon.

NIXON AND PRIVILEGE

According to the young Karl Marx, "the general ethos of bureaucracy is secrecy."[42] There is a Herblock cartoon in which two high-ranking bureaucrats are discussing a blunder on their part. "We certainly bungled that one," says one to the other. "How shall we label it, 'Secret' or 'Top Secret?'"

Though published before Mr. Nixon became president, this cartoon characterizes the Nixon attitude toward executive privilege. The privilege doctrine was expanded by the Nixon administration beyond all previous limits, and this was done to enable the doctrine to be used as a principal executive instrument to avoid disclosures of improprieties, not only in the departments, but within the White House itself.

Though Nixon, like other recent presidents, made a commitment not to invoke executive privilege unduly,[43] he asserted it more than

41. Quoted in Bernard Schwartz, *Law and the Executive in Britain* (New York University Press, 1949), p. 167.
42. David McLellan, *Karl Marx: His Life and Thought* (New York: Harper & Row, 1973), p. 72.
43. See Berger, *Executive Privilege*, p. 253.

any other president. It was estimated in 1973 that two-thirds of the occasions on which the executive refused to furnish information to Congress occurred in the previous twenty years.[44] The vast majority of these occurred during Nixon's presidency. A study prepared by the Library of Congress shows that executive privilege was asserted six times under Presidents Kennedy and Johnson and nineteen times during President Nixon's first term.[45]

The Nixon notion expanded executive privilege not only quantitatively but also qualitatively. Nixon asserted a complete immunity from disclosure requirements for the White House. On March 12, 1973, he directed that no "member or former member" of the White House staff shall appear before Congress.[46] A month later his attorney general asserted the extraordinary claim that this immunity extended to all federal employees. The president, the attorney general declared, is empowered to forbid federal employees from testifying before congressional committees under any circumstances and to block congressional demands for *any* document within the executive branch.[47]

We now know that these extreme assertions were blatantly cynical tactical moves in the White House endeavor to frustrate the Watergate investigations. The publication of the White House transcripts has given us an unprecedented insight into the inner operations of the president's office. They show that the executive-privilege doctrine has been a major element of the various "scenarios" rehearsed by the president and his staff to meet public pressure but still avoid full disclosure.

On April 10, 1973, Attorney General Kleindienst put forward his already-referred-to claim that executive privilege covered all federal employees. A conversation between the attorney general and the president on April 15 demonstrates that this was only a tactical device designed to limit the Senate Watergate Committee probe. As Nixon put it, "After your hard lining the executive privilege I think we ought to make a deal with the Ervin Committee provided the ground rules are proper."[48] The Kleindienst "hard line" was the

44. Anthony Lewis, *The New York Times*, August 20, 1973, p. 31.
45. The study is reprinted in Berger, *Executive Privilege*, p. 373.
46. Ibid., p. 254.
47. Ibid., pp. 254–255.
48. *The New York Times, The White House Transcripts* (New York: Bantam 1974), p. 471.

means to secure "a bargain—the thing by which you are going to work that out."[49] In an earlier conversation, John D. Ehrlichman, a top aide, conceded to the president, with regard to the attorney general's claim, "Now that was a tactic. Kleindienst took a hard line up there . . . because if he had softened it at all, that would have really hurt our negotiations."[50]

The extent to which the White House was willing to go in using executive privilege as a cover-up tactic may be seen from a discussion on making two former White House staff members implicated in Watergate "consultants" in order to shield them with executive privilege:

HALDEMAN: Say, did you raise the question with the president on Colson as a consultant . . . ?

DEAN: The thought was as a consultant, without doing any consulting, he wants it for continued protection on—

HALDEMAN: Solely for the purpose of executive privilege protection, I take it. . . .

PRESIDENT: What happens to Chapin?

DEAN: Well, Chapin doesn't have quite the same problem in appearing as Colson will.

HALDEMAN: Yeah—you have the same problem of Chapin appearing as Colson.

PRESIDENT: Well, can't—that would [be] such an obvious fraud to have both of them as consultants, that that won't work.[51]

CASE LAW

The 1954 attorney general's memorandum asserts categorically that "courts have uniformly held that the President and the heads of departments have an uncontrolled discretion to withhold the information and papers in the public interest."[52] This assertion is all the more remarkable, since neither the attorney general nor the Wolkinson article cites any cases in support. The truth is that there is no authority in federal court decisions for uncontrolled executive withholding of information from Congress or the courts.

49. Ibid.
50. Ibid., p. 314.
51. Ibid., p. 93.
52. Quoted in *The White House Transcripts*, p. 68.

Until 1974, the Supreme Court case in point was *United States* v. *Reynolds.*[53] It rejects the claim of absolute discretion in the executive. Though decided a year before the 1954 attorney general's memorandum, the *Reynolds* decision is not even mentioned in the memorandum, which emphasizes the already-made point about the quality of scholarship in the memorandum. *Reynolds* arose out of the crash of a military aircraft on a flight to test secret electronic equipment, in which certain civilian observers were killed. Their widows sued the United States under the Federal Tort Claims Act. Plaintiffs moved for discovery of the air force's official accident investigation report, but the secretary of the air force filed a claim of privilege objecting to production of the document. The Supreme Court adopted the view that the determination of privilege, even where military secrets are involved, is a judicial function: "The court itself must determine whether the circumstances are appropriate for the claim of privilege. . . . "[54] *Reynolds* went a long way toward putting to rest the view stated by presidents and attorneys general "that the President's final and absolute assertion of Executive privilege is conclusive on the courts."[55] Under *Reynolds* it is for the judge to determine whether privilege is validly claimed. "The court itself must determine whether the circumstances are appropriate for the claim of privilege."[56] If examination of a document is necessary before the judge can decide whether it should be disclosed, he can and must make such examination. As a more recent federal case puts it, "Any claim to executive absolutism cannot override the duty of the court to assure that an official has not exceeded his charter or flouted the legislative will."[57]

WATERGATE TAPES CASE

It was essentially the *Reynolds* approach that was followed by the Supreme Court in *United States* v. *Nixon*[58]—the *Watergate Tapes*

---

53. 345 U.S. 1 (1953).
54. Ibid., p. 8.
55. Nixon v. Sirica, 487 F2d 700, 714 (D.C. Cir. 1973).
56. 345 U.S. at 8.
57. Committee for Nuclear Responsibility v. Seaborg, 463 4F2d 788, 793 (D.C. Cir. 1971).
58. 418 U.S. 683 (1974).

case. President Nixon there claimed that no court could require him to produce tape recordings pursuant to subpoena on motion of the Watergate special prosecutor for use in a criminal prosecution on charges of conspiracy to defraud the United States and to obstruct justice. He was asserting an absolute executive privilege, which disabled the courts from even inquiring into whether privilege was applicable to the subpoenaed evidence, since the president, rather than the courts, had final authority to decide whether privilege applies in the circumstances. Under the president's claim, the executive's mere assertion of privilege was sufficient to overcome any need (even that to enforce criminal statutes) for the subpoenaed materials.

The *Watergate Tapes* decision categorically rejected the president's claim. Though there may be an executive privilege in maintaining military and diplomatic secrecy, the applicability of the privilege is a judicial, not an executive, question; "it is 'emphatically the province and the duty' of this court 'to say what the law is' with respect to the claim of privilege presented in this case."[59] Neither the separation of powers nor the need for confidentiality of presidential communications can sustain "an absolute unqualified presidential privilege of immunity from judicial process."[60]

The interest in confidentiality of presidential communications is not diminished by production of such material for *in camera* inspection by a court. The president's need for confidentiality is general in nature, while the need for production of relevant evidence in a criminal case is specific and central to the fair decision of the criminal case. The generalized interest in confidentiality cannot prevail over the demands of due process in criminal justice. "The generalized assertion of privilege must yield to the demonstrated, specific used for evidence in a pending criminal trial."[61]

CONCLUSION

The *Watergate Tapes* decision should put to rest the claim of an uncontrolled presidential privilege. It has already played a major role in the constitutional process as a prime catalyst in inducing Mr. Nixon's resignation.

59. Ibid., p. 703.
60. Ibid., p. 706.
61. Ibid., p. 713.

It may, nevertheless, be doubted that even a unanimous Supreme Court decision can by itself restore the constitutional balance. "If not good law, there was worldly wisdom in the maxim attributed to Napoleon that 'The tools belong to the man who can use them.' "[62] In political, as in natural science, nature abhors a vacuum. If extreme executive claims are not resisted by Congress, they tend to take over the field. Executive privilege may be only a "myth," but myths can become reality if enough people can be made to believe in them. For every *Watergate Tapes* decision that rejects presidential pretensions, there is a mass of administrative practice that has gone unchallenged. If presidential performance during the Nixon administration has provided an opportunity to redress the organic imbalance, one would have to be oversanguine to expect the needed congressional resurgence as a result.

Of course, the abuse of executive privilege constitutes but one aspect of the movement toward an "imperial Presidency."[63] The nation has in recent years heard arguments on behalf of the presidency such as have not been presented in the English-speaking world since the time of Charles I. As Senator Javits put it, "Watergate came about, at least in part, because the Presidency had become an office of such awesome authority that those close to an incumbent Chief Executive seemingly could be led to believe that they were above the law, especially when they felt able to cite 'higher' grounds of loyalty to the President . . . as justification for their actions."[64] In executive privilege as in other areas of political power, the overriding constitutional need has become that of somehow reducing the presidency to "life-size." The alternative is the view attributed to William H. Seward over a century ago: "We elect a king for four years and give him absolute power."[65]

62. Jackson, J., concurring, in Youngstown Sheet & Tube Co. v. Sawyer, 343 U.S. 579, 654 (1952).

63. See Arthur M. Schlesinger, *The Imperial Presidency* (Boston: Houghton Mifflin, 1973).

64. Jacob Javits, *Who Makes War: The President Versus Congress* (New York: Morrow, 1973), p. xx.

65. Quoted in Edward S. Corwin and Louis W. Koenig, *The Presidency Today* (New York: New York University Press, 1956), p. 61.

9

Canada

G. BRUCE DOERN

Because of its liberal democratic traditions, Canada has shared many of the ambivalent principles and contradictory practices that surround government secrecy in contemporary democratic politics. In recent years this has been reflected, among other ways, in two governmental studies, the 1969 Royal Commission on Security and the 1969 Task Force on Government Information,[1] and in the general orientations of Prime Minister Pierre Elliott Trudeau, a political leader fond of conceptualizing politics in the modern idioms of cybernetics and information theory.

The Royal Commission on Security tended to focus on the more traditional concerns of governmental secrecy as they relate to matters of international and domestic security. The Task Force on Government Information tended to stress the need for governments to utilize the full range of technological modes of communication to ensure that the public had more complete knowledge of governmental programs and that governmental authorities were in turn conscious of the grievances, demands, and needs of its citizens. Hence it titled its report to Prime Minister Trudeau *To Know and Be Known*.

1. See *Report of the Royal Commission on Security*, abridged (Ottawa: Queen's Printer, 1969; hereafter called Canadian Report) and *To Know and Be Known*, Report of the Task Force on Government Information, vol. 1 (Ottawa: Queen's Printer, 1969).

While these reports indicate a concern for the two halves of the democratic equation and hence mirror similar concerns in other states, there are other factors in the Canadian political environment, which, in part at least, differentiate the politics of secrecy and information in Canada from other states. First, Canada's bilingual status requires the development of political communication in both English and French. The continuing legitimacy of federal institutions, particularly in the view of French Canadians, is dependent upon the development of language policies and practices that will both increase their individual and collective influence and improve the information they possess about public policies and programs. Recent political history has been concerned with the political accommodation of French Canadians through such policies as the Official Languages Act, regional economic development incentives, and changes in cultural and social policy.

A second factor is the importance of, and difficulty in, communicating in a country that is geographically immense, but relatively small in population, and that has developed strong regional bases of power in provincial governments as a reflection of its diversity.[2]

Canada's political history has also witnessed the emergence and persistence in federal politics of so-called third political parties, which have often been based on regional or provincial protests against the Canadian Ontario-based centers of power. In recent years even the Progressive Conservative party, the official opposition to the governing Liberal party for most of the past four decades, has reflected a regional base of power centered in western Canada and in the eastern maritime provinces.

The power of provincial governments both reflects and reinforces these patterns but is augmented by the considerable formal constitutional power they possess over such policy fields as natural resources, education, and social welfare. The place of secrecy and information *within* provincial governments reflects similar traditions in that cabinet-parliamentary systems of government exist at the provincial level. This means that while there is, of necessity, considerable exchange of information between the federal and provincial levels of government, there is also a considerable amount of strategic withholding of information for policy analysis purposes. These factors,

2. See R. Van Loon and M. Whittington, *The Canadian Political System* (Toronto: McGraw-Hill, 1971).

plus the relatively small number of provincial governments and the power they possess, mean that intergovernmental politics in Canada is sometimes accurately compared with international diplomacy, with the political exchanges occurring at federal-provincial conferences of ministers. The conferences are usually (though not always) held in camera and hence escape the direct exposure of the mass media.[3]

As in all states with a liberal tradition of democratic government, Canada has strong traditions of freedom of the press. While its record of vigilant criticism has been a major factor in opening the processes of government, Canada has not had the tradition of a truly national press, in the sense of national newspapers such as *The New York Times* or the *Washington Post*. The development of the electronic media has been featured by the state itself intervening to create, though not control, national outlets for electronic communication. Thus the publicly owned Canadian Broadcasting Corporation provided the first national broadcasting service, and more recently Telesat Canada launched the world's first domestic satellite communication system.

Canada's position as neighbor of the powerful United States is reflected in the above policies of state intervention, particularly in recent years. The impact of the American mass media and the constant demonstration effect of the apparently more open processes of the congressional system are important influences on attitudes toward governmental processes.

All of these factors have resulted in a profound gap between the constitutional and official legal policies regarding secrecy and information and the realities of the political marketplace.

CONSTITUTIONAL AND LEGAL POLICIES

Governmental secrecy in Canada is based largely on British parliamentary practice:[4] the common-law doctrine of crown privilege, the traditions of ministerial responsibility and of an anonymous civil service, the principle of the freedom of the press, the Canadian version of the British Official Secrets Act, and a system of classifica-

3. See Richard Simeon, *Federal-Provincial Diplomacy* (Toronto: University of Toronto Press, 1972), and J. S. Dupre et al., *Federalism and Policy Development* (Toronto: University of Toronto Press, 1973).
4. See chapter 10, "Great Britain," by Colin Seymour-Ure.

tion for government documents. The prevailing view among scholars is that Canadian public bureaucracies are excessively secretive and that Canada's official information policies reflect traditional concepts and a slavish adherence to bureaucratic secrecy.[5]

Common-law traditions of crown privilege recognize the right of the crown to refuse to disclose classified information where it is felt that disclosure would be detrimental to the public interest. The concepts of ministerial responsibility and civil service anonymity have, in part, contributed to the general assumption that all documents are secret unless they are specifically declared to be public. These concepts also mean that opposition politicians are less able to question or criticize public servants than in other systems of government.

While the largest part of the Canadian practice of administrative secrecy has been based on informal constitutional tradition, it has also been influenced by the more specific statutory influence of the Canadian Official Secrets Act, as well as the Criminal Code of Canada. As Maxwell Cohen points out, the Canadian Official Secrets Act, like its British counterpart, is

> designed to cover spying in its generally understood sense of obtaining information not otherwise in the public domain in order to make it available to a foreign government or agent. Perhaps more important, section 2 of the British Act and section 4 of the Canadian Act embrace in intent almost any form of information obtained in the course of service or contract of employment, or otherwise, and then passed on without authority to any other person whatever his status and whatever the purposes of the transfer of information may be, however unclassified the information may be, if obtained from sources available because of holding a government position or having a government contract.[6]

Although disclosures of 1945 regarding a Soviet spy ring and a subsequent report by a Royal Commission on Espionage represented the zenith of public concern about secrecy in the area of espionage,

5. See D. C. Rowat "How Much Administrative Secrecy?" *Canadian Journal of Economics and Political Science* 31 (1965):477–498; and Louis Rivietz and John Jordan, "Administrative Secrecy and Departmental Discretion at the Federal and Provincial Levels in Canada" (Paper presented to Canadian Political Science Association, Montreal, 1972).

6. See Maxwell Cohen, "Secrecy in Law and Policy: The Canadian Experience and International Relations," in *Secrecy and Foreign Policy*, eds. Thomas M. Franck and E. Weisband (New York: Oxford, 1974) pp. 355–356.

other influences of the Official Secrets Act are less spectacular and more subtle. It continues to exert influence on practice precisely because it fails to distinguish the periodic serious offenses from the minor potential offenses that are likely to be the product of the day-to-day exercise of administrative discretion.

The high point in the governmental enforcement of secrecy in peacetime arose during the 1970 Quebec October Crisis. The possibility of seditious violence had been anticipated by the 1969 Royal Commission on Security in its analysis of separatism in Quebec. The October 1970 kidnapping of James Cross, the U.K. trade commissioner in Montreal, and of Pierre Laporte, the Quebec labor minister, and the subsequent murder of Mr. Laporte resulted in the proclamation of the War Measures Act on October 16, 1970. Under its severe powers, over 400 persons were arrested. In addition, regulations prohibited the media from publishing anything that threatened security or supported the Front Liberation de Quebec (FLQ), the organization believed to be responsible for the violence. Maxwell Cohen has captured the historic impact of these events:

Nothing in postwar Canada provided such drama or seemed to pose such threats to order as these almost "revolutionary" events. They affected the very image of societal stability in the Province of Quebec and particularly in Montreal. The Provincial authorities invited the "co-operation" of the national Government—or were compelled to accept it—and the air was filled with fear, enough to have influenced calculations by either the national or the Quebec Government. Anyone living in the Montreal area at the time, with some "feel" for the psychological realities, must admit to the sense of physical fear that haunted the region. It was fear, personal and institutional, fear for self and fear for society.

Serious debate has since taken place both among students of politics and public law, and among political parties and the public in general, as to the significance of this recourse to maximum force—unusual for Canada—and the suspension in substantial part of the role of the civil authority during a period of the crisis. Coming as the kidnappings and murder did, as climax to almost a decade of mounting violence and intense nationalist fervour (especially among the intellectuals and the youth in Quebec), the crimes at the time were not easy to evaluate for purposes of determining objectively the amount of force needed to meet the challenge. There are some, particularly on the left, who now argue that panic caused both Governments to resort to extravagant measures of control. This assessment has gained momentum since the actual number of revolutionary cell members involved was revealed to be not the three or four thousand terrorists estimated by one Federal Cabinet Minister, but only, at most, a few hundred.[7]

The Official Secrets Act influences the classification of government documents, particularly with respect to national security and external relations. The classification of documents as top secret, secret, or confidential is also influenced, however, by the important need to prevent the invasion of the privacy of an individual as well as to ensure the tendering of frank advice on policy options and strategies. Despite these restrictive provisions and the frequent difficulty in interpreting them, a considerable amount of government information is available or can be released.

INFORMATION LEAKAGE

In recent years there has been an increasing incidence of information leaks to the media. These leaks are in addition to those that cabinet ministers themselves sometimes strategically arrange. The strength of public-service norms regarding confidentiality and integrity has not prevented information leakages. Reports and studies dealing with foreign investment policy, bilingualism and biculturalism policy, and copies of cabinet policy documents have been leaked to and published in the press. The motivations for the leaks seemed to range from an attempt to expose and influence policymaking to a desire to merely embarrass the government. The reasons for increased incidence of information leaks are clearly connected to the disenchantment and alienation of individuals and groups with the status quo. They are also related to the burgeoning, and less easily controlled, growth of policy and planning branches of government departments whose tentacles extend, via contracts, to university academics and other external consultants.

The question of leaks and secrecy was addressed by Gordon Robertson, clerk of the privy council and secretary to the cabinet. Referring to the recent leaks, he comes down firmly on the side of the public servant's official responsibility.

7. Ibid., p. 363.

If we believe that representative and responsible government is the best way we have so far been able to work out to provide a degree of participation that is consistent with effective action and to give expression and reality to the general will in determination of the interests and wishes of the people as a whole, we cannot accept as permissible a liberty by those in the service of the state to place their convictions about policy, or about the public right to know, ahead of their official responsibility.[8]

The Robertson statement, however, merely begs a series of larger questions. There is clearly a very fine line between conviction-motivated leakages and official leakages, wherein the sharing of information by public servants with the media or with interest groups is not only tolerated but encouraged as a positive aid to consultative and participatory policymaking.

Because of the vagueness of the classification system and because of widespread awareness of the practice of discreet sharing of information between agencies and their clientele, the public servant is placed in the position of developing his own guidelines. The Royal Commission on Security noted the strong tendency, especially among junior officials, to overclassify documents in order to play it safe.[9] This may occur regardless of the official policies regarding secrecy. Even the liberal policies of classification and declassification that have been urged in Canada will have little effect if the necessary intrabureaucratic resources and support are not forthcoming to make such policies a practical reality.[10]

THE POLITICS OF SECRECY AND INFORMATION

The broader context of secrecy and information in Canada can be seen in the ambivalent approaches taken by the Trudeau government. To say that the approaches have been ambivalent is merely to point out the inherent importance of information as a politically strategic commodity. There is evidence in recent Canadian experience to

8. Gordon Robertson, Clerk of the Privy Council (mimeographed paper presented to the Royal Society of Canada, June 6, 1972), p. 25 and quoted in ibid., p. 365.

9. Canadian Report, pp. 71–72.

10. See Rowat, "How Much Administrative Secrecy?"

support both those who suggest that governmental processes reflect a more open and even information policy and those who suggest that the supply of information is increasingly controlled by the political executive and the bureaucracy.

Prime Minister Trudeau and his closest advisers, especially during the 1968 to 1972 period, tended to publicly conceptualize politics with metaphorical references drawn from information theory and cybernetics. Thus Trudeau sought to bring more "rational" policy processes to government. He defined the role of political parties as society's "radar":

> We . . . are aware that the many techniques of cybernetics, by transforming the control function and the manipulation of information, will transform our whole society. With this knowledge, we are wide awake, alert, capable of action, no longer are we blind, inert pawns of fate.[11]

The basic approach of Trudeau and his closest advisers seemed to be congruent, on a philosophical plane, with those political scientists who have argued that we ought to view the political system as a goal-seeking and error-correcting information system that will "learn how to learn."[12]

It is because of this view that the Trudeau government accepted both the substance and the reasoning of the 1969 Task Force on Information. The Trudeau government found the Task Force's assessment of the information imbalance to be persuasive, particularly the opinion that a large segment of the population was "thoroughly uninformed of Canadian political life."[13] It noted, moreover, the "remarkable failure of government to understand and exploit such technological miracles as television."[14] Both of these (and other) findings were related to the increasing demands for participatory democracy, a demand very much encouraged by the "coronation" atmosphere of the 1968 Trudeau electoral victory. The basic philosophy of the task force regarding the "right to know" was also endorsed by the government, and the task of implementing it was

---

11. Quoted in G. Bruce Doern and Peter Aucoin, eds., *The Structures of Policy Making in Canada* (Toronto: Macmillan, 1971), p. 65.
12. See especially K. Deutsch, *The Nerves of Government* (New York: Macmillan, 1963).
13. *To Know and Be Known*, p. 3.
14. Ibid., p. 2.

given primarily to Information Canada. As we have previously observed:

> In an earlier model of politics and policy processes such a structure would tend to be relatively illegitimate. For a politician with a cybernetic model of politics, such a structure becomes obvious and essential. While critics might view it as a propaganda agency, the Trudeau philosophy endorses it with great fanfare as an essential precondition to the effective development and implementation of public policy. The Trudeau shift in emphasis is symbolized, both metaphorically and structurally, by the creation of Information Canada.[15]

Quite predictably, the new agency became the center of controversy. The government, for example, was strategically selective. It sought to improve the citizens' knowledge of policies and programs but failed to establish a proposed survey research unit, which would presumably have brought together data (some of it undoubtedly critical of the government) on citizen attitudes toward government programs.[16] The initial appointment of an official from Trudeau's own Liberal party to head the agency also did little to dissuade opposition critics from their initial suspicions that Information Canada would become a propaganda arm of the governing political party. Opposition leader Robert Stanfield vowed to dismantle Information Canada arguing that "it is nonsense for this ministry to talk about setting up elaborate information services until the Prime Minister and his ministers are prepared to discharge their fundamental responsibility of answering questions in this chamber."[17]

The above reference to the parliamentary question period takes us into other realms in which the politics of secrecy and information was in operation. For while Information Canada was being launched with great fanfare, Trudeau had broken with long-standing parliamentary tradition by putting his ministers on a rotating roster system. Rather than having all ministers available in the House of Commons every day for questioning by the opposition parties, only some ministers would be available each day. While motivated by the desire to give ministers more time to attend to their ministries, the

15. G. Bruce Doern, "The Development of Policy Organizations in the Executive Arena," in Doern and Aucoin, *The Structures of Policy Making in Canada*, pp. 65–66.

16. *Globe and Mail*, February 11, 1972, p. 7.

17. Quoted in *Globe and Mail*, February 12, 1972, p. 7.

practice clearly had the effect of managing criticism and the exchange of information to suit the government's convenience. The practice of rotating ministers was dropped in 1972 when Trudeau was returned with a minority government.

In parliamentary systems there is a great imbalance between informational resources of the government on the one hand and the opposition groups on the other. This imbalance is much more marked in Canada than in the American congressional system. The Trudeau period witnessed a further ambivalence on this question, which draws particular attention to the different political uses of information. The opposition parties were granted generous increases in public funds in support of parliamentary research offices for each party caucus.[18] The Trudeau government wanted the parties, or so it seemed, to do better research on their policies and to participate more rationally in the parliamentary process. While the opposition parties gratefully accepted this largess, it was doubtful that they would use it as intended by the government. The research resources of opposition groups are still so puny in relation to that of the state that opposition groups are more likely to find greater marginal utility in using such resources not for policy research but rather for strategic party and organizational communication.

In addition there are at least four other areas in which the politics of secrecy and information have emerged in Canada. These areas include the experimentation with the white-paper process, the government's creation of its own critics, the use of royal commissions and task forces as instruments of governing, and the question of governmental access to corporate information.

The use of white papers as a prelegislative instrument of information has its Canadian origins in the post–World War II period.[19] In general the process involves the preparation of a document outlining the government's basic policy on an issue. In the early Trudeau years this device was transformed from a strictly informational instrument to a process around which greater consultation and participation would emerge. There was a greater implication that the government would be prepared to alter its policies if the process generated

18. See E. R. Black, "Opposition Research: Some Theories and Practices," *Canadian Public Administration* 15, 1 (Spring 1972):24–41.

19. See Audrey Doerr, "The Role of White Papers," in Doern and Aucoin, *The Structures of Policy Making in Canada*, pp. 179–203.

a different consensus or set of views. Again the white-paper process demonstrated mixed political results depending upon one's point of view and the political value one places on the strategic relationship between timing, information, and participation.

One assessment of the lengthy consultation that took place on the White Paper on Tax Reform pointed out that the individuals and interest groups that were most likely to benefit from the proposal were the least able to be mobilized or to participate in the process.[20] On the other hand, important information was generated that helped avoid serious problems with some of the proposals. The length of the consultation process and the complexity of the subject matter also resulted in a long period of uncertainty as to what final policy would be. This experience can be contrasted with the White Paper on Indian Policy, where a similar process of consultation permitted the affected Indian constituency to virtually reverse the government's policy.[21] The unpredictability of the process and its policy outcomes seem to have put the use of white papers into a state of suspension. The experiment was not repeated in such important areas as foreign investment policy, resource policy, or the status of women.

During the past decade, policy advisory bodies have been established in which the government has virtually created its own critics. Bodies like the Economic Council of Canada and the Science Council of Canada, to name two of the most important, have been created to bring debate in their respective policy domains out of the closed executive-bureaucratic deliberation process and into a somewhat broader public arena. Although composed of individuals from various sectors of the economy, these bodies must be seen in some respects as a form of intermediary buffer between the well-established interest groups and the executive. The publication of council reports has been an important addition to public debate, although the real influence of the councils has been limited. These agencies have found their political strategies as external advisers and critics very much dependent on their own access to information, most of it housed in regular government departments. Thus they must constantly weigh the strategic advantages of being either an aggressive public critic

20. Ibid., pp. 195–200.
21. See Audrey Doerr, "Indian Policy," in *Issues in Canadian Public Policy*, eds. G. Bruce Doern and V. Seymour Wilson (Toronto: Macmillan, 1974), chapter 2.

and therefore being unlikely to get the necessary information, or a quiet behind-the-scenes advocate, a strategy more likely to secure the necessary information and influence.[22]

More constant and influential information exchanges occur between interest groups and the executive-bureaucratic machinery. In cabinet systems the cabinet and the bureaucracy, rather than Parliament, are clearly the arenas of operation for interest groups.[23] In recent years, influenced by consumer advocates and other emerging "interests," government agencies have provided funds to such groups to enable them to develop the capacity to assemble the necessary information and expertise and to challenge other agencies of government.

In their strategic political use, white papers and advisory bodies must be seen, in part, as being similar to the historic Canadian use of royal commissions and task forces. Among the range of governing instruments, the Canadian political process has always included the utilization of symbolic informational outputs either to precede, or to substitute for, other governing outputs such as more substantive spending and regulative programs. This can be seen as a basically manipulative practice, which distorts democracy. But from the point of view of governing politicians, it is likely to have a less Machiavellian connotation, reflecting instead such day-to-day political realities as uncertainty, lack of financial resources, cabinet conflict over priorities, and the desire to give the appearance of doing something, rather than the appearance of doing nothing, or of not knowing what to do.[24]

The appropriate information balance will also be central in the area of governmental ability to acquire information needed for the regulation of power exercised by private corporations. Recent debates in Canada on energy policy, the regulation of multinational firms, and the regulation of transportation and communications indicate the excessive degree to which Canadian governments have been almost wholly dependent upon information generated by private companies for the making of vital public policy. Recent developments in transportation regulation indicate that the federal government will

22. See Doern and Aucoin, *The Structures of Policy Making in Canada*, pp. 263–265 and 278–279.

23. See Robert Presthus, *Elite Accommodation in Canadian Politics* (Toronto: Macmillan, 1973).

24. See Doern and Wilson, *Issues in Canadian Public Policy*, conclusions.

pass a transportation information act to secure better governmental access to private information.

CONCLUDING OBSERVATIONS

As with other democratic countries, Canada will undoubtedly continue to experience difficulties in striking an appropriate balance between the public's right to know and to participate, and government's preference for confidentiality.

Having in mind the foregoing review of Canadian law, politics, and practice, it would appear that Canada is ripe for legislative change along the lines recently proposed by Professor Maxwell Cohen. Cohen proposes a single statute, which would combine a liberal concept of access to information, a modernized official secrets act, standards for classification of documents, provisions for a classification review mechanism, and time scales for the release of material.

A single statute thus could incorporate (1) the right to information that it is not necessary to keep secret, and—after a period of years—virtually all information; (2) the criminal law prohibitions on disclosure of information that it is necessary to keep secret; (3) a classification system to distinguish between what must, and what need not, be kept secret; and (4) an independent body to review the way this distinction is applied in practice. This proposal has the virtue of combining complementary ideas within a single legislative project. It would also have to reconcile clearly antagonistic positions, and would moreover require considerable skill in draftsmanship to incorporate statements that liberalize the disclosure of information with the subsequent sections dealing with prohibitions on communication and disclosure. The virtues outweigh the difficulties. In a single statute the public, the bureaucracy, and the courts could all see more readily the balancing of interests: the liberalizing provisions regarding access, and the restrictive rules for the protection of confidentiality.[25]

In the realm of political practice, as distinct from legislated policy, there will be a need for a more extensive political use of both the old and the newly tried devices of political consultation and participation. Such increasing experimentation will require a more candid admission

25. Cohen, "Secrecy in Law and Policy," p. 354.

by both politicians and citizens of the need to trade some control over the timing and content of decisions for the achievement of more legitimate, and hence ultimately more effective, public policies. In the foreseeable future the capacity of the Canadian government to regulate private, especially corporate, power in the public interest is likely to require acknowledgment by government of the unsatisfactory extent to which it has relied on private information supplied by such centers of power. In short, the realm of political practice in Canada will have to acknowledge more openly the strategic political importance of information as a scarce political commodity.

10

Great Britain

COLIN SEYMOUR-URE

INTRODUCTION

"The right to know" is not a value deeply entrenched in British political culture. The editor of the Sunday *Times,* a paper that has thrived on investigative journalism in the last decade, commented in 1974: "Our philosophy and, in turn, our law and our attitudes have been conditioned to defend free speech rather than free inquiry."[1] British government is highly secretive: a result of the marriage between modern, large-scale bureaucracy and an oligarchic political tradition. The bureaucracy swells with the ever-widening scope of government activity, while the tradition (increasingly meritocratic) has survived because of an enduring homogeneity of political culture. Government has been granted ready legitimacy, perfectly symbolized by the absence of a written constitution; and it has not been expected to carry on its business in a glare of publicity.

Now, however, there are pressures against secrecy. Some are in the political institutions themselves; some are discernible in popular attitudes, shifting forms of political behavior, and pressures for change in the law; and some derive from changes in mass media. It

1. Harold Evans, "The Half-Free Press," in Granada Guildhall Lectures, *The Freedom of the Press* (London: Hart-Davis, MacGibbon, 1974), p. 37.

is upon these pressures, set out under the various headings below, that the bulk of this essay concentrates.

THE EFFECT OF CONSTITUTIONAL AND LEGAL PRINCIPLES

Collective and Individual Ministerial Responsibility

Much government secrecy follows from a few bedrock constitutional principles. First, there is the convention of collective cabinet responsibility.[2] The point of this in the eighteenth century was to protect individual ministers against the king, who could ill afford to ignore the advice of a united ministry. With the gradual nineteenth-century displacement of the king's power the convention became equally effective in maintaining a government's majority in the House of Commons. Members of Parliament thought twice about voting down a minister if that meant turning out the whole government. Cabinet secrecy—a bare list of the names of those attending is all that anyone is officially supposed to know—is an obvious instrument of collective responsibility. It permits uninhibited private argument to precede the cool unanimity with which decisions are made public. The Opposition has no chance to exploit disagreements; neither do dissident government supporters. The convention is strengthened by its application to ministers outside the cabinet, who may have had nothing to do with most policy decisions yet must remain loyal to them. In 1969, a junior minister, Jeremy Bray, was obliged by Harold Wilson to resign because he published a book containing criticism of government policy.[3] The convention therefore covers at least fifty ministers (depending on the government's size).

A second crucial convention is individual ministerial responsibility.[4] A minister is responsible to Parliament for every action carried out by officials in his department. Exactly what "responsible" means is a matter of dispute. But if nothing else it means "answerable," and the principle has the important corollary that no one else is answer-

2. See E. C. S. Wade and G. Godfrey Phillips, *Constitutional Law*, 6th ed. (London: Longmans, 1963), pp. 75 ff.

3. Mr. Wilson said in the usual exchange of letters that he had "no alternative but to uphold the principles which every Prime Minister must maintain in relation to the collective responsibility of his Administration." *Times* (London), September 25, 1969.

4. Wade and Phillips, *Constitutional Law*, p. 75.

able. The civil servants themselves who make most of the decisions remain anonymous and invisible. They are not accountable directly or personally to the public or to any system of administrative courts. They appear before parliamentary committees only with the approval of their ministers and cannot be obliged to answer questions. In this way the logic of Parliament's right to control the executive, ultimately through the purse, is maintained. Even information that is to become public is conventionally presented to Parliament first. The report of a royal commission or a parliamentary select committee, or the contents of a white paper expounding government policy, may be ready for some time but cannot be published by the press until Parliament has received it. Indeed, premature publication of a select committee report, which is the property of the House of Commons, is a breach of privilege—potentially endangering the proper performance of the House's functions—and as such it is in principle punishable as contempt.[5]

Party Discipline

Collective . responsibility is buttressed by, and itself encourages, party discipline. This discipline is further increased by the competitive party context. While the government party remains united for fear of losing its majority, the Opposition must be united in order to present a credible alternative at the next general election. The fact that for at least fifty years now the Opposition cannot have expected to defeat the government in the House and that the government decides the timing of the next election (within the five years limit) puts a particular priority on long-term unity. Presenting a united front in opposition thus also entails secretiveness. As far as possible, the inevitable squabbles about policy and personalities must be carried on in private, and the parliamentary party meetings in which these take place carry strong informal sanctions against disclosure.

A "Westminster Bias"

Ministerial responsibility and party discipline have a double effect. They put the weight of publicity about government very firmly upon

5. T. Erskine May, *Treatise on the Law, Privileges and Proceedings of Parliament*, 17th ed. (London: 1964), p. 119.

the forum of Parliament, but they make information difficult to get. Westminster is the turnstile of the government amusement park; yet many of the merry-go-rounds are tucked away in Whitehall. The parliamentary bias may give a distorted image of government activity. The problems facing the Opposition provide a good example of the consequences. Opposition is the time for formulating fresh policies. Yet precisely when access to official information is important, a party in opposition is cut off from it. In a very few areas, like defense, the virtue of a well-informed Opposition is recognized. By convention, too, Opposition leaders maintain contacts with civil servants to discuss administrative questions touching on their prospective policies. Near an election the initiative may even come, as in 1964, from the civil servants.[6] Apart from this, the financial poverty of British parties makes Opposition spokesmen almost literally helpless. In the latter period of the 1970 Conservative government the Labour shadow cabinet had six modestly paid research assistants, financed by a research foundation, the Rowntree Trust. There were a few other ramshackle arrangements: one shadow minister, for instance, had an assistant paid for by a publisher. The research department of the Labour party outside Parliament could offer only limited help due to its own shortage of resources.[7] The Conservative party, being wealthier, does better. The result of these shortcomings is that Opposition spokesmen cannot even make effective use of what official information is available in routine but important forms like departmental reports and the estimates.

Legal Provisions

The main bugbear of those concerned at the extent of government secrecy is the various official secrets acts.[8] The chief act, dating from 1911, defines secret or confidential information so widely that the civil servant's conventional cup of tea is covered. Particularly un-

6. See the *Times* (London), April 22, 1970, and George Brown, *In My Way* (Harmondsworth: Penguin Books, 1972), p. 88.

7. R. M. Punnett, *Front-Bench Opposition* (London: Heinemann, 1973), pp. 272–278. Cf. Brown, *In My Way*, p. 89.

8. The best history of the Official Secrets Acts is David Williams, *Not in the Public Interest* (London: Hutchinson, 1965). See also Harry Street, *Freedom, the Individual and the Law* (Harmondsworth: Penguin Books, 1964), and Jonathan Aitken, *Officially Secret* (London: Weidenfeld and Nicolson, 1971).

popular with journalists is section 2, which makes it an offense to receive and retain information as well as to disclose it. The effect of this act is said to be arbitrary and unpredictable, liable to the temptation of "political" use, and grossly inhibiting to reasonable journalistic inquiry. In 1973, for instance, the act was threatened against an inconspicuous specialist publication, *Railway Gazette,* for publishing an official document discussing drastic reduction in the railway network.

The best proof of the breadth of the various secrets acts is that without official guidance about what will in practice be prosecuted as an offense, they could not work at all. This guidance is provided by D (Defense) Notices, issued by a joint committee of civil servants and representatives of the mass media.[9] The notices are cast in fairly general terms and constitute in effect a warning, not a prohibition against publication. They are wide enough to need interpretation themselves; and the person who gives it, the secretary to the committee, is thus a key figure—all the more so since newspapers are evidently willing on occasion to refrain from publishing something at his request, even though he admits that no D Notice is strictly applicable.

The D Notice system has generally worked well since 1912. There have been modifications and periodic rows—the last being in 1967, when the Wilson government disagreed with the secretary to the committee about whether the meaning of one notice did or did not cover a *Daily Express* story about government appraisal of overseas cables. More important than that, however, was a major prosecution under the acts brought against the editor of the Sunday *Telegraph,* another journalist (Jonathan Aitken), and an army officer who had been senior British government observer in Lagos during the Nigerian civil war in 1969. The paper had published an official appreciation of federal Nigerian prospects by a colleague of the officer, Aitken being one of several intermediaries. All were acquitted after a four-week trial. The judge declared that it was time section 2 was "pensioned off." The new Conservative government (the Labour government had initiated the case but strongly denied any party political bias against the *pro*-Conservative paper) set up an inquiry into the Official Secrets Act of 1911 under Lord Franks. This pronounced section 2

9. See the works cited plus Colin Seymour-Ure, *The Press, Politics and the Public* (London: Methuen, 1968), chapter 4, and Charles Wintour, *Pressures on the Press* (London: André Deutsch, 1972), chapter 12.

a "catch-all provision" and "a mess" and proposed a new official information act, much more tightly drawn. It would cover the obvious categories of defense, internal security, cabinet documents, information given to the government by private individuals or concerns, matters affecting currency and the reserves, and so on. The attorney general's sanction for prosecutions would normally be replaced by that of the director of public prosecutions, a figure less involved in party matters. Publishing information knowing it to be leaked would, however, remain an offense.[10]

Reactions to the report were moderate. Some commentators would have preferred the introduction of a defense of publication in good faith and in the public interest. Some liked the idea of a Swedish or American kind of "freedom of information" act. The Conservative government ensured itself hostility by proposing to extend the Franks categories (to include budget plans, for instance). The press felt that the old uncertainty in application would remain essentially unchanged. In any event, no new legislation was brought in before the government left office in 1974.

Another related branch of law is contempt of court. This has achieved potential new importance with the growth of investigative journalism into areas where the government may be indirectly involved in matters before the courts. The Criminal Justice Act (1967) permits newspapers in preliminary hearings to report only the bare details of a charge unless the defendant chooses to have publicity. The general rule against comment while matters are *sub judice* means that in a British Watergate, for instance, the entire story would have been bottled up once the original charges against the defendants in the bugging case were made, which in practice would have meant some seven months. Contempt of court applies also in civil cases. The Sunday *Times* found that ten years after the thalidomide drug tragedy it still could not publish its dossier on how that came about, since the courts were even then seized of the matter.[11] Appealing to the House of Lords, the most that the paper won was a majority opinion that the press may argue a moral case while litigation is pending, but not produce the evidence on which it is based.

A special form of legal constraint is the so-called Thirty-Years

10. *Report of the Departmental Committee on Section 2 of the Official Secrets Act 1911* (London: H.M.S.O., 1972), Cmnd. 5104.

11. Thalidomide, a drug introduced in the early 1960s for pregnant mothers, led to the birth of deformed and limbless babies.

Rule, which hampers inquiry into actions of bygone governments. Under this, official documents do not become generally available for public examination until thirty years have elapsed. The main exceptions in practice have been the memoirs of former cabinet ministers who have been able to secure approval for publication.[12] More seriously, the controversial doctrine of crown privilege gives ministers the right to prevent disclosure of documents or other information on the grounds that it would be against the public interest. The rule extends even to disclosure that certain information exists, where that alone might be injurious. A series of cases, often involving home office and police affairs, has limited the application of the doctrine in the 1960s; but the effect has been largely to transfer to the courts the right to decide whether disclosure should be permitted, rather than to reduce such restrictions dramatically altogether.[13]

Counterpressures in Government and Party

The pressure toward secretiveness and a "Westminster bias" produced by constitutional practices is increasingly matched by counterpressures. These have always existed, of course. Every government and Opposition want favorable publicity: It is mainly the processes of decision, and not decisions themselves that they wish to conceal. There is no British Ministry of Information, but since the 1930s departmental information and press offices have been developed on a large scale. There is also a central office of information, whose activities include a wide range of publicity about government activities on a nonpartisan basis. This sort of institutionalized publicity necessarily creates its own kind of concealment by seeking to focus public attention on certain types of government activity. But in an informal way most politicians enter exchange relationships with journalists, and the price of good publicity is, now and again, bad publicity. Some arrangements become routine, like the twice-daily briefings for lobby correspondents from the prime minister's public relations adviser and the weekly meeting with the leader of the House of Commons about forthcoming parliamentary business. Others are

12. See, for instance, the memoirs by Winston Churchill, Anthony Eden, and Harold Macmillan.
13. See S. A. De Smith, *Constitutional and Administrative Law*, 2d ed. (Harmondsworth: Penguin Books, 1974).

on an individual basis, perhaps between a minister and a journalist from his constituency. In any cabinet or party, moreover, conflicting views will always find an outlet. Rival ministers will make sure their perspective on a problem is leaked. Dissenters from a cabinet decision will want their dissent registered.[14]

Collective responsibility is not about to crumble without a fundamental change in constitutional practice, but in recent years a few cracks in cabinet secrecy have been worth noting. In the Wilson government of 1966–1970 two ministers, Frank Cousins and, more important, James Callaghan, publicly made known their disagreement with government policy. More recently a junior minister, Eric Heffer, made no bones about his disapproval of the minority Wilson government's policy toward Chile in 1974. But unlike Jeremy Bray in 1969, he was not asked to resign. Again, the problem of the Opposition's sources of information is beginning at least to be recognized: In July 1974, the Wilson government announced its intention to set up a committee to make recommendations for help for the Opposition from public funds.

GOVERNMENT MACHINERY AND THE INFORMATION MARKETPLACE

Cabinet and Civil Service

The effects of the secretive constitutional principles can be seen in the level of public ignorance about the machinery of the cabinet and civil service. The cabinet, for example, works through a series of some forty standing and ad hoc committees, on which sit not only the twenty-odd cabinet ministers but other ministers, civil servants, and service chiefs. Parallel committees of officials exist for some of them. Yet virtually nothing of this has been public knowledge, even in academic texts.[15] Here, too, however, pressures against secrecy are beginning to work. Perfectly in keeping with its spirit the authoritative source for this part of the British constitution is now the *Times*.

14. See Seymour-Ure, *The Press, Politics and the Public*, chapters 5 and 6; and Jeremy Tunstall, *The Westminster Lobby Correspondents* (London: Routledge, 1970) passim.

15. See, for example, John P. Mackintosh, *The British Cabinet*, 2d ed. (London: Methuen, 1968); Patrick Gordon Walker, *The Cabinet*, (London: Jonathan Cape, 1970).

On May 3, 1973, it published in a leading article the most complete available account of the organization of the cabinet, quoting in aid a statement in the Conservative government's 1970 election manifesto: "We will eliminate unnecessary secrecy concerning the workings of the Government."

That statement was simply a declaration of goodwill. So, too, was the same government's adoption of the TV phone-in. One of its periodic fifteen-minute party political broadcasts in 1973 was given over to live telephone calls to Prime Minister Edward Heath.[16] The chances of one's call being chosen were naturally almost nil. Even so, the program could fairly be regarded as an assertion that citizens of a democracy ought in principle to have the opportunity of direct access to the chief executive.

The Civil Service

A declaration against secrecy was also voiced in the report of the Fulton Committee on the Civil Service in 1968, the most systematic overhaul of the service in this century: "We think that the administrative process is surrounded by too much secrecy. The public interest would be better served if there were a greater amount of openness."[17] This paragraph generated only a vacuous and ineffectual white paper.[18] But in modest ways the Civil Service—and especially the work of the 3,000 members of the policy-making administration group—has become more visible in the 1970s. Partly this was through the development of parliamentary committees, discussed below, but it also involved significant innovations in TV and radio. Civil servants started appearing on radio to explain departmental reports or to talk about their role in policymaking. In the fall of 1973, Granada, one of the big commercial TV companies, networked a three-part program about Parliament called "The State of the Nation," which

16. Each year the main British parties agree between themselves and the broadcasting authorities to a number of free radio and TV broadcasts not exceeding about one-and-three-quarter hours per party per annum.

17. *The Civil Service: Vol 1, Report* (London: H.M.S.O., 1968), Cmnd. 3638, p. 91.

18. *Information and the Public Interest* (London: H.M.S.O., 1969), Cmnd. 4089. Samuel Brittan, a one-time temporary Treasury economist, describes it as "thoroughly perverse and unsatisfactory" in his *Steering the Economy* (Harmondsworth: Penguin Books, 1970), p. 61.

was expensively researched and promoted. One part traced the preparation of a consumer protection bill in the Department of Trade and Industry, exposing to public view for the first time discussions between civil servants, ministers, and representatives of interest groups.[19]

A rather different form of openness, less liable to the objection of tokenism (however well-intentioned), was the increased use of temporary civil servants at policy-making levels.[20] The first major influx came with the 1964 Wilson government, keen to follow thirteen years of Conservative rule with a burst of indicative planning and research-based policies for growth. Academic economists flowed into George Brown's Department of Economic Affairs, charged with preparing the National Plan.[21] Under the Heath government of 1970 the Central Policy Review Staff was set up. This, too, was staffed in part by temporaries, including its chairman, Lord Rothschild. It reviewed the policy options in such diverse matters as the Concorde airliner and British population trends. On returning to office in 1974, Wilson kept the CPRS and added a personal policy unit of seven, led by a political scientist from the London School of Economics. In addition eighteen political assistants—far more than in 1964—were brought in to help ministers in their private offices, usually staffed exclusively by career civil servants.

The point about these developments, apart from the publicity they attracted as innovations, was that sooner or later temporaries left again, carrying with them into the senior levels of academic life, journalism, or commerce a familiarity with the central government machine, which, however diluted and immeasurable the result, constituted a clear bridge between the Civil Service and other branches of the political elite. A new tendency to approve similar moves by career civil servants may have been marked by the fact that Sir William Armstrong, head of the Home Civil Service, was appointed chairman of the Midland Bank immediately upon his retirement instead of after the conventional three-year "quarantine period" designed to

19. Granada published a book of the programs: *The State of the Nation* (London: Granada Television, 1973).

20. See Brittan, *Steering the Economy*, pp. 55–60.

21. For a full description, see Brown, *In My Way*. The plan (London: H.M.S.O., 1965, Cmnd. 2764) sank without a trace, a victim of the deflationary measures necessary to correct severe balance-of-payments difficulties in 1966.

prevent firms from generally poaching men from departments with special responsibilities in their fields.

Counterpressures in Parliament

The most regular form of increased public accessibility to civil servants has come through the proliferation of specialized House of Commons committees. These had their roots in the Select Committee on the Estimates, which annually studied government plans for departmental expenditure, and in the Select Committee on Nationalized Industries, which since 1958 had examined in turn the operations of each of the public corporations—railways, coal, electricity, and so on. Two new committees were set up in 1966: one on agriculture and one on science and technology. Committees on education and science, race relations, overseas aid, and Scottish affairs were later added. The Agriculture Committee ran into immediate difficulty by deciding to visit Brussels to explore the implications of British entry into the European Economic Community. The Foreign Office was extremely uncooperative. When the committee was disbanded in 1969 to make room for a new one, some members felt the reason was just a pretext for removing a body that aggravated civil servants. Many aspects of the committees were controversial, but they did examine civil servants closely and made available in a convenient form a large amount of information that could be useful to interest groups and was hitherto concealed.[22]

A major development of the system took place in the early 1970s. Following the adoption of the Public Expenditure Survey techniques (PESC), the estimates of future government expenditure were presented to Parliament in a new form based on functional categories and projected over five years. A white paper published near the beginning of the parliamentary year sets out the government's overall expenditure strategy.[23] This move in itself represents a substantial step toward making government spending policy more comprehensible and "open." In addition the Heath government replaced the old Estimates

22. On the committees generally, see Donald R. Shell, "Specialist Select Committees," *Parliamentary Affairs* 23, 4 (1970):380–404. A jaundiced view of the Agriculture Committee is by John P. Mackintosh, a member, in *New Society*, November 28, 1968, pp. 791–792.

23. For details see *Public Expenditure: A New Presentation* (London: H.M.S.O., 1969), Cmnd. 4017.

Committee and most of the new specialist committees with the single, much larger Public Expenditure Committee of fifty members. This has worked through six subcommittees covering the major fields of government and with full authority to deliberate on policy. In practice these have behaved like the earlier committees and have seized on particular topics, sometimes quite narrow (for example, private practice in the National Health Service hospitals). One subcommittee carried on a highly sophisticated dialogue with the Treasury and the Department of Applied Economics at Cambridge University of a kind that simply could not have been conducted in the public domain before. The committee's reports have not made much visible difference in government behavior. The Opposition has failed to exploit them, and their work has not on the whole caught the imagination of the national press. But a great deal of information about matters of substance and of Whitehall procedures has been generated. At least it is available even if it is not yet widely used.[24]

Two other parliamentary reforms reducing secretiveness are also worthy of note. One was the innovation of Green Papers, now an accepted routine. These represent policy proposals to which the government is deliberately not committed but upon which it wants discussion and comment before proceeding to a decision. Secondly, the Parliamentary Commissioner for Administration is firmly established. Appointed in 1967, he is limited by a fairly restrictive statute. He cannot initiate inquiries except at the request of an MP on behalf of a complainant. Nor can he himself publicize the results of particular cases. The interpretation of "maladministration" has in practice been fairly limited. No *causes célèbres* have been exposed. Yet the office fills a hole left originally by the particular cast of the terms of reference of the Franks Committee of 1955, which molded the current practice of tribunals and inquiries. That committee was set up after the Crichel Down affair.[25] Much of the disquiet in this case was

24. An authoritative commentary on the Public Expenditure Committee and its context is by Sir Richard Clarke, a former permanent secretary in Whitehall: "Parliament and Public Expenditure," *Political Quarterly* 44, 2 (1973).

25. Land at Crichel Down was requisitioned by the Air Ministry in 1940. An undertaking to give the owner first chance of taking it over again after the war was ignored. The owner's persistence led to a public inquiry and the minister of agriculture's resignation. See the Franks Committee *Report* (London: H.M.S.O., 1957), Cmnd. 218. On the parliamentary commissioner for administration, see Frank Stacey, *The British Ombudsman* (Oxford: Clarendon Press, 1971).

because the Civil Service had not done anything strictly illegal, yet the Franks Committee's terms of reference prevented them from making proposals to cover such cases. It is precisely these that the parliamentary commissioner can investigate.

Counterpressures from Nongovernmental Agencies

Extra pressures to publicity come from the widening range of nongovernmental agencies involved in policymaking. This again is difficult to measure. But in many important policy areas of the 1970s—management of the economy, industrial relations, social services, education—trade unions, employers' organizations, and such research institutions as the National Institution of Economic and Social Research, Political, and Economic Planning as well as the research efforts of the greatly expanded British university system (some of it funded by the government's research councils) have all made direct or indirect contributions.[26]

Advisory boards have been a feature of departmental consultation with outside organizations for many years. The Annual Farm Price Review, superseded when Britain joined the European Economic Community, was the classic case of a department dealing directly with its constituency: Representatives of the National Farmers' Union and the Ministry of Agriculture settled in conclave the level of government support for agricultural products for each successive year. The British Medical Association's relations with the Ministry of Health were similarly close. As economic management has become more complex, the Confederation of British Industries and the Trades Union Congress have become more directly involved with government, both on an *ad hoc* basis when particular crises arise (strikes, financial difficulties for major industries like aerospace, shipbuilding, and so on) and in routine forms like membership of the advisory National Economic Development Council. The activity of interest groups of all kinds has expanded dramatically, complicating the policy-making process in the department and decreasing the likelihood of decisions being taken without certain groups finding an opportunity to put their point of view.

26. A good study of the fresh air let into one department, education and science, is in Edward Boyle and Anthony Crosland, *The Politics of Education,* ed. Maurice Kogan (Harmondsworth: Penguin Books, 1971).

The machinery of government, these developments imply, is becoming more pluralist. Departments are aware of competing constituencies that they must satisfy. Interest-group activity has overtaken the political parties as a source of policy and day-to-day pressure both on the cabinet and the Civil Service. While the more complex machinery may obfuscate still further the processes of decision, for the wealth of special groups concerned access to information is increasing.

MASS MEDIA

Organization and Values

Getting information about the government to Parliament lifts a veil but does not tear it off. This is the business of mass media. It is important to realize that the routines and values of Great Britain's media system themselves encourage certain kinds of publicity more than others. The system as a whole is dominated by London. The London-based national daily press has twice the circulation of the combined morning and evening provincial press and takes a metropolitan view of government. Occasionally a provincial scandal—often police or town hall corruption—will attract national attention, particularly if it ramifies like the affair of architect John Poulson in the early 1970s.[27] In general, however, the ninety-three provincial morning and evening papers lack the will or resources to develop investigative journalism, and it is quite likely that at least part of the good reputation of British local government rests upon the silence about its activity. Even the government of London, covering a population of 8 million, receives negligible attention in the national press. Broadcasting has always been dominated by London; and although commercial television is organized in fourteen areas (some

27. John Poulson built up a large and successful architectural practice, which included many major development contracts for local authorities. He was convicted in 1974 on corruption charges. A senior Scottish civil servant was jailed, too, and also a leading member of the Labour party in the northeast of England. Previous—though innocent—associations with Poulson also led Reginald Maudling, the home secretary, to resign from the Heath government when inquiries leading to the corruption charges were being carried on. Poulson's activities came to light very slowly and only on any scale once the long-drawn-out bankruptcy inquiry started after his business became overextended.

small), the companies themselves are mainly controlled by national interests (including the press); there is extensive networking; and the main news is provided by a separate London-dominated organization, Independent Television News.

Within this system, news values impose a particular pattern. Academic research confirms the commonsense impression that media are interested in clear-cut, concrete, short-run topics—"clashes," "crises," negative events; the unexpected and unpredictable. Routine, complex, or abstract government action is less likely to attract attention. Television, which is now the prime news source of most people, has the added biases, moreover, of a "visual" medium. It is difficult to film dirty water, foul air, and smells. A program on pollution or the international monetary system is more difficult to dramatize than civil war in Nigeria or starvation in Ethiopia.[28]

Some of these values are linked to the panting twenty-four-hour cycle of the daily press and TV news programs. Others stem from rigidly defined news-gathering routines. In the early 1960s, when transport policy was a matter of urgent government thinking, most "transport specialists" in the media were motoring correspondents with an obsession for high performance in new cars. Only when transport and "environment" impinged did the emphasis shift and a public debate develop. Subjects are often divided, moreover, according to source relationships, and a topic can wriggle away fishlike between the dangling hooks of different specialists. Economic journalism provides a good example. Until the early 1960s government economic policy was not subjected to regular, well-informed, and detailed scrutiny in the national press. Subsequent increased coverage has been hampered by the fact that the appropriate journalist needs to be part reporter, part analyst, part commentator. Also, because certain subjects like incomes policy, about which the politicians, civil servants, trade unionists, and industrialists concerned do not necessarily wish to be at all "secretive," he has to cross the boundaries of several journalistic specialists. None of these "subject specialists" has a perspective on the whole topic, and all of them are likely to stress in an incomes policy story those aspects relevant to their own speciality (trade union affairs, the City, and so on).[29] Secretiveness

28. For useful insights on such questions, see John Whale, *The Half-Shut Eye* (London: Macmillan, 1969).

29. Peter Jay, "On Being an Economic Journalist," *The Listener*, August 24, 1972.

about management of the economy, therefore, may certainly be a function of bureaucratic attitudes, but it is just as certainly a function of media news values and organization.

The political (or lobby) correspondents take part also in this process. The secretive pressures discussed earlier require clandestine procedures in news gathering at Westminster. Lobby correspondents attribute their stories opaquely to "government circles" and "informed sources." They have also been criticized for their concern with day-to-day events, their lack of specialist skills (they have to deal with any subject that may enter the Westminster arena), and occasionally, for being "managed" by governments.[30]

The other substantial factor inhibiting media coverage of government for many years was the severe restriction of political broadcasting. This is best symbolized in two facts. Until 1959 there was no mention of election campaigns on radio and TV at all during the three weeks before polling day. The only election programs were the modest ration produced (at public expense) by the parties themselves.[31] Second, the Fourteen-Day Rule, abolished in 1955, prohibited discussion on the air of any subject due to be debated in Parliament within the next fourteen days.

Counterpressures

The cause of the restrictions on political broadcasting was the politicians' and broadcasters' obsession with broadcasting neutrality and "balance"—defined by reference to time given to spokesmen of different parties. In the 1960s these principles were interpreted much more loosely. Ministers and backbenchers broadcasted with increasing frequency between and at elections.[32] It could be argued, indeed, that since Parliament refused to broadcast its own proceedings, it began to be bypassed by television. Current affairs programs developed

30. See Tunstall, *The Westminster Lobby Correspondents*, especially chapter 8, pp. 89–97.

31. Colin Seymour-Ure, *The Political Impact of Mass Media* (London: Constable, 1974), chapter 8.

32. Cf., the *Guardian*, January 9, 1974: When Parliament is not sitting, ". . . the normal processes of democracy are supplanted by letters to Ministers . . . , press statements, occasional speeches, and supremely by radio and TV appearances. Over the last seven days, no fewer than ten Ministers, Opposition front bench spokesmen and party leaders have appeared on the *World at One* and its associated programmes (*PM* and *The World This Weekend*) . . . ."

their coverage of political issues; and though the "political neutrality" ethic cramped investigative tele-journalism, the probing political interview became a fine art. Long set-piece programs on major issues like Ireland and the European Economic Community, loosely modeled on parliamentary styles and with senior parliamentarians taking part, perhaps began to displace some of the functions of Parliament itself.[33] Secretiveness in a general sense was thereby reduced. But of course, the television medium falls easy victim to superficiality, and the case can plausibly be made that such developments gull the public into thinking they perceive the fire of government when all they really see is the smoke.

There has been no growth in the press to match the expansion of political broadcasting. Two less dramatic but important shifts should, however, be mentioned. First there is a broad, if intangible, orientation in the national press away from the loyalty to party, which characterized it for a century. It is replaced by an antigovernment ethic, which is by no means new but has increased since the late 1950s. This is linked to the second shift—the growth of investigative journalism, best typified in the work of the Sunday *Times.* Teamwork journalism and plentiful expertise turned that paper (and others that adopted its techniques more modestly) into a kind of surrogate legislature, scrutinizing the executive with an intensity (inevitably selective) that MPs lack the resources to match.

Cooperation between press and parliamentarians is often explicit. A highly publicized case was the Sunday *Times* campaign to raise the level of compensation for the victims of the thalidomide drug disaster. The campaign produced from Harold Wilson, leader of the Opposition at the time, a letter to the *Times* affirming that, without the Sunday *Times,* the parliamentary debates ". . . would have been uninformed and lacking in decisive content, and the result which in fact flowed from those debates would never have occurred."[34] In another case the *Guardian,* shocked at the low level of wages paid by British firms operating in South Africa, provided the impetus for a thoroughgoing inquiry by a subcommittee of the Public Expenditure Committee.

The press gets help from other groups, too. The late 1960s saw a huge proliferation of organized grass-roots activity in social policy fields. This coincided with the growth of policy concerns that crystal-

33. Seymour-Ure, *The Political Impact of Mass Media,* pp. 144–147.
34. *Times* (London), July 24, 1973.

lized rapidly into concepts like "the environment" and "consumer affairs," which would have been unintelligible to the wider public in 1965, but a few years later could be incorporated into the names of government departments. Homelessness, enduring poverty (and new definitions of it), poor schools (and preschool facilities), pollution —all the range of now familiar issues, the backside of affluence, and the cobweb corners of the welfare state generated interest groups. Most of these, like Shelter, the Child Poverty Action Group, and the Runnymede Trust (a race-relations group) were highly geared to cooperation with the mass media. Increasingly, too, they spawned their own magazines. A problem in which government was active, therefore, might be ventilated in the national media—with subsequent government reaction—as the result of a two-step process: crystallization at the local level or in a special-interest group, followed by a filtering process to national media.[35]

As well as the growth of specific organizations, wide changes can be seen in public attitudes to government secrecy. Just as the Franks Committee of 1955 had articulated a public demand for "openness, fairness, and impartiality" in the conduct of administrative tribunals, so for a subsequent generation "the rights of third parties" at tribunals were acknowledged. The introduction of a parliamentary commissioner for administration was followed by successful demands for a health service commissioner and local government commissioners.[36] Legislation about minimum standards of manufactured goods was increasingly oriented toward the demands of the consumer, not the interests of the producer. The system under which the police are responsible for the investigation of complaints against themselves met mounting criticism.

Such examples can be said to reflect a declining confidence in bureaucratic competence—not necessarily in bureaucrats themselves, but in the relevance or effectiveness of a cumbersome bureaucratic structure. There were signs, too, of increased willingness to seek social explanations for individual predicaments and to place responsibility on government. These developments in turn were reflected in new kinds of media stories. Lead levels in the air of a new highway interchange system in Birmingham were found by the Sunday *Times*

35. The fortnightly satirical magazine *Private Eye* had an especially impressive record of this kind.
36. An unspecified number of local government commissioners was provided for in the Local Government Act of 1974.

in 1973 to be dangerously high for the neighborhood population. It does not seem too fanciful to contrast this kind of community-based grievance, probably not attributable to the dereliction of a particular civil servant, with newspapers' concentration in the past upon precise individual grievances like the Crichel Down case. The same developments were also reflected in the formation of community action groups and "neighborhood law clinics" designed to give greater meaning to the notion of equality before the law and to ensure that citizens in poor areas were aware of—and received—their rights from the bureaucracy.

CONCLUSIONS

Is Britain moving to a new assertion of the "right to know" and of "freedom of inquiry" as well as freedom of speech? Britain formerly had a homogeneous political elite whose members understood one another. In 1950 a correspondence went on in the *Times* about the power of the crown to refuse a prime minister's request for a dissolution of Parliament. An anonymous letter on May 2 set out an authoritative view. Anyone who "needed to know" sooner or later discovered that the author was a former private secretary to the king. ("Where do you find the British Constitution?" "In the *Times*. Among the letters. Anonymous ones.") Now the elite has changed. At the very least it has to justify and explain itself to a wider public. Much can be achieved by organized group activity and resourceful mass media. A good deal of government information is inaccessible, not because it lies beneath ground marked Keep Out, but because citizens lack spades. Hard legal barriers seem the most difficult to change: They need deliberate, formal change and their sanctions can be crippling. There is a danger, too, of an indiscriminate pressure for publicity, from which the subjects less capable of organization around a lobby or of capturing public attention will be excluded regardless of their merits. The British press, furthermore, has some good watchdogs, but its overall economic situation is precarious. TV may supplant it at the national level; yet, as we have seen, TV still lacks investigative thrust and political freedom of movement. British government, in the widest sense, is less secretive now than it was ten years ago. But the change is slow, and there is still a long distance to travel.

11

Israel

ITZHAK GALNOOR

There is a "secrecy paradox" in Israel. Government affairs are formally very secretive, yet a great deal of confidential information gets into circulation, occasionally concerning sensitive matters of security and foreign relations and quite regularly concerning internal deliberations on domestic issues. Consequently, accusations of both excessive secrecy and excessive disclosure often emanate from the same event. References to a "credibility gap," government manipulation of information, and abuses of "security" for internal political purposes are quite common, yet so are complaints that too much gets published, that the government (especially the cabinet) is incapable of guarding vital information, and that the whole state apparatus not only leaks but actually resembles a sieve. The paradox continues when those in favor of openness argue for stronger laws aimed at curtailing secrecy, while those in favor of confidentiality point out that even the existing measures aimed at protecting official information are not observed.

The foregoing suggests that Israel confirms the hypothesis presented elsewhere in this volume that secrecy is the *added value* of the information commodity in the political marketplace, wherefore access should be examined in terms of the internal political process.[1] Accordingly, the first three sections in this article describe the more

1. See chapter 5, Itzhak Galnoor, "The Information Marketplace."

formal elements of secrecy in Israel in order to provide the basis for the fourth section, in which the politics of information and secrecy is discussed. In the last section I shall speculate about current political trends in Israel and their impact on government secrecy.

THE CULTURE OF SECRECY

All democratic societies deviate to some degree from the principle of the people's right to know, but it is difficult to judge whether secrecy in Israel is any more or less "pathological" than in other democracies.[2] Nor can we distinguish between secrecy processes that are inherent in the domestic political culture and those that are influenced by the external (and, in Israel's case, hostile) environment. The following list of characteristics is aimed only at presenting those factors that clearly influence the "secrecy paradox" in Israel.

First, Israel has inherited from the British Mandate era the prohibitive approach to state secrets. This is reflected not only in the rigid official secrets laws, but also in symbolic codes of political and administrative behavior. And so lip service is paid to the ideal of a cohesive, loyal, and anonymous Civil Service speaking publicly with only one voice, while the real purpose of public relations officers who exist in every ministry is often denied. This perceived "British way of governing" is foreign to the realities of Israeli politics and administration, but it supports the claim for confidentiality in state affairs and confuses discussion of whether or not secrecy is legitimate in Israel.

Second, behavior is still influenced by the prestate practice of leaders using intimate and confidential modes of operation. The habit of working in a small caucus, facilitated by the common ideology and the solidarity of the pioneer groups, was further reinforced by the need to conceal activities from the Turkish, and later from the British, authorities. This behavior was so thoroughly transferred to state organs that one observer has alleged that the country is still run as "one vast underground movement."[3] But here, too, the influence of this habit is not so obvious. At this point it will suffice to

2. See Carl Friedrich, *The Pathology of Politics* (New York: Harper & Row, 1972), pp. 175–209.
3. G. E. Caiden, *Israel's Administrative Culture* (Berkeley: Institute of Governmental Studies, University of California, 1970).

say that in order to run a whole country as an underground movement, critical information cannot be confined to a very small circle.

Third, the general legitimacy of secrecy is reinforced by external pressures. Security and foreign affairs are such sensitive matters and their implications for the country's survival so obvious that there is a near-general consensus that the government is entitled—indeed, obliged—to keep security information secret in the public interest. Consequently, arguments over what is really security information extend not only to military and foreign affairs or the strategic economic capacity of the country, but also to data regarded as innocent or trivial in other countries, for example, transportation routes, water resources, commercial links with countries and firms that do not want to be identified, immigration, nondefense items in the national budget, possible targets of indiscriminate terrorist activities, and many more. Controversy in this area focuses upon the blurred border line between security and nonsecurity affairs and on the tendency of the government to use "security" as a blanket for covering up blunders and politically embarrassing information. Conversely, there have been numerous cases in which the government was accused of *releasing* security information for political maneuvering.[4]

The legitimacy of withholding information about security and foreign policy contributes to general secrecy and creates opportunities for government manipulation of information. Yet, again, this is only one part of the general picture. Despite the fact that little official information is published on security issues, many people are able to

---

4. One quite typical case occurred during the negotiations on the establishment of a new cabinet after the December 1973 general elections. Up to March 4, 1974, "Rafi," a faction within the Labor party headed by then-Minister of Defense Moshe Dayan and Shimon Peres, refused to join a new coalition cabinet headed by then-Prime Minister Golda Meir. On that night the cabinet was convened for a special meeting to discuss the situation along the Syrian lines. The next day both Dayan and Peres changed their positions and announced their willingness to join the new cabinet because under such tense conditions, "Israel cannot afford the abnormal situation of not having a Cabinet." A few days later the major opposition party accused the leaders of the Labor party of abusing security information. An editorial in *Maariv*, a newspaper not known for opposing Dayan, presented the secrecy issue in this affair in the following way:

Despite the secretiveness of the security information the public has the right to know what happened between the end of the Central (Labor) Party's meeting and the end of the Cabinet's meeting which caused Dayan and Peres to change their position 180 degrees (*Maariv*, editorial, March 7, 1974).

read between the lines of general references in the press or laconic government announcements. Excluding highly secretive military information, it is impossible to contend that Israeli citizens—many of whom are called up for active military duty every year—are ignorant about security affairs.

Fourth, having their own government is a new experience for the Jewish people. Less than three decades of national sovereignty has not sufficed to develop firm norms for regulating the political process and guaranteeing individual rights. Thus, the boundaries between state privileges and civil freedoms are still ill-defined and rules of the democratic game are still evolving. Israel has no written constitution. There are instead several Basic Laws slowly enacted over the years. The one concerning civil rights and aimed at merely consolidating existing ordinances was debated in the Knesset (Parliament) only in 1975 and quickly disappeared from the agenda.[5] The prospects of gradually developing a consensus about civil rights are hindered by external pressures, the lack of an established tradition, and bitter disputes over the role of religion in the state.

Lacking any constitutional or legal guidelines, the people's right to know is not formally recognized in Israel; in fact, it is not even established on the symbolic level discussed elsewhere in this volume.[6] Israeli citizens are not known for their insistence on their rights as recipients of public services or as consumers. There is mutual reinforcement between officials who use regulations and sheer harassment to discourage citizens' formal attempts to gain access and citizens who are used to seeking information and preferential treatment through an acquaintance (a practice known as *protekzia*).[7] Where *protekzia* reigns, the people's right to know is not taken seriously. Public opinion can seldom force the government to release information. In this regard, the high rate of voting turnout in Israel should not be confused with active public participation in governing processes. General adherence to democratic forms has been accompanied by civic passivity and disbelief that public opinion can

5. In the 1973 elections a new "Civil Rights party" entered the Knesset with three members, but this relative success in Israeli politics is also related to the 1973 war and not only to the public support for the party's civil rights platform.

6. See chapter 4, Rozann Rothman, "The Symbolic Uses of Public Information."

7. Brenda Danet, " 'Proteksia' Orientation toward the Use of Personal Influence in Israeli Bureaucracy," *Journal of Comparative Administration* 3, 4 (February 1972):405–434.

influence policy.[8] But this does not mean that total secrecy always prevails. As will be pointed out later, there are many who know alternative routes for gaining informal access.

Fifth, Israel is a small society of about 3 million people with a huge public sector and intensive intervention of government in all aspects of life. How does this effect secrecy? On the one hand, smallness helps government establish central control and manipulate information by monopolizing or dominating the main channels of communication. On the other hand, in a small society it is difficult to prevent a high proportion of the population from knowing many secrets, no matter what the regulations say. Moreover, the clannishness of a small society, the relatively direct face-to-face relationships have led to a more open and, as a rule informal, exchange of information. Israel is a country where there is a high degree of citizens' emotional (*not* political) involvement, where men serve in the military reserves until the age of fifty-five, and where the "nonprivate sector" employs in one way or another about 50 percent of the labor force.[9] Under these circumstances, it is simply impossible to keep many things secret for a long time. In short, size, like the other four factors listed in this section, can influence secrecy and access to information in opposite directions, and there are many intervening variables that control the degree of openness in a given social system.[10]

THE LEGAL FRAMEWORK

Along the lines of British tradition, the secrecy and publicity laws in Israel prescribe everything official to be secret unless disclosure is

8. Based on Alan Arian, *Consensus in Israel* (New York: The General Learning Press, 1971), p. 7. On changes that occurred in the last years, see the last section of this article.

9. Based on Haim Barkai, *The Public, Histadrut and Private Sectors in Israeli Economy* (Jerusalem: The Falk Institute, 1964 [in Hebrew]). The figures are outdated, but the general structure has not changed much.

10. The assumption among laymen and political scientists alike is that the smaller a community, the more visible (and accessible) is government. Secrecy and manipulation of information are not discussed directly. Dahl and Tufte tentatively suggest that the smaller the scale of the society, the more likely it is that the differences in the directness of communication between citizens and leaders be reduced to a minimum. They quickly add that factors other than size, such as political culture, may change this likelihood and even though they are not concerned with information flow or content, this last comment seems to apply to the Israeli case. See Robert A. Dahl and Edward R. Tufte, *Size and Democracy* (Stanford: Stanford University Press, 1973), pp. 87–88.

specifically permitted. There is no local equivalent to Great Britain's official secrets acts, but the fifth chapter of the Israel Penal Revision Law (State Security), 1957, is concerned with official secrets. The same law deals with espionage, treason, and damage to the state's security and foreign affairs on the one hand, and with preventing disclosure of official information by civil servants on the other. This proximity of concerns indicates the general prohibitive approach. Section 23 deals with espionage, but it also forbids the disclosure of information that pertains to issues that the cabinet, with the approval of the Knesset Defense and Foreign Affairs Committee, has declared to be secret matters. Sections 27–30 of the same law impose up to three years' imprisonment on employed and retired public officials who disclose to unauthorized persons any official information (not necessarily classified) that has come to their knowledge *ex officio*. This is further supplemented by very detailed regulations of the Civil Service Commission.[11]

Still in effect are the Defense Regulations (Emergency) issued by the British authorities in 1945. The Censor is authorized to prohibit the publication of any material that "in his opinion would be, or be likely to be, or become prejudicial to the defense of Israel or to the public safety or to public order" (87[1]). The Censor also enjoys unlimited authority to prevent publications by ordering any publisher to submit for inspection any item intended for printing (97[1]). Accordingly, he can prohibit publication by just stating one of the general reasons mentioned above without providing concrete justification. He can even prohibit publication of the fact that censorship was applied.[12]

Since the early 1950s there has been a voluntary arrangement whereby the Editors' Committee (composed of the chief editors of the daily newspapers in Israel) serves as a mediating forum between

11. *Civil Service Regulations*, sections 41.2, 62.1, and 69.1.

12. A short report in *The New York Times,* May 13, 1975, revealed that the Israeli military censor prohibited the publication of a book written by an Israeli journalist, because it contains secret information about the diplomatic negotiations between Secretary of State Henry Kissinger and Israeli ministers. According to this report, the decision to censor the book was also secret and was made by the military censor upon the personal direction of the prime minister. The act of censorship was disclosed by the Israeli military spokesman only after the publication abroad and after the rest of the story appeared in Israeli newspapers (*Haaretz*, May 13, 1975). In due time the author received permission to publish a censored version. There are many other examples of privileged information about Israeli affairs that are first published abroad.

the government and the newspapers. It is usually to this forum that an act of censorship is justified and a request for self-restraint made. The editors are frequently briefed on sensitive matters and meet government and military officials for off-the-record discussions. The entire arrangement is often described (1) favorably because of its voluntary nature or (2) unfavorably as a means of co-opting the newspapers into a secrecy conspiracy against the public.[13]

Section 28 of the Basic Law: Government, 1968, restricts the publication of cabinet decisions pertaining to state security, foreign affairs, and other subjects vital to the state that the cabinet announces to be secret. This law is reinforced by the Cabinet Internal Work Regulations, according to which only the secretary can act as a spokesman for the cabinet and make announcements about subjects discussed and decisions made. Section 28 has been the subject of much debate in Israel because of attempts to impose penalties on those who *publish* the secret information rather than on those who *leak* it. In practice, a great deal of what transpires in cabinet meetings is leaked immediately or eventually. One preventive measure used frequently is to define a particular cabinet meeting as a session of the Ministers' Security Affairs Committee. The espionage section in the Penal Law applies to leaks from this committee, but they still occur.[14]

13. There were a few cases in which an editor refused to follow the "advice" given in the closed meetings of the committee. In 1966, *Haaretz* published the fact that Prime Minister Eshkol visited Iran secretly and again in 1969 that the U.S.A. agreed to sell Phantom jets to Israel. Another controversial example occurred during the 1973 war. While the public was kept in the dark regarding the military situation, Defense Minister Moshe Dayan met with the editors' committee a few days after the war started and presented a realistic appraisal of the events. His account was in great contrast with the public announcements made by the prime minister, the chief of staff, and the military spokesman. Parts of this briefing leaked informally and increased the confusion regarding the real war situation. When Defense Minister Dayan was accused of breaking down during the meeting, he released, contrary to the established precedents, the whole discussion. It appeared in print about four months after the war (*Haaretz*, February 15, 1974) and created further criticism because there was nothing really secret about the information as such, except for its possible negative effect on public morale.

14. There is nothing inherently Israeli in this system of leaks, nor in the recurrent debates about them that occur "when Governments try to have it both ways—to use the leaks to their own advantage and to suppress and condemn them when it discloses truth they don't like" (James Reston, "In Defense of Leaks," *The New York Times*, June 21, 1974, p. 37). The edge is usually in favor of government officials who, armed with legal sanctions, can use leaks more than they could be used against them. Leaks delight journalists in Israel

Another example of a rigid approach combined with informal arrangements is the document classification system. There is no law prescribing document classification and the various regulations are somewhat contradictory, but always in the direction of overclassification. The classification of official information is based on a pamphlet published by the General Security Service and adopted by the Civil Service Commission,[15] but in practice there are many more categories and each ministry has developed different regulations. The law states that everyone may see material deposited in the state archives, but there are no automatic declassification procedures or legal time limitation, such as the British "thirty years" rule, and release can be restricted by regulations pertaining to the content of the material.[16] Thus the documents that are deposited (and many are not) arrive with their classification and remain so classified unless otherwise specified. Anyone who wants to study the documents about the establishment of the state in 1948 or certain decisions of the Jewish authorities in 1936 would quickly discover that they are still classified. Yet, "classified" information about these and other events does get published. One notable example are the diaries of the late Prime Minister Ben-Gurion, which include official documents or quotations from them.[17] On a selective basis appointed scholars with the "proper" credentials can also gain access.[18]

---

who regard them as a safety valve against excessive secrecy. On balance, however, directed information probably outweighs unplanned leaks in both significance and amount, creating, therefore, the same opportunities for distortions as secrecy.

15. General Security Service, *Procedures for Safeguarding Documents*, Civil Service Commission, 1964. There are three main classifications:

1. Top secret—to prevent *very severe* and *continuous damage* to the state's security, foreign affairs and economy;
2. Secret—to prevent *severe damage* to above state's interests;
3. Restricted—to prevent *damage* to above state's interests, to the orderly management of government bureaus and their execution of policies and manpower management.

16. Archives Law of 1955 as amended in 1964.

17. David Ben-Gurion, *The Restored State of Israel*, 2 vols. (Tel Aviv: Am Oved, 1969 [in Hebrew]).

18. One example is the court order that confirmed the censorship of a book about the Latrun battle, 1948, on the grounds that the author gained access to the information as a public official. The court order revealed, however, that the authorities granted permission to three military officers to use the same information for research and publications. (Itzhaki v. Minister of Justice, Supreme Justice Order No. 159/73, vol. 28, 2d part, 1974, pp. 692–700).

RELATIONSHIPS BETWEEN THE GOVERNING BODIES

The structure of government in Israel resembles the British model. The cabinet must retain the support of the Knesset, but in practice the loyalty of party members in the legislature makes room for a very strong executive. The Knesset serves as an arena for presenting information to the public and is very effective as such because of the mass media attention. The plenary does not have the legal right to demand specific information from ministers. This is left to Knesset committees and individual members.

The committees conduct their affairs in camera, and information secured from ministers and civil servants reaches the public indirectly through the mass media. The principle according to which each minister is politically responsible for whatever happens under his administrative jurisdiction prescribes certain channels for the flow of information from officials to Knesset committees and the public. The executive in Israel, very much like that in Britain, is formally assumed to be monolithic and to maintain a strict separation between politics and administration. Civil servants therefore appear before the Knesset committees mainly to present a departmental point of view.[19]

There are no parliamentary hearings in Israel, but each committee can decide to open its meetings. Such a rare case occurred in 1971 when the permanent Knesset Economic Committee headed by a member of the Opposition party decided to open its investigations concerning the state-supported automobile industry (the Autocars Company). This episode demonstrated, above all, that the committee had few independent and effective sources of information. Another resort of the Knesset to secure information is to set up a parliamentary committee of inquiry,[20] but this instrument has not been tested since its legislation in 1958.

The individual Knesset member is as helpless as a committee to find out what goes on in a ministry.[21] He can use the Knesset question

19. The Knesset Rules (13.b) state: "The Committee *may* request the Minister concerned for explanation and information pertaining to a subject which is discussed or which falls within its jurisdiction and the Minister, himself or through his representative, *must* provide the explanations and information requested" (translation and emphasis mine, I. G.).

20. Basic Law: The Knesset, section 22.

21. Under the Israeli proportional representation voting system, there is no constituency representation. Citizens vote for nationwide fixed lists of party candidates.

period, or write to the minister, or develop informal connections with civil servants. But the question period has not been very successful, for responding ministers seldom share with the Knesset information that they are reluctant to divulge. And letters to ministers are rarely sent, because Coalition members do not need them and the Opposition cannot gain much political mileage out of the discreet replies.[22] Instead, members of the Coalition and the Opposition alike use their personal political connections to establish informal channels of communication with ministers and public officials. These channels are probably very effective, but in using them, Knesset members do not act as legislators and representatives, or even as recognized mediators between the executive and the public; they operate instead on the level of "those in the know"—a higher level of *protekzia*.

The state comptroller is an extension of legislative control over the executive. In addition to more traditional supervision, the comptroller in Israel is required by law to investigate waste, inefficiency, and improper behavior in government departments and public organizations. He is entitled to demand confidential information from public officials, but only his conclusions and recommendations are presented to the Knesset in public reports. The comptroller's ability to conduct his investigation independently of the executive has gained him a great deal of influence in Israel. His reports are probably the best source of independent information (unlike government publications), thorough (unlike journalistic reports), and regular (unlike special investigations). Their impact is both preventive and remedial. Nonetheless, the information secured by the comptroller is post factum and limited to administrative aspects. He does not probe policy or day-to-day issues, nor does he guarantee the citizens' right to know. In March 1971, the state comptroller was given the additional role of ombudsman.[23] He now has the formal authority to require any kind of official information needed to answer a citizen's complaint. Every citizen is thus provided with a formal channel for finding out how and why a certain decision affecting him was made. The ombudsman's probe, however, is issue-oriented. He cannot deal with the more general aspects of hidden governing processes.

In addition to the Knesset and the comptroller, the law courts

22. See A. Diskin, "The Time Dimension and the Efficiency of the Questions in the 6th Knesset," *State and Government*, 1, 3 (Jerusalem: Hebrew University, 1972), pp. 162–67 (in Hebrew).

23. State Comptroller Law (Amendment no. 5), 1971.

demand information from the executive when it is needed for the judicial process. But the right of the state (known as executive or crown privilege) not to reveal official secrets even in court is recognized. The questions here are: (1) whether certain types of information given in evidence (documentary or oral) held by the state to be secret should be presented in the courts and (2) *who* should not see this information—the judges, the parties to litigation, or the public that has the right to see that justice is done?[24]

Until 1968, the practice in Israel was based on the British Crown Proceedings Act, 1947. This was widely used in matters of security and foreign relations, but the tendency of some ministers to use it in other areas was not always accepted by the Supreme Court.[25] Since an amendment enacted in 1968, the *final* decision about whether evidence should be made public or not is in the hands of the judges. Where the evidence pertains to security or foreign relations, a document signed by the concerned minister is presented to the court stating that disclosure would be harmful to "state security or foreign relations." In such a case, evidence will not be disclosed unless a member of the Supreme Court decides that the need for justice should prevail over secrecy. In other cases, a document signed by the minister is presented to the court stating that disclosure would be harmful to an "important public interest." Here again, evidence will not be disclosed unless the judge decides that the need for justice should prevail. In all cases, the reasons for preventing disclosure are given in camera, and the judge determines who should be present at this juncture.

The implications of this law go far beyond the limited scope of information demanded by the courts. It establishes two important principles. First, the executive has no monopoly on determining what the public interest is and when secrecy is needed in order to preserve it. Second, the law recognizes that the conflict inherent in government secrecy is usually between two legitimate public interests: the people's right to know versus the need to preserve state security and governmental efficiency.

Yet, despite the changes in these laws and other institutional

24. For a discussion of these general questions see Eliahu Harnon, "Evidence Excluded by State Interest", *Israel Law Review* 3 (July 1968):387–415. See also chapter 8, Bernard Schwartz, "The United States: The Doctrine of Executive Privilege."

25. See, for example, Ha'etzni v. Ben-Gurion, 11 P.D. 403 (1957); and Harnon, "Evidence Excluded by State Interest," pp. 400–441.

arrangements, the real amount and content of information that the public, or, more precisely, certain members of the public, get to know is not determined by law.

THE POLITICS OF INFORMATION AND SECRECY

I have argued elsewhere that there is no such thing as total government secrecy, that only a small amount of information can be fully monopolized by a few officials, and that information is a commodity in the political marketplace whose "price" is determined on an exchange basis.[26] The political culture and the legal structure will set some broad guidelines for transactions in this marketplace, but the actual information flow is determined by a system of exchanges. Total secrecy is therefore a systemic residue, an outcome of rare situations when exchanges have not taken place. Partial secrecy is much more common, and it occurs when bargains include provisions for the exclusion of outsiders. In Israel the existence of such a marketplace with unwritten "rules" is quite apparent.[27] Information requests based on abstract right-to-know demands are easily ignored, and the harsh secrecy laws are applied only when an exchange is impossible or undesirable. Information is restricted even though its release could not possibly endanger the state's security, such as when mayors manage to ban the publication of the city comptroller report. At the same time, reports that circulate in newspapers or on the social grapevine (and the two are closely intermingled) show that regardless of the legal provisions, truly sensitive information is divulged time and again to selected confidants, while "unauthorized" people regularly gain access to the most confidential sources. A typical example was the leakage in 1971 of a secret memorandum written for the Foreign Affairs Ministry by a senior official in the Jerusalem municipality. The document presented various options regarding the future position of Jerusalem, and the leak occurred during an internal debate on that issue.[28]

26. See chapter 5 in this volume.
27. For a list of these rules, see ibid.
28. Published in *Maariv*, April 27, 1971. The memorandum was paraphrased and there were quite a few omissions including the crucial fact that it had been written three years earlier. The leak was clearly intended to influence internal political debates at that time. The event was followed by an unprecedented publication of the original memorandum (*Maariv*, May 4, 1971) and a complaint to the Press Council.

Is there a pattern in all this? Obviously, there are channels of communication that certain people belonging to certain circles know how to tap. Who are those people? How do they gain access? Why they and not others?

Segmentation

Israeli society is a segmented one. The standard joke that for every Israeli there are two political parties is statistically incorrect, but quite indicative of the complexity of the internal bargaining process.[29] On the one hand, the society is very small, bound by common values and external threats and governed by the same political elite for more than fifty years. On the other hand, it is a society in transition, coping with both lack of cohesiveness and the centrifugal forces of modernization.[30] Israel's political system is sometimes described as a "consociational democracy," namely, fragmented but stable. Most factors listed by Arend Lijphart as conducive to this type of system can be found in Israel, except that a very sharp division into subcultures does not exist and multiple memberships are common.[31] Hence it is better to refer to the Israeli system as segmented rather than fragmented. Israelis themselves speak of "sectors"—public versus private, "workers" organized in the Labor Union Federation (Histadrut) versus "independents," agriculture versus industry, religious versus nonreligious, Jewish versus Arab—and these are further subdivided into a maze of overlapping factions, organizations, and groups. The term *segments* denotes these various circles that vary in size, power, and unifying subject matter. They are of interest to us because they operate as two-way transmitters of information between individual citizens and government.

The main subdivision in Israel has always been the political parties, which existed before the state was established and which come to dominate many other affiliated organizations and therefore provide a central channel for recruitment into the political elite. When the

29. In the 1973 elections twenty-one parties competed for the 120 seats in the Knesset to be determined by the votes of about 2 million eligible voters.

30. By 1973, 52 percent of the Jewish population were immigrants. *Statistical Abstract of Israel, 1974*, Central Bureau of Statistics, no. 25, 1974, p. 23.

31. Arend Lijphart, "Consociational Democracy," *World Politics* 21, 2 (January 1969):207–225.

state was established, it provided the framework as well as new opportunities for additional elites, especially those based on ethnic background, occupational and regional criteria. Notable among these are the bureaucratic, military, and professional groups.[32] The state organs thus became a new focus for fierce internal competition over power, resources, and prestige. In the process, access to information became a crucial means of maintaining or strengthening the position of a segment. Conversely, monopolization of critical information became in itself evidence of influence.

Segmentation, coupled with the small size of the society, has created the secrecy paradox in Israel. Despite the culture of secrecy and the laws requiring it, the system is relatively open. The doors are unmarked, but those who know about their existence can use them.

The main reasons for this *functional openness* are that the political elite is in fact a "cartel of elites,"[33] that the decision-making process is complicated and must incorporate many actors, and that a segmented society attempting to retain stability must resort to the politics of accommodation. The rules are such that the well-established segments are familiar with the communication network, have regular access to the relevant channel, and can obtain a certain piece of information if it is vital to their interests. This generalization applies mainly to segments such as agriculture or the collective settlements and increasingly so to private economic interests such as banking or industry. The "price" a segment pays for becoming established and for gaining access (and influence) is only partly tangible: votes, money, support, information. The other part is intangible—giving up adversary lobbying and agreeing to confidential exchanges. Functional openness thus makes the established segments partners to government secrecy. There are, however, a number of groups that are less established in the sense that they have no fixed commitments in their relationship with government. They can opt for either giving support in exchange for access to information (and influence) or using open pressure tactics and public campaigns. To this category belong some private economic groups such as the merchants and the farmers associations; professional associations such as those of lawyers, engineers, and accountants; and a few

32. See S. N. Eisenstadt, *Israeli Society* (New York: Basic Books, 1967), especially pp. 154 ff.
33. Lijphart, "Consociational Democracy," p. 213.

voluntary organizations such as the Council for a Beautiful Israel. Most of them are firmly plugged into the communication network via partisan affiliations and memberships on boards of directors of public corporations and advisory bodies.

Truly nonestablished groups are very few and lack real political significance. Public interest and promotional groups are not common and the handful that exist are mainly political protest groups that have been established recently. Most independent groups, including nonpolitical voluntary associations, have had a very short life span in Israel. Those that endure may seem to be independent, but are actually affiliated with one of the established segments or with government directly. Consumer protection organizations, for example, belong to the Histadrut, local authorities, and the Ministry of Commerce.[34]

To summarize, the main reason why a great deal of official information becomes known in Israel is that there are many established segments, almost all of whom are part of the communication network.[35] Circulation, however, is determined on a functional need-to-know basis, for the guiding principles of the information flow within the channels is *selectivity* (of the information passed on to each segment) and *exclusion* (keeping this information from outsiders and other segments). Obviously, the complexity of the network hinders tight central control, and many leaks have nothing to do with the arrangements described above. Nevertheless, the aggregate sum of information that circulates within this network does not correspond to the democratic axiom of the *public* right to know. The "public" as such is by definition outside the network.

34. A typical example is MALRAZ (acronym of Council for the Prevention of Noise and Pollution). The council was established as a voluntary organization with the blessing and funding of the Ministry of Health and received support from local authorities and established groups. When it became too noisy and started to campaign against government projects, the funds were cut off, access to relevant information became practically impossible, and attempts to raise money from the public did not succeed. The council still exists, but it cannot function effectively outside the established channels through which resources, including information, flow.

35. I am indebted for ideas in this section to Dan Horowitz and Moshe Lissak's forthcoming book, *The Origins of Israeli Politics* (in Hebrew). On politicization in Israel, see Dan Horowitz and Moshe Lissak, *From Yishuv to State: Change and Continuity in the Political Structure in Israel* (Jerusalem: The Kaplan School, Hebrew University, 1972 [in Hebrew]).

Politicization

Small size plus segmentation have influenced the information market-place in the direction of functional openness. Now we have to introduce the factor that has regulated a great many contradicting pressures—the political parties. Israeli political parties have been active in the absorption, of immigrants, health services, housing projects, transportation cooperatives, sports clubs, student associations, voluntary groups—to mention but a few examples. Israel can tolerate a high degree of segmentation because the parties—until recently, at least—provided for internal political cohesion of the numerous subsystems. The parties have carried out this role by virtue of their strong grip on the most important resources—money (partly raised abroad), jobs, status, prestige, and information. Internal bargaining has been carefully structured through the so-called partisan key method, namely, an understanding between the dominant Labor party (previously known as Mapai) and the other parties, including those in opposition, about their proportional share of the various resources.

The actual competition over resources has been by no means smooth, but by and large developments since 1948 may be described as a constant and successful attempt of the political elite to maintain these arrangements against all pressures. One reason for their success has been the ability of all the parties—especially those that joined Labor in the coalition cabinet—to retain and develop their control over the various segments.

If we turn now to the secrecy aspects of politicization, we notice that the right to know is less exercised in Israel on the plane where "the public" or the mass media or individual citizens confront government officials and more through the political parties and their affiliated satellites. The parties have served until very recently as the clearinghouse for a two-way flow of information between government and various active groups. The mayor of a developing town, the local secretaries of workers' councils, or members of the religious councils could easily use partisan contacts to gain advance intelligence and promote their respective interests. They could also meet friendly counterparts in government bureaus who readily recognized their "jurisdiction" in a specific area. Conversely, leaders have had no need to resort to the strict secrecy laws to maintain their monopoly on critical information. Information, like other resources, could be controlled and distributed according to flexible arrangements rather than on the basis of fixed rules. For instance, it is not uncommon for two parties to sign an agreement with secret clauses to seal coalition negotiations.[36] Thus the mosaic of segments linked to the parties, and especially to the Labor party, has helped the political elite to consolidate their power by becoming gatekeepers of information. They were also able to justify this situation on the grounds that they saw the whole picture as opposed to the fragmented knowledge of other nonpolitical elites.

There are no detailed studies of the political elite in Israel. Those who belong to the elite's inner core are usually veterans whose families immigrated from Europe. They do not belong to the same class nor do they follow an identical pattern of mobility, but they do share common values, dedication to the state, and a willingness to work within the existing structure. They see each other very frequently in their official capacity and in informal meetings, and are used to the internal friction of a segmented society. They usually wear more than one official hat and serve as links between the inner circle, the party, and the affiliated segments. Their status is determined to a great extent by their intimate knowledge of what is going on and their ability to share this information selectively.

It is through this far-flung political elite that official information is publicized and secrecy laws circumvented. There is little difference in this respect between a cabinet minister who shares confidential information with members of his kibbutz, a military officer who talks freely with "his" confidential newsman, and a senior bureaucrat who is willing to disclose privileged information to coopted or self-appointed guardians of particular interests. Of course, there is nothing peculiarly Israeli in this phenomena, but the results here are different. Selective release of information strengthens the power of the inner core, but because of small size and great segmentation, it also contributes to the "functional openness" mentioned above. The political affiliation process is rather inclusive and encompasses most groups in society, but not every group is linked to the network, and not every linkage is really democratic in the sense that it enables participation. Oddly enough, in Israel the system of functional participation through highly organized groups is more refined than

36. The coalition agreement between the National Religious party and Mapai in the Tel Aviv municipality in 1969 included secret provisions on religious matters that were later revealed.

direct democratic representation through political parties. The diary of the late Prime Minister Moshe Sharett for the years 1953–1957 reveal how most groups were "in the know" only in a limited way, how little the public knew, and how often information was used to deceive public opinion.[37]

Mass Media

News media exercise wide-ranging influence in Israel. Radio and television receive great attention even though they are controlled by a public broadcasting authority and can afford only a narrow margin for controversial issues. For controversy, Israelis turn to twenty-three daily newspapers (in 1975), mainly to three independent ones (*Haaretz, Maariv,* and *Yediot Aharanot*) and to a few weekly magazines. The other news publications all belong to the Histadrut, political parties, and affiliated organizations.

In the prestate period, the news organs of the Jewish community expressed the opinions and aspirations of the political "movements." Much of this educational activity and missionary zeal still exists, with the result that most of the media not only belong to the political "network" described above, but also provide an indispensable service as brokers of information for the "publics" within the segments. Many messages in Israeli media are not directed to the general public but to insiders who possess the ability to interpret them. Generally speaking, then, we see a mass media system, which, reflecting segmentation and politicization, strengthens the ability of the government to control the information marketplace[38] and encourages the creation of the "manipulated consensus" discussed by Lowi elsewhere in this volume.[39] A great deal of self-restraint is exercised by the media, especially in security matters. In addition, the existence of state-run broadcasting services and partisan newspapers gives

37. Excerpts from the diary were published weekly in *Maariv*, April 3, 1974–July 26, 1974.

38. See Reuven Cahana and Shlomit Knaan, *Press Behavior Under Conditions of Security Tension and Its Influence on Public Support of the Regime* (Jerusalem: The Eshkol Institute, Hebrew University, 1973), especially, pp. 104–108 (in Hebrew).

39. See chapter 3 by Theodore Lowi, "The Information Revolution, Politics, and the Prospects for an Open Society."

politicians and administrators an effective weapon to fight media independence. Sanctions include preventing access to government sources and even applying economic pressures.[40] These relatively controlled channels also provide officials in government and in the affiliated segments with ample opportunity to get their information and views published. The network of established segmental organizations and groups serves also as alternative channels to mass media. The power of those "who know" lies not only in excluding but also in deciding in whom to confide. Official information and leaks can be distributed directly through this network and not only via the media. Consequently, newsmen in Israel are constantly on guard to find out what is going on in closed circles and often they solve the problem by becoming bona fide members with all the rights (access) and duties (secrecy) involved.

From this first glance, the uninitiated reader might get the impression that there is no free press in Israel. Yet, in reality, mass media and especially the three independent newspapers enjoy so much attention from officials and the public alike that they can play a central, albeit restricted, role in the information marketplace. In the early 1970s, the independent newspapers shared among them more than 80 percent of the general circulation of the daily publications.[41] They exercise a strong influence on the standards and quality of the mass media and can be viewed in many cases as the only viable opposition to government. Thus in addition to their usual difficult position on the horns of the secrecy dilemma (cooperative versus adversary relationship with government) newsmen in Israel face another hurdle. Compared to their counterparts in several other democratic countries, the Israeli mass media are not fully autonomous; but compared to other subsystems and segments in Israeli society, certain parts of the mass media enjoy a great deal of relative independence as well as influence. Their position has been strengthened in the last years because of the new kind of exposure provided by television (started in 1968) and because of the recent trends described in the next section.

---

40. Stopping the advertisements of government departments, public institutions, and parties in a certain newspaper is a real economic sanction for newspapers in Israel. The issue was raised publicly by *Haaretz* in an editorial on January 26, 1972.

41. Cahana and Knaan, *Press Behavior Under Conditions of Security Tension*, p. 104.

CURRENT TRENDS

So far I have observed that there are few unaffiliated citizens in Israel, and that in practice much is known on an exchange need-to-know basis and not because of the people's-right-to-know norm. However, government secrecy in Israel has begun to change in recent years, especially as a result of the October 1973 war. Even the casual observer will notice that the ability of the government and more generally of the inner core of the elite to perform through tacit agreements and internal bargains has diminished considerably. On the symbolic level, the public is no longer confident that no matter what the government does domestically, it can be relied upon in security matters. On the pragmatic level, government can no longer count automatically on the support of the political parties, the Histadrut, the various segments, and the established groups within them. Examples abound. The cabinet in Israel always leaked mainly because top officials needed to maintain the support of the established groups. But in recent years leakage has become the rule rather than an exception. It is enough to compare the very limited public knowledge of the negotiations for the withdrawal of Israeli forces from Sinai in 1957 and the extent of information and military detail that was published about the disengagement agreements in 1974/1975 to realize the change that has occurred. The change can be only partly attributed to new leadership styles.[42] The more profound reason is that members of the elite need now to share information, not only with their own groups, but also with the public in order to secure wider bases of support. Concomitantly, opposition to the political elite has grown stronger, more vocal, and is less inclined to exercise its influence through confidential exchanges. In the past, the general distribution of power between the main partisan blocs has remained remarkably stable in the eight elections since 1948, despite the numerous internal splits and realignments. The relatively new phenomenon is that for the first time the probability of a real political change has increased considerably. The increasing political fluidity

42. Among the reasons usually mentioned for these developments are the lack of dominating leaders who could replace the founding leaders; the relative decrease of the ruling elite's monopoly on resources such as money, positions, and prestige; and the inherent difficulties of running a modern economy through anachronistic federative arrangements between sectors that originated in the prestate era. Also, the system of cooptation that brought into the ruling elite prominent members of other elites (especially the military) has also weakened loyalty and internal cohesiveness.

has weakened considerably the ability of the party system and especially of the Labor party to maintain discipline and perform its mediatory roles.

The 1967 and 1973 wars did not initiate this process, but they certainly accelerated the trend by provoking urgent and painful debates over the country's goals and ability to survive. The result in terms of the information marketplace is a sort of vacuum created by the weakening of the Labor party and other parties as coordinating devices. The Labor party is no more the same forum where members of the various elites synchronize their positions. What could replace it is still unknown and some new clusters revolving around a powerful personality may emerge. This was the case with Golda Meir's famous "kitchen" in security and foreign affairs and the circle around former Finance Minister Sapir in economic affairs. Yet they were loyal party members and the disappearance of these two towering leaders and of Moshe Dayan from state affairs after 1973 made all arrangements more fluid and further diminished the power of the party. The Labor party is subdivided into so many factions that support—let alone the results of internal bargains—has become quite unpredictable. This is true also with regard to the other two major parties—the Likud and the National Religious parties.[43] Secrecy prevailed as long as the parties were strong enough to maintain loyalty on a discretionary basis and to recruit to key positions on the basis of reliability. Now the parties' political resources required for co-opting people and groups have decreased, and so the number of those who do not want to exchange their independence for confidential cooperation has increased.

The ruling party is often referred to as a political supermarket. Previously it could sell different commodities to divergent groups, but somewhere there was a discreet "register" that kept a record and coordinated distribution. Now the supermarket is still there, but the register has either disappeared or is not keeping up with the ongoing transactions. For outsiders, the result is more openness. Official information is no longer channeled through one distribution network only, and the multiplicity of uncoordinated sources creates more

43. The symptoms of this new development can be seen when members of the ruling party demand information on the Knesset floor from ministers from the same party; or when members of the Religious party voted in 1975 for changing the Defense budget that was approved by their own ministers in the cabinet.

opportunities for access. Consequently, the political process itself has become more transparent, leading to many revelations of hidden exchanges, irregularities, illegal activity, and corruption.

For insiders, namely, those who were part of the previous segmented network, the effect has been toward more adversary relationships with government. The exchange relationships have become strained because groups tend to act independently and to prefer public campaigns over discreet agreements. One recent example is the reform in the income tax system, aimed at replacing the previous tacit arrangements between groups of taxpayers and the state income administration. In the last few years many details about these arrangements, some of them illegal, appeared in the press. The government finally yielded to demands for reform, but it did not enjoy enough credibility to initiate changes through the Civil Service machinery. Instead, a group of independent experts was nominated to prepare a reform proposal, enabling the government to defend it against the pressures of undisciplined groups.[44] This procedure signifies a departure from the previous practice of appointing committees composed of representatives of the established sectors to work out an agreement through an internal process of bargaining. Another manifestation of the new trend is the increasingly open debates over allocations of resources through the state budget. Debates between two ministries, or even within one, are now carried on publicly in the press or on the air. This occasionally happened before, but not so intensively and without revealing all the relevant information. Greater exposure did not exclude even the defense budget, the details of which are secret and not presented to the Knesset as a whole.

These changes could not pass without affecting the conduct of civil servants. Israeli bureaucrats are more loyal to their departments than to the Civil Service as a whole, and because of the perennial coalition government they are further subdivided into domains of political party influence. Senior civil servants have not been reluctant to express their opinions publicly, but usually it signified the tip of some internal (especially interministerial) feuds. The gradual increase of professionalism has somewhat changed this situation, but civil servants have retained their bureaucratic inclination to prefer arrangements according to which they could confine their interaction

44. The reform law was enacted with minor changes in July 1975.

to recognized pressure groups or a few knowledgeable middlemen. Yet here, too, there have been some changes recently. For instance, the emergence of popular radio programs and newspaper columns dealing with citizens' complaints proved to be very effective in circumventing the bureaucratic maze and in forcing officials to reveal information. Even more illuminating perhaps is the fact that the Civil Service has started to leak in the lower levels. This is a new phenomenon, because leaks have usually been the privilege of the politicians and the higher officials.[45] The kind of information that gets published nowadays must come from dissatisfied or idealistic clerks.[46] On a higher level, an attempt is now being made to reinforce a regulation that prohibits immediate transfers from the civil service and the military to public corporations and the private sector. If this is strictly applied, the "network" would be denied the valuable liaison services of people who can transmit information from one segment to another.

The cumulative effects of these trends can strengthen the ability of the public to participate more meaningfully in the political process and to exercise its right to know. It might also foster the emergence of new groups and segments or even new political parties with different modes of operation. What has certainly weakened is the imperative that to gain access to information (and to influence) one must work through the established network. To state that the old route is no longer viable is premature. There are indications, however, that circulation of information is not rigidly confined to the prescribed channels. If our thesis is correct, that secrecy in Israel is a function of collaboration among the elite, the ruling parties, and the segments, then it is probable that uncoordinated fragmentation may lead to greater openness. It might also influence the stability of the system and effect other structural variables, but these possibilities are beyond the scope of this summary. Thus small size plus segmentation minus established arrangements may influence the information marketplace in the direction of systems' (right-to-know) openness as opposed to the previous functional (need-to-know) openness.

45. A famous exception is the case of Hai Hasidoff, a low-level official in the Justice Department who was sentenced to a two-month prison term because he passed on an official document to the weekly magazine *Haolam Hazeh* in 1960.

46. One such revelation alleged that the minister of housing used the department's funds to write a check as a personal gift. In other cases officials in public corporations stepped forward and testified against their superiors.

The established arrangements have been visibly shaken as a result of the 1973 war. It is possible to deduct some evidence of disintegration as early as the 1960s, especially around the bitter internal fight in the ruling party over the so-called Lavon affair. The resignation of Prime Minister Ben-Gurion in 1963 and the split within Mapai belong also to this trend. Nevertheless, no breakdown took place then, and the 1965 elections could be viewed as "a victory of the institutional setting of the existing regime."[47] The great military victory in 1967 may have reversed or halted the trend and enabled the consolidation of the existing arrangements. Yet some of the changes described above and especially the weakening of the party system occurred during the powerful and relatively stable premiership of Golda Meir. Attempts to freeze the institutional setting by giving more to the established groups were only partly successful at that time, and various social tensions forced the government to respond hastily to the demands of new and nonestablished groups.[48]

The 1973 war sent a tremor throughout the whole social, economic, and political structure of the country. Much like the aftermath of an earthquake, some things remained intact, others were destroyed immediately, still others may tumble down later. Aside from the war's direct informational credibility aspects, there have been also long-range repercussions on government secrecy. The trend toward fragmentation resulting in more openness has been accelerated. For instance, the Agranat Commission was appointed in 1974 to investigate the military aspects of the war. The bulk of the commission's report remained secret, but the published parts revealed information of a nature that was hitherto not permitted in Israel.[49] More open-

47. See Eisenstadt, *Israeli Society*, p. 357.

48. For instance, the emergence of the vocal and sometimes violent group of the Black Panthers with a strong ethnic background of deprivation; or the attempt of young couples to get organized outside the existing structure in order to change government housing policy. See Itzhak Galnoor, "Social Indicators for Social Planning in Israel," *Social Indicators Research* 1 (1974): 46–48.

49. The committee itself was aware of this aspect when it stated that despite secrecy considerations it is desirable to publish part of the report "for both reasons of the public right to know and misunderstandings and distortions in various publications" (*The Agranat Commission Report* [Tel Aviv: Am Oved, 1975], p. 57, unauthorized translation from the Hebrew, I. G.). This did not prevent the commission from criticizing the "public climate" and the publication of information about their work. (One member dissented from this opinion, pp. 65–66.)

ness and more revelations are also to be found in the information published on foreign and domestic affairs, including the policy-making process and the internal politics within the parties and the various segments.

How the new climate surrounding government secrecy will develop and what new processes will emerge in the information marketplace are difficult to predict. There are various possibilities.

1. Consolidation and the maintenance of the previous arrangements could take place. After all, this political structure and its communication network survived many tremors before.

2. On the other extreme there might be a transfer of political power and an entirely new internal alignment. External pressures and internal fragmentation could drastically alter most of the alliances built since the state was established.

One possibility here is that the state will grow stronger as the parties and the segments decline or even disappear as a buffer between citizens and government. If this were to occur, secrecy and propaganda might prevail to an extent unknown hitherto in Israel. The "secrecy paradox" in Israel is based, among other things, on the need of the political elite to share information (and other resources) with others. These arrangements, albeit deficient, are still preferable to the total information monopoly in the hands of the state and its official organs. The disappearance of mediators without the emergence of substitutes would signify a real danger for Israeli democracy.

3. It is also possible that still other arrangements will emerge, partly new and partly old. There might be a restructuring of the segments in the network and consequently new rules for the information marketplace. This possibility seems the most probable to this writer. New kinds of credentials would be required to gain access, and the result might be a chance for utilizing the interim confusion to strengthen citizens' partnership in the political process. Then there would be a higher probability that the aggregation of information that circulates publicly in Israel be partly based on a functional demand and supply exchange, and partly on the legitimate right of the public qua public to know. This would also signify a more desirable equilibrium between secrecy and publicity in one small democracy.

12

The Netherlands

H. A. BRASZ

Statehood came to Holland in the sixteenth century more or less by chance, with institutions functioning more as instruments of reaction against foreign oppression than as exemplars of an orderly inner rule. Further developments of the body politic were strongly influenced by neighboring countries such as France, England, and Germany. Thus the Napoleonic era saw the introduction of a distinctive administrative system styled on the centralized French model.

Although the unitary state was firmly established, in the nineteenth century there was also a long-standing trend toward political decentralization and away from bureaucratization, so that the institutions of representative democracy were adopted and developed with great caution. Nevertheless, by the end of the century the necessary group of full-time, salaried officials was well on its way to becoming one of those large, complex organizations for which modern states are notorious. These developments paved the way for the incorporation of German-style institutions, and two decades later the Dutch machinery of government resembled the famous Weberian model of bureaucracy. More openness in the meetings of representative bodies was accompanied by more secrecy on the part of administrative institutions within which information piled up.

PRECARIOUS SECRECY AS A CULTURAL TRAIT

The particularities of the Dutch case in the management of secretiveness and publicity should be sought in the cultural and political environment and not in the bureaucratic system.[1] The life of the burghers in their moderately sized towns was for centuries a peaceful one, rarely bothered by any form of tyranny. Even during the 1568–1648 war against the Spanish oppressors, the country was ruled not by the nobility but by the wealthy and enlightened merchants, and by the end of the seventeenth century the descendants of these merchants had consolidated their power. But even so they did not set themselves apart from the people. In such a context, legitimation of power has a low-secrecy threshold. The burgher's own privacy was uncertain: In a small town nothing remains long hidden from prying eyes. Today the Dutch houses still evidence this cultural trait. At dark the lights are switched on and the curtains usually remain open; walking down the street one can look into the rooms and into the lives of the occupants. But if the householder feels it is necessary, he draws the curtains and shuts out the eyes of his neighbors.

Governmental institutions reflect this cultural flexibility. The Dutch public generally respects the need for privacy, secrecy, and information storage, but this does not stop it from expecting to be kept informed about the essential details of government business. The social environment and the political culture do not favor neatly formulated laws for regulating the openness or secretiveness of government. Pragmatically, and with some slight degree of practical deception, the Dutch situation allows mild chaos with regard to the accessibility of public information. These cultural traits of Dutch institutions are probably related to the small size of the country and they may be fairly typical of other small countries.[2] Secrecy, although easily introduced, is always uncertain. The greater part of the information simply remains in the files and is not classified. Thus data as such is hidden, but the barrier is insecure: Information is neither publicized nor protected by particular measures. This might be called *formal filing*, that is, the neutral and technical process of storing paperwork and other material in public organizations. All this applies to general

1. Frank E. Huggett, *The Dutch Today* (The Hague: Ministry of Foreign Affairs, 1974).
2. Compare with the discussion of the influence of size on secrecy in Israel in chapter 11.

government papers. In some sectors, however, attitudes and expectations may be different, for example, in foreign affairs and national security.

STAGNATING POLITICAL SYSTEM

Notwithstanding the tolerance shown by the Dutch people, the situation has deteriorated as the administration has become more complex. The nonaccessibility of government and administration probably reached its critical point in the 1930s, but the search for more openness did not gain political momentum until the middle 1960s, leaving a gap of three decades. How is this delay to be understood? Two types of interpretations are possible: structural and accidental.

The Dutch political system is pluralistic due to the long tradition of freedom. No political party can hope to form a majority government alone and coalition is inevitable. Lijphart interprets the stability of Dutch politics as a process of accommodation.[3] Decision making is usually done by committees in which all parties are represented, in which businesslike bargaining is incessant, and which meet behind closed doors, while political leaders and their adversaries assail each other in public. This pragmatic process of policy formation enables mutual concessions that are only little reflected in official declarations and public reports. This process would be impossible without a mix of arrangements that include restricted public access to the administration's files, a little genuine secrecy, a selective ventilation of information, and flexible handling of public information by the leadership. A leader of a political party will tend to consult his followers whenever he opens a public debate, but he will not be inclined to disclose to them any concessions that he may make in the closed committee rooms. Such a structure is necessarily very flexible and has helped to stabilize Dutch political life, particularly during the 1930s–1960s. During this period, the social systems themselves came under heavy external pressure, but the secrecy-publicity mechanism and bureaucratic nonaccessibility were never questioned since any changes in this area might have shaken the country's stability.

The preoccupation with the economic crisis of the early 1930s

3. A. Lijphart, *The Politics of Accommodation: Pluralism and Democracy in the Netherlands* (Berkeley: University of California Press, 1968).

foreclosed structural changes in government and in governing practices such as secrecy. The crisis did not even entail revelations about the dysfunctioning of large and complex organizations. Later, developments toward liberalization of information were brought to a complete standstill by the Nazi occupation of the Netherlands. The Dutch people were deprived of their freedom, experiencing totalitarian foreign rule and the practical oppression of almost all that was dear to them. The Nazi system of total control stifled the dissatisfaction with Dutch institutions that had been gradually increasing and provided practical experience of how cruel a government apparatus can really be.

It would be an exaggeration to say that the government of occupation provided an effective scapegoat for the prewar inefficiency of the national administration. However, the immediate postwar task was one of reconstruction. The dominant theme was the restoration of almost all prewar institutions, including the system of accommodation in the pluralist parliamentary democracy. The flexible but relatively closed structure, whose legitimacy had been badly affected under Nazi bureaucracy, was again strengthened.

In the 1960s external pressures diminished, institutions were subjected to critical examination, and the arena of political discussion and practical politics was permeated by a quest for openness. The crisis in Dutch politics started almost unnoticed in the late 1950s. By 1966 it had penetrated so far into individual voting behavior that at one stroke a new political party, Democrats 1966, or D'66, which favored intensive structural change by nonsocialist means, became a significant new factor in Dutch political life. Since then, voting behavior has been unusually versatile and political stability has diminished: Rather than accommodation, political polarization and politicization of administration, propagated by the communications media, have become trends. In its turn, Parliament has demanded that the government provide more information more quickly, and the methods of the Opposition have become increasingly aggressive. Publicity increases the significance of reprehensible activities, and it becomes more difficult thus to hide these events behind locked doors. In such a setting leaders are easily deprived of their influence, traditional political parties run the risk of decimation, and more people come to realize that it is undemocratic to bargain in closed committees and to store information away in government files. As these developments have taken place in Holland, numerous articles, scientific studies, and political speeches have critically addressed the problem of openness versus secrecy. Actions were undertaken in favor of more openness and in order to protect individual privacy from the dangers of data banks and the new information-gathering technology. It was in the context of the rather confused period of 1968–1972 that the case of "open-minded Barend" (discussed in a following section) developed and unfolded to its somewhat disappointing conclusion.

REGULATION OF SECRECY

The Dutch have no legal right to know what is contained in government files, but the constitution lays down freedom of the press, stating: "No person shall be required to obtain permission prior to publishing his opinions or sentiments, with the exception of every person's duty before the law."

With the exception of the postal services, the written constitution of the Netherlands makes no mention of secrecy, nor has any specific act of Parliament been passed in this respect. A few acts contain special provisions regarding secrecy, for example, the Civil Registry Act or the Public Records Act. Government records are transferred to special repositories after a period of fifty years and are then made public unless otherwise resolved. In effect, this means that decisions regarding the disclosure of official papers are dependent on executive regulations.

Although departmental internal instructions as to the classification of files and other information may be precise and specific, general instructions given to public officials by their superiors are vague. The following rules may be derived from the civil service statutes, which regulate the legal status of central government officials. A public official is required by statute to maintain secrecy regarding information in his office insofar as this follows "from the nature of the matter" or from an order given by a superior. This does not apply to his relationships with his superiors, or to cases in which he has official permission to publicize information or to make it available to certain individuals. He has to be diligent and accurate and to behave in a manner commensurate with "a good officer."

But what does *good* mean in this context? This is defined in each case, in each service, in each ministry and may even differ from person to person, according to individual interpretation.

Accordingly, secrecy depends on the particular case. In exceptional circumstances the ministries sometimes leak instructions about the classification of documents and data. My request to the minister of interior for information in this respect was unavailing. As far as I have been able to ascertain from older publications, official documents are classified into four ascending categories.[4]

Official classifies a document as inaccessible for "reasons of policy" even though its contents in the hands of private individuals cannot be considered as endangering the state or its interests. More strict is the classification *confidential,* which is applied to information that might be disadvantageous to the safety or interest of the state or its allies if it fell into the wrong hands. The classification *secret* implies possible severe disadvantages. Documents classified as *very secret* contain information that could be seriously damaging to the state or its allies if wrongfully used. No information is available on period of classification and procedures for declassification.

A public official accused of violating secrecy may be subjected to internal disciplinary action, starting with a warning and in serious cases ending with dismissal. He has the right to appeal to the independent Civil Service Court on grounds of legality or of general principles of good administration and reasonableness. Penal law includes general provisions for severe punishment if a serious misdemeanor is committed against the safety of the state. Special provision is made for penitential punishment if a civil servant should violate official secrecy. The specification of the offense may include self-interpretation and an intention to violate secrecy as part of the duty to maintain secrecy.

The constitution of the Netherlands prescribes publicity for meetings of representative assemblies (first and second Chambers of Parliament; and the provincial and local bodies). At the same time, however, these bodies are allowed to use discretion in deciding whether or not to open their doors to the public. The Chambers have the legal right to require information from the ministers and to institute investigations in order to acquire necessary information. The

4. A. de Swaan, "Geheimhouding van de openbare zaak" [Secrecy in public affairs], *De Gids* 129, 6 (1966):3–26.

minister is obliged to give the Chambers the information and to submit official records to a committee of investigation, unless he is of the opinion that this would be contrary to the interests of the state. This is known as the right of interpellation. In this respect, civil servants may also plead interests of state or that they have acted in accordance with orders from superiors.

Every member of Parliament has the right to question a minister. This is usually done in writing, and questions and answers are published in the official *Gazette*. However, the minister is not obliged to answer. The number of questions asked in this way has increased of late, as have the complaints regarding tardy or obscure replies by the government.

The judiciary is equally unable to do much to decrease secrecy. The government may always plead the official oath of secrecy and the magistrate has no power to infringe the curtain thus applied.

There are no special laws in the Netherlands regarding censorship or prevention of espionage. In addition to the freedom of the press, radio and television are mostly in the hands of private institutions. The government may exercise an after-the-event control of radio and TV programs, but it rarely makes use of this power. Prior approval is precluded by law.

From the legal point of view, the rights of the Dutch in limiting government secrecy cannot be called extensive. On the other hand, the legal protection of classified information is also limited and the status of most government records on the secrecy-publicity continuum is uncertain. The records may be inaccessible even though they are not legally classified as secret. The law gives little insight into the wide freedom of using information given to the government.

This situation combined with the political structure remains unchanged to the present day (1975). The following case illustrates the constraints of the system and their institutionalization in Dutch society.

THE "OPEN-MINDED BAREND" CASE

In the mid-1960s a new style of politician started to emerge, less conciliatory than the type that had dominated the Netherlands' politics for many years. At that time politicians felt the need to strengthen their personal image with respect to openness of character, political attitude, and practical ideals. On the political scene it also seemed attractive to advocate more open government, illustrating this argument with examples of the blatant wrongs of secretive administration. This brought publicity to the politicians, showing them to be professionally interested in making government processes and files accessible. Even within the bureaucracy the disparaged and timorous State Information Services acclaimed the quest for more openness.

In 1968 the government appointed a Committee on the Reorientation of Publicity in Government, chaired by Mr. Barend Biesheuvel. This move was made under verbal declarations favoring more openness. The committee's terms of reference were vague and this, together with the accompanying publicity, justified both a general and a narrow interpretation of its task. The members were mainly representatives of the mass media, the universities, and the information services. They favored more general openness but—as the name of the committee indicates—they were mainly committed to the narrow task of reorganizing the information services. With a few exceptions, generalists from the civil service were not represented, nor were other strata of society that might have exercised a mitigating influence. Given the general demand for institutional changes in these years, the committee reached a consensus on the need for exercising the principle of openness in government affairs. This consensus was reflected in the committee's draft Statute on the Publicity of the Public Services in the Netherlands.

In the draft's opening clause, all government ministers are made responsible for publicizing and explaining, whenever feasible or relevant:

1. all decisions with general applicability
2. all other administrative acts or intentions, even when not in final form, whenever "good and democratic" government necessitates public discussion and the formation of public opinion
3. reports and recommendations given to government by certain committees

The draft provides for the following exceptions:

1. security of state (military secrets)
2. good relations with foreign powers (international relations)

3. the economic and financial interests of the state, if severely threatened

4. constraints imposed by criminal investigations

5. disproportionate damage or favor to individuals (threats to privacy, corruption, or leakage of classified information)

Within these boundaries, all individuals are granted the legal right of access to information.

The government in power reacted quickly, and negatively, to the proposals. Rumor has it that the professional civil servants (heads of ministries) almost unanimously rejected the Biesheuvel draft, principally because the consequences of introducing such a system could not be predicted. The draft was acclaimed by the public, and the main ideas were propagated by the mass media.

An image of radical openness descended on Mr. Biesheuvel, who did not find it disagreeable. He was then a member of Parliament and did not bear direct administrative responsibility. Shortly afterward, however, a general election was held and the inevitable and long negotiations to find a team of ministers with sufficient parliamentary backing brought Mr. Biesheuvel to the post of prime minister. He now bore full responsibility for government secrecy and publicity and was obviously affected by his reputation for openness. The contradiction between this and the political realities imposed on a leader of a not-so-progressive and narrowly based government soon caused difficulties. Leakage of classified information to the press occurred and on one occasion an angry prime minister openly advocated *ad hoc* secrecy. He had no choice, but his "open" image inevitably collapsed.

The internal weaknesses of the Biesheuvel government caused such conflict that it fell after one year. Biesheuvel had been no more successful than his predecessor in the matter of publicity. In fact, he had had to check his own radical proposal.

How should we interpret the "open-minded Barend" case? It was but an incident within the context of the all-embracing changes in the political and cultural subsystems of Dutch society. The committee was a response to the general feelings of the time, and openness was a popular theme. However, as a proposal for action the draft statute was insufficiently prepared and therefore serious errors were made in reorganizing the State Information Services and in changing the process of publicity and secrecy. In 1968 there was insufficient understanding of the issue for decisions to be taken. The presentation in the committee's report of government openness as an absolute principle did not satisfy the requirements of logical analysis.

The report helped to justify a plea for more openness in government and as such had a favorable response. But the search for a fitting mode of application and a satisfactory definition of the limits of "more openness" remained unsolved. In 1974 the whole issue was in the hands of a new coalition government in which the parties of the Left are predominant. The interest in government secrecy has continued, but by fall 1974 no substantive action had yet been taken.

A LITTLE THEORIZING AND THE REALITIES OF GOVERNMENT SECRECY

The phenomenological effect of the receipt of information regarding government processes has to be the focal point in any discussion of openness. Let us start with the premise that availability of information benefits the citizen and promotes the democratic quality of governmental institutions. However, in order to assess the ultimate effect of openness, it is necessary first to distinguish between two concepts of consciousness.

Civic consciousness is the citizen's appreciation of government processes and public issues. A high level of civic consciousness is a precondition for a high degree of participation. *Private consciousness* is the citizen's appreciation of governmental actions and information that affect his personal interests.

The *openness* of a government unit refers to the degree of *accessibility* of its documents, for example, the practical possibility of obtaining written or oral information about their contents.

Publicity as a process is intended to increase accessibility. The more accessible the documents, the greater the openness of the unit and the greater the degree of civic and private consciousness among citizens at given levels of receptivity. Publicity is a means for enhancing all these qualities by making documents accessible, units open, and citizens conscious.

The main phases in the life cycle of documents in the Netherlands are shown in figure 1. In the *opening phase* (0), the document is under consideration by authorities or *in statu nascendi*. Routine and other administrative processes govern its accessibility. In the subsequent phases the bulk of documents is neither publicized nor classified but merely put away in the files. This storage technique has already been referred to as *formal filing* (F). A considerable part is *destroyed* after some years (D). Formally filed documents, which are not destroyed, have to be sent to the archives (A) after fifty years. They are recycled to phase 0 if reference is made to them in new administrative processes. However, some documents are classified in the opening phase as secret (S) and are stored in special places. *Secrecy* is the process of withholding information through these storage procedures and of proscribed publicity. It is a phase in the life cycle of a document, which may afterward:

1. be destroyed
2. after fifty years or more be filed in the archives
3. be declassified within fifty years, rerouting the documents to the *formal files*
4. continue to exist in the archives as a *permanent secret* (PS)

The general archives in principle allow access to the documents, but exceptions are easily made. The accessibility of documents in different phases of their life cycle is as follows: Accessibility is nonexistent for documents that are destroyed (D). Exceptions may be possible, but generally speaking the contents are lost forever. Secret documents are concealed, but this does not mean that they are entirely inaccessible, or that a document is never open to public discussion. Secret documents are stored in guarded places and are made available only to particular people. But leakages and declassification, whether or not due to political pressure, can cause a document to be taken out of the secret file and to be made accessible. In the Netherlands very few government documents are classified as S.

Most documents are formally filed in phase F and their accessibility differs from case to case. To a scoop-hunting journalist they are almost as well-protected as secret documents. A formal right to peruse such documents does not exist, but representatives of pressure groups and *ad hoc* action groups, politicians, and the interested parties in a certain case are usually allowed to see them. Moreover, copies of such documents are usually available elsewhere

1. because they were written by nongovernment individuals and associations who have copies in their own files;
2. because during the opening phase the original government

FIGURE 1

LIFE CYCLE OF GOVERNMENT DOCUMENTS IN THE NETHERLANDS

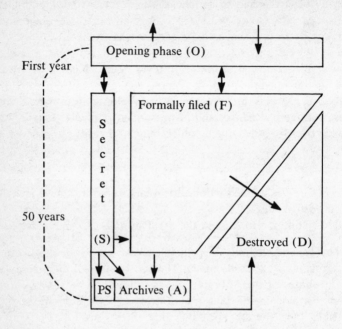

document or copies thereof were sent to individuals or nongovernment organizations;

3. because they are public records of a representative body;

4. because in one way or another they have been open to the public, for example, during an administrative process or the preparations for a hearing;

5. because during an earlier stage they were published in one form or another, for example, in the official *Gazette*.

It is my impression, unfortunately not founded on empirical research, that in the Netherlands formally filed documents have a considerable degree of accessibility to government officials and to others. In all probability government could most effectively enhance its openness by instructing its officials to further increase accessibility to such documents.

A greater degree of availability is given to those documents that circulate or are drafted during administrative processes (phase 0).

Such processes are usually concerned with social or personal problems. The interested parties naturally know a great deal about such cases, irrespective of the formal degree of accessibility or publicity, and they also receive notification of the decision reached and the motives therefor. In negotiating with another party the government also exchanges documents, otherwise the negotiations would have little chance of success. Another example is that of the pressure groups that are represented on various committees to which documents are submitted. Directly or indirectly, and even if they are considered confidential, these documents are available to these groups.

Finally, government documents end up after a period of fifty years in the archives and are open to the public if an exception is not made. The actuality of such documents is minimal after fifty years, since most of the interested parties are long dead. Accessibility to the archives is of the greatest significance to the historian, but even he is not allowed to see all the filed documents.

CONCLUSION AND SOME ANTICIPATIONS

This general overview shows that legal rights to accessibility are restricted. Rumor has it that in practice accessibility is also restricted by the selfishness of authorities and bureaucrats. Nevertheless, the Dutch situation has extensive latent openness. The tendency toward politicization of the government apparatus means that civil servants may give information with impunity to politicians and nongovernment partisans. Communications media in the Netherlands are privately owned and biased government propaganda has little chance. Even the education of the masses by means of selective commentaries on the contents of government documents is in private hands. The government's manipulation of information does not enable it to control public discussion of the major problems of the day. To the contrary, latent openness entails that in time a great deal becomes known to the public or to certain groups. Organized interest groups make use of that latent openness and find it worth their while to organize efficiently. During the last few years, more *ad hoc* action groups have joined the public information market. They specialize in compiling data with a limited view in mind and their sources are frequently better than those of the authorities. Moreover, they are given a great deal of help by the mass media.

Privacy, as the right to be left alone, is widely recognized in Dutch culture, notwithstanding the low threshold between privacy (protected by secrecy) and publicity. Government files frequently contain information pertaining to private matters. Individuals desire full information regarding events that affect their personal interests, but at the same time they usually regard such information as a matter of privacy and demand restricted openness by denying accessibility to others. The degree of openness of a government service is frequently in discord with the individual's right to privacy. Secrecy in certain matters is therefore not to be despised. Too much is undesirable, too little invades privacy.

More relevant to our thesis is the regulation of access, which is also the clue to an operational solution to the secrecy dilemma. Conflict between openness and privacy cannot be solved by general priority rule: Circumstances have to provide the right answer, and authorities must make their decisions *ad hoc,* giving the individuals concerned the right to appeal. The opening or closing of a system under certain circumstances should not be considered unusual, nor is there any a priori preference for openness. In fact, an alternation of secrecy and openness is a common state of affairs, and flexibility in this respect is a healthy phenomenon in a complex and differentiated government organization. In the Netherlands, the greater the openness of administration and government, the more rigid is secrecy and the protection of privacy.

More organized openness entails more secrecy. This paradox is explained when we realize that more openness is necessary for the mass of information in the administration's files that is not in itself classified as secret. If we permeate the technicalities of formal filing with which the material is surrounded, we also undermine the administrative and political function of the mere fact of storage. Secrecy and restricted access must then replace the impersonal character of bureaucratic information processing.

It is my anticipation that the urge for more openness and yet for greater protection of privacy will gain momentum in the Netherlands, and that restrictions to access will consequently be eased. At the same time, the protection of privacy will become more formalized and rigid. Differentiation and discretion will be reduced somewhat, but little procedural unification is likely.

Seen in its broad cultural context, the recent shift toward more openness seems functional as Dutch tradition rejects a high threshold between secrecy and openness. In the past the pendulum has swung too far toward bureaucratic imperviousness; it now has to swing back to its "rightful" place.

Seen in the political context, the drive for greater openness is part of a trend toward less accommodation in Dutch society. From the viewpoint of individual consciousness little is likely to change; even under conditions of greater openness, the government will continue to be regarded as a powerful "monster," difficult to understand, and almost impossible for the powerless citizen to influence. Civic consciousness may grow a little. But the effect of being better informed about one's lack of power is perhaps not so beneficial as some advocates of more openness seem to think.

Greater openness will do little to affect the equilibrium of the Dutch system. It is not an alien element, and its results will not be particularly inordinate.

13

The Federal Republic of Germany

JUERGEN REESE

Since the existence of the Federal Republic of Germany, legislation and jurisprudence have repeatedly had to tackle the problem of secrecy. Compared to other countries, the legal norms in Germany play a considerably more important role. Here, the legalistic form of argument has been preferred over any other form. We shall see later how some ground has been gained for the democratic principle of the right to know through an increasing liberalization of criminal law. The incidents, often unpleasant, that have hastened this change afford an insight into the fundamental attitude of the political elite. They can be cited as evidence of the political culture, keeping in mind, however, that legal rules and their application form only one part of the political culture. More significant, perhaps, are the relations between the leaders and the critical public—relations whose terms elude codification. These relations roughly can be characterized by an underlying conflict between government and the public.

In democratic regimes a distinction should be made between *state secrets*, which are legitimate and are aimed at protecting the public interest, and the *secrets of the ruler,* which are attempts to cover up facts and actions in order to avoid criticism. The problem is that under the shroud of state secrets the government tends to legitimize the secrets of the ruling elite.

As a result of this, two questions arise concerning the analysis of secrecy: How successfully do the government, public administration, and parliamentary groups in power conceal secret information from the press, the Opposition, and academic groups? What function does government public relations serve in terms of deliberately screening information? When examining government secrecy, we are always dealing with policies that are "defensive" (through monopoly and restriction) and "offensive" (through leaks and manipulation of selected information).

Full answers to these questions cannot be found in the internal structure of a political system. The answers are subject to variations resulting from changes in leadership and in political issues. The last twenty-five years of democratic history in the Federal Republic of Germany are still too limited to enable us to present reliable generalizations on the political culture of government secrecy.

Nevertheless, in the first part of this chapter, the historical connection between the change of the elite, the outstanding political issues, and government secrecy is discussed. The second part concentrates on the institutional and legal aspects of restrictive information policy. In the third part, the relationship between efficiency of the governmental processes, information to the public, and control of the government will be elucidated by means of a few institutional examples in the Federal Republic of Germany. This part will also present the offensive aspects of government information policy. Finally, an attempt will be made to evaluate the significance of government secrecy for the future development of democracy. The basic thesis of my exposition is that as politics becomes increasingly complex and internationalized, government secrecy becomes less and less a problem of restrictive information policy and more and more one of offensive information policy.

THE POLITICAL CULTURE

If there is such a thing as continuity in the development of political cultures, it is manifested in the ethos of the Prussian state, which set the tone of political discourse in Germany until the 1960s. The days of the Weimar Republic had demonstrated that this ethos could survive even without a monarchy. The old elite of the state bureaucracy and the army weathered the crisis and retained its high degree of uniformity in fundamental attitudes and conduct.[1]

Formally, the Weimar Republic was a democracy, but substantially it could not have become one because of the sociological structure of its ruling class. Political freedom, openness, and publicity were all totally contrary to the ethos of the ruling class, which instead valued solidary alliances, discretion, and absolute loyalty toward a superior. The solidarity of the members of the elite constantly renewed itself by the common contempt in which they held ordinary people and the quarrels among the numerous parties in the Reichstag. The leaders of national socialism knew exactly why they had to protect the old elites. These elites guaranteed continuity in completing the state's business and could, at worst, be neutral toward an authoritarian leadership.

But as a result of the breakdown of 1945, the ruling class (leadership of the National Socialistic party, the military and administrative elite, and the managers of the war economy and heavy industry) became a nonelite overnight. The new official maxim kept the doors of political offices shut to them.

Since the relatively homogeneous ruling class had been dissolved, the formation of political parties from the local up to the federal level took a long time. The Social Democrats (SPD), a party with a long tradition, had lost many of their best leaders in the Third Reich. The Christian Democrats (CDU) were a new party with a middle-class and religious orientation. The Liberals (FDP), who also have played an important role in the recent history of the Federal Republic of Germany, traditionally supported principles such as free enterprise and governmental restraint in the economy and society.

Old and new members of these parties had to learn their roles in a situation that was ideologically identified in a negative manner: to avoid goals and actions that could be remindful of the Third Reich. The result was a political pragmatism with differentiated but few real controversial goals. In this manner the new political leadership caused the formation of an ideological vacuum, inviting a renewed authoritarian style of leadership.

Traditionally, there have been several dominating principles in the

1. Theodor Eschenburg, *Die improvisierte Demokratie* (Munich: Piper, 1963); Karl Dietrich Bracher, *Deutschland zwischen Demokratie und Diktatur* (Bern: Scherz, 1964).

German civil service: hierarchical organization, strict division of competency, absolute discretion and secrecy, and tenure. These principles survived the Third Reich intact, enabling the civil servants to pursue their careers in the Bonn state.[2] Political leaders, public administrators, and trade association officials rediscovered their common interests and emerged as a powerful veto bloc in foreign affairs, domestic policy, and administration, thus establishing the so-called CDU state.[3] This period began with Konrad Adenauer's chancellorship in 1949 and is best characterized as one of restoration supported by the reestablishment of business, the farmer's associations, and the organizations of German deportees.

The government of this state operated on the conviction that it alone knew the one best way of governing. It also knew how to convey this conviction to the people and managed to get itself reelected on platforms that rejected innovations. Two factors favored this development: the spectacular and continuing economic growth that, to a large extent, spared the government difficult distribution struggles, and the cold war, which, by conjuring up a perpetual enemy abroad, created solidarity with the government at home.

A propaganda which portrays the opponent as fundamentally evil, the conflict irreconcilable, and the danger deadly, allows for no differentiations. The arguments of the other side must neither be made known nor refuted; they are settled without interference, owing to their provenance.[4]

The same applied to the intellectual treatment of communism as well as to the handling of political opponents in Parliament and in the press.

Many potential opportunities to start anew in dealing with the urgent societal issues of the industrial society were thrown away, among others the possibility of demonstrating political fair play in party competition. The widespread impression that politics is a shady

2. *Basic Law of the Federal Republic of Germany*, promulgated by the Parliamentary Council on May 23, 1949, as amended up to August 31, 1973 (Wiesbaden, 1973), art. 33, para. 5.

3. Gert Schäfer and Carl Nedelmann, eds., *Der CDU-Staat 1, Analysen zur Verfassungswirklichkeit der Bundesrepublik* (Frankfurt: Suhrkamp Edition, 1969).

4. Gerhard Schoenberger, "Meinungslenkung contra Information," in *Information oder Herrschen die Souffleure?* ed. Paul Hübner (Reinbek: Rowohlt, 1964), pp. 57–72, 62 (unauthorized translation—J. R.).

business was confirmed. This also hindered the development of citizens' participation.

In a climate of relative political indifference combined with authoritative power politics and traditional civil service allegiances, one could normally expect an extensive application of official secrecy. It seems all the more surprising because as early as the fifties Bonn enjoyed the reputation in press circles of being one of the few capitals in the world where the government was ready to issue information.[5] There must be some truth behind this reputation since even a critical state secretary admitted that Bonn did not overdo discretion.[6] What, then, are the underlying causes of this unexpected ambivalence?

The question points to a particular contradiction in the handling of government secrecy in the Federal Republic of Germany. On the one hand, the insistence on the reunification of Germany, as well as the struggle for sovereignty, had to increase the still existing distrust abroad. Because of this bow-wash effect of German foreign policy, credibility became one of its essential problems. Added to the necessity of overcoming distrust were above all feelings of guilt and political insecurity. One can speculate that these resulted in a liberal information policy toward foreign correspondents and foreign governments. In the course of time it also became a good public relations practice.

On the other hand, however, the CDU state reacted with utmost irritation to criticism from within. It initiated a restrictive information policy as well as an aggressive ideological campaign.[7] Thus the isolated dissenter was naturally portrayed as a traitor. The most spectacular trials, related to so-called public treason, took place during the time of the CDU rule.

A good example of this is the Spiegel affair, which started with the publication about a military exercise. This report contained criticism of the government's conception of defense in 1961 and led to the detention of half the editorial staff of the German magazine *Der Spiegel*. They all were found innocent, but under the public pressure

5. *Stuttgartner Zeitung*, August 31, 1972.
6. Karl Carstens, *Politische Führung, Erfahrungen im Dienste der Bundesregierung* (Stuttgart: Deutsche Verlagsanstalt, 1971), p. 25.
7. Arnulf Baring, *Aussenpolitik in Adenauers Kanzlerdemokratie* (Munich: Oldenbourg, 1969), pp. 293–328; Alfred Grosser and Juergen Seifert, *Die Staatsmacht und ihre Kontrolle* (Freiburg and Olten: Walter-Verlag, 1966), p. 18.

a minister had to resign.[8] Further, the Paetsch case can be cited, which dealt with the secret tapping of telephones of private citizens by the Office for the Protection of the Constitution. German law did not allow this practice. Believing this to be an abuse of power, a member of the office, who was sworn to secrecy, disclosed the tapping in 1963 and was indicted for this reason. The Federal Court agreed with him and contradicted the government's opinion.[9]

However, this authoritarian style has faced increasing difficulties since the end of Adenauer's chancellorship. Even earlier, social scientists had criticized the unsatisfactory conditions brought about by these practices. For instance, Theodor Eschenburg pointed out the extent to which associations had absorbed state power;[10] Juergen Habermas diagnosed a lack of critical publicity within private (and very secretive) organizations such as the vocational and professional associations with a membership of several million people.[11] Instead of exerting a "pressure for publicity" the CDU state preferred mutual adjustment with the associations and the exclusion of the public. Under the shroud of a symbol-loaded foreign policy, the power processes in domestic affairs took place for the most part in the darkness of secrecy. This must be the reason why citizens of the politically unprejudiced postwar generation identified themselves with the functioning and achievements of the elite and not with the political structure as such. The political power that rose with the first significant issue of postwar domestic politics (the education crisis) unfolded not within the established structure of parliamentary democracy, but outside in the extraparliamentary opposition.

Such was the case of the students' rebellion in the late sixties.[12] Although this development did not last long on the federal level, it has had a strong impact on local and regional politics in the form

8. See Juergen Seifert, *Die Spiegel-Affäre* (Freiburg and Olten: Walter-Verlag, 1966).

9. See the Paetsch case (Federal Court, St. 20, Karlsruhe, November 8, 1965).

10. Theodore Eschenburg, *Herrschaft der Verbände?* (Stuttgart: Deutsche Verlagsanstalt, 1956).

11. Juergen Habermas, *Strukturwandel der Öffentlichkeit* (Neuwied: Luchterhand, 1962).

12. Uwe Bergman et al., *Rebellion der Studenten oder Die neue Opposition* (Reinbek: Rowohlt, 1968). Since the beginning of the 1970s the ecology problem has aroused the same public interest as the education problem; however, it has so far led only to locally limited citizen initiatives, which in a proper sense cannot be called extraparliamentary.

of citizen initiatives.[13] Before that the duty of the citizens was to maintain political tranquillity; now the politics of protest came into fashion. *Ad hoc* initiatives of citizens are still springing up in great numbers, particularly concerning traffic planning and housing programs.

In a persistent conflict with politicians and public agencies, citizens have become increasingly aware of the impact that government secrecy has on their daily lives. Questions such as whether citizens are informed adequately and in time about political moves now form the substance of the most bitter controversies. For instance, citizens supported by the press were interested in the preservation of the royal gardens and buildings in Munich. They stopped the implementation of a very important part of city planning so effectively that in 1968 the City Council created a half-official agency named Muenchner Forum. Its duty is to organize debates on potentially controversial planning moves of the political and administrative leaders.[14] It seems that this agency has also increased some problems of communication between political leaders and the public. It is like the Cartesian problem: You must know something to become conscious that you know nothing. In any event, this institutional way of handling the public interest has rarely been imitated elsewhere.

It still remains to be seen whether parliamentary democracy will succeed in linking this newly strengthened interest to an institutional framework. The chances for such a development are also undermined by the relative weakness of the political and administrative system compared to the economic one.

Because they understand the limited control capacity of the political system, academics and practitioners have taken a growing interest in reforming state management. A good example is the Project Group on Governmental and Administrative Reforms set up in 1968 by the federal government. Different proposals for organizational reforms within the public administration have been prepared by this group. Above all, they have aimed at improving the inner circulation of information and at institutionalizing middle- and long-range planning.

---

13. See Heinz Grossmann, ed., *Bürgerinitiativen, Schritte zur Veränderung?* (Frankfurt: Fisher Taschenbuch, 1971); Pierre Hoffmann and Nikitas Patellis, *Demokratie als Nebenprodukt* (Munich: Hanser, 1971).

14. Juergen Reese, "Widerstand und Wandel der politischen Organisation" (Stuttgart: Frommann-Holzboog, 1976).

Setbacks of these joint efforts in the fields of planning and administrative reform lead to an ever more skeptical attitude toward the feasibility of reforming the political and administrative system on the part of the academics and practitioners.[15] In turn, the fear of criticism and its delegitimatory effects may cause the government to draw its shroud of secrecy even tighter. Already there had been some indications of such an attitude on the part of Willy Brandt's government (1969–1974). The evidence includes the fact that the federal government is often unprepared to agree to the publication of certain government-sponsored opinions concerning governmental and administrative reform.[16] Furthermore, the government unsuccessfully attempted to prevent the distribution of a paper that a former member of the Federal Ministry for Urbanization and Habitation had prepared for the Scientific Congress of the German Association for Political Science in October 1973.

Germany, like other Western countries, is trying to cope with the problematic connection between limited political control capacity, economic crisis, and delegitimatory processes. These exogenous conditions set the stage for the information policy of most governments. Germany has come a long way in having surmounted the "cartel of fear"[17] of its leadership and in having liberated itself to some extent from the constant pressure of "the German question."[18] Yet apart from the influence of exogenous conditions on government information policy, the degree of secrecy and publicity is also determined by the traditional attitudes and habits of the administrative establishment. Here the conservative and monopolistic power of administrative lawyers seems to be decisive. Now as before, they

15. Volker Ronge and Günter Schmieg, "Einleitung," in *Politische Planung in Theorie und Praxis*, eds. V. Ronge and Günter Schmieg (Munich: Piper, 1971), pp. 7–25; Fritz W. Scharpf, "Politische Durchsetzbarkeit innerer Reformen" (Göttingen: Otto Schwartz & Co., 1974).

16. For instance, the publication of Renate Mayntz-Trier and Fritz W. Scharpf's *Programmentwicklung in der Ministerialorganisation* (Bonn, 1972) was stopped.

17. Ralf Dahrendorf, *Society and Democracy in Germany* (Garden City, N.Y.: Doubleday, 1969).

18. The intensive parliamentary controversies over the *Ostpolitik* of the social-liberal coalition once again pushed the German question into the center of political attention. In view of numerous indiscretions regarding secret treaty negotiations, the government permitted a criminal prosecution of journalists who had published secret papers. See the second section of this chapter.

constitute a relatively closed group capable of defending their privileges successfully.[19] Hierarchy and absolute loyalty toward superiors still dominate because of a stubborn adherence to the traditional incentive system, even in those areas such as integrative long-range planning and cross-sectional programs where new forms of administrative cooperation are long overdue. Outside experts are hired when one cannot do without them, but their narrow professional orientations prevent them from contributing notably to the openness of the administrative system.[20] Moreover, because there are so few instances when experts are called in, they have relatively little influence and are fully exposed to the pressure of administrative socialization and the obligations of secrecy that go with it.

Since the change of government in 1969 there have been indications of more openness, but for reasons quite different than in the past. The social-liberal coalition headed by Willy Brandt was in desperate need of politically loyal personnel within the administration after twenty years of uninterrupted CDU rule. This need was met in part by appointing younger staff members of the party to government positions. These new people established channels of communication to the party and exposed government and ministerial internal deliberations to public discussion in the party.[21] In general, officials and experts with no party affiliation still favor a restrictive information policy. But this new group of party-affiliated civil servants could contribute in the future to a significant change in the conservative uniformity of the administrative system.

CONSTITUTIONAL AND LEGAL ASPECTS

The tendencies toward greater publicity of administrative actions discussed above confront a rather restrictive theory of political and administrative law in the Federal Republic of Germany (FRG). Max

---

19. Thomas Ellwein and Ralf Zoll, *Berufsbeamtentum—Anspruch und Wirklichkeit* (Düsseldorf: Bertelsmann Universitätsverlag, 1973); Wilhelm Bleek, *Von der Kameralausbildung zum Juristenprivileg* (Berlin: Colloquium-Verlag, 1972).

20. W. R. Scott, "Professionals in Bureaucracies—Areas of Conflict," in *Professionalization*, eds. H. M. Vollmer and D. L. Mills (Englewood Cliffs, N.J.: Prentice-Hall, 1966), pp. 265–275.

21. For instance, civil servants with party affiliations participated in developing the first long-term program of the Social Democrats.

Weber, whose ideal model of bureaucratic domination was most certainly influenced by the Prussian approach, saw in the official secret a basic characteristic of modern bureaucracy.[22] German administrative law has followed this principle up to the present. Between the principle requiring disclosure unless secrecy is specifically required and the principle requiring secrecy unless disclosure is specifically permitted, it insists on the latter.[23] Peter Duewel points out that German law, according to concurring opinion in the jurisprudence literature, does not recognize a general and unconditional right of a citizen to obtain information from the state, but as a general principle leaves it to the discretion of the public agencies and civil servants to allow inspection of records and to release information.[24]

According to the Basic Law of the FRG, all state power comes from the people. Inherent in this principle is the precept of publicity in the exercise of state power.[25] This is reinforced by the constitutional guarantees of freedom of speech and liberty of the press.[26] State secrecy is not specifically mentioned in the Basic Law and one can argue that it can be legitimate only as an exception to the rule.

But there are other laws pertaining to secrecy and they can be divided into two categories:

1. Laws aimed at protecting *state secrecy*. State secrets are protected by a very detailed section of the Criminal Law[27] and are defined as "facts, objects, or knowledge which are accessible only to a limited number of persons, and which must be kept secret in order to avert the danger of serious harm being done to the FRG" (section 93,1). Facts infringing on the free and democratic basic order of the FRG are not state secrets (section 93,2). These laws are mainly against the distribution of information to other states.

22. Max Weber, *Economy and Society: An Outline of Interpretive Sociology*, eds. G. Roth and C. Wittich, (New York, 1968).
23. Peter Duewel, *Das Amtsgeheimnis* (Berlin: Duncker & Humblot, 1965), p. 113.
24. Ibid., p. 114.
25. Helmut Ridder, in Helmut Ridder and Ernst Heinitz, eds., *Staatsgeheimis und Pressefreiheit* (Hof: Oberfraenkische Verlagsanstalt, 1963), pp. 33, 43; Adolf Arndt, *Landesverrat* (Berlin: Luchterhand, 1966), p. 36.
26. *Grundgesetz für die Bundesrepublik Deutschland*, May 23, 1949, art. 5.
27. *Achtes Strafrechtsänderungsgesetz* from June 25, 1968, Bundesgesetzblatt no. 43, 1968.

They are concerned with preventing disclosure of security secrets, the publication of which will violate an important public interest.

2. Laws aimed at protecting *official secrecy*. These laws prohibit the distribution of official information from the government to the public. Official secrecy is regulated by the Federal Civil Service Law (*Bundesbeamteg nesetz*) and by the German Criminal Law (*Strafgesetzbuch*):

—The Civil Service Law binds the public servants to keep all official business secret. The civil servant who violates this risks disciplinary proceedings (section 61 of the Civil Service Law).[28]

—A public servant who does not abide by this law can be imprisoned for up to five years (section 353 b of the Criminal Law).[29]

—Unauthorized distribution of a paper that is classified can lead to imprisonment for up to three years, if an important public interest is concerned (section 353 c of the Criminal Law).

As we can see from the third article above, the distinction between state secrets and official secrets is not clear and the two can often be overlapping. Apart from the legal confusion, there is also the political reality.

Governments in representative democracies tend to exploit any form of domination, including secrecy. In some countries leaks represent an important counterbalancing factor. In Germany the traditional disciplinary and penal sanctions are strong enough to prevent officials in general from taking the risk and from not recognizing beforehand the consequences of unauthorized disclosures. This creates an attitude that encourages the use of secrecy to avoid criticism and to conceal facts that need not be concealed.

Because of its partisan interest, the formal system of document classification, according to which information should be kept secret for reasons of state security, provides little guidance for the definition of state secrets. The secrets of the ruling elite that owe their existence entirely to the interest of perpetuating government power should not be regarded as state secrets and thus be protected by

---

28. *Bundesbeamteg nesetz* from 1953, reissued on October 1, 1961.
29. *Strafgesetzbuch des Deutschen Reiches* from 1871, reissued on August 25, 1953.

criminal law. But in reality this distinction between bona fide state secrets and self-motivated government secrets is not observed.

It is part of the inconsistency of the German Criminal Law that in spite of this, a penalty is imposed on the distribution of classified information, that is, of both state and ruler's secrets, not only on civil servants, but also on journalists and private persons. The article concerned (353 c) dates back to the time of national socialism and has survived all criminal law reforms almost intact. The public prosecutor must prosecute each infringement when it becomes known to him. But there are a few exceptions to this rule. If the prosecution uncovers state secrets in the course of its investigations, there is a regulation that permits the government to withhold consent to the prosecution in order to protect a state secret. The political common sense not to use this regulation was broken in 1972 by the government;[30] however, recent experience has shown that this article does not please public prosecutors or judges and that they will try any legal means to repeal it. This possibility of repeal results from the necessity for the court to estimate whether the information still had been secret when published and if the publication violated an important public interest.

Due mainly to the vagueness of the notion of secrecy and the extensive practice of secrecy, different legal and political problems arise. This holds especially true for the so-called public treason cases when state secrets are made available to a foreign power through unauthorized publications. Careful investigations by a clever journalist will time and again yield information that is classified. How is he to differentiate between state secrets, the publication of which will be punished severely; official secrets, the publication of which can, but generally will not, be punished; and illegal secrets (secrets concealing illegal actions and conditions), the publication of which is a duty to the citizen?

Since the Spiegel affair in 1962 the professional public has been continually concerned with these questions. The debate has subsided for the present as a result of the Eighth Criminal Law Reform of June 25, 1968.[31] In this law the idea of establishing a privilege for journalists was rejected. This would have required a careful examination of the journalist involved in order to establish his motives in

30. Review of the Public Relations Office of the Federal Government (November 8, 1971), appendix 7.
31. See note 27.

publishing a state secret.[32] Today, at least, the publication of a state secret is punishable only if it intentionally "causes damage to the Federal Republic of Germany or favors a foreign power,"[33] or if through negligence the publication of the state secret seriously endangers the security of the country.[34] Thus the professional risk to journalists of publishing a state secret erroneously has been significantly reduced. The much smaller risk of being punished for publishing an official secret still remains.

Another important complication was the question of how a citizen should (or may) react when he realizes that the government is acting illegally under the protection of the state secret.[35] This danger exists especially in the secret services and in the administration of the chancellor's secret budget. It is no wonder that political scandals start from and come to an open end with these institutions time and again. Due to historical developments, there can scarcely be foreign interventions by the German secret services like that, for example, of the CIA in Chile. Today the danger connected with the secret services in Germany is much more one of abuse in domestic politics. For instance, it is considered a fact that Konrad Adenauer let a few of his political opponents be shadowed by the services.

Where secrecy is daily routine, control by the government (and even more so by the Parliament) is relatively ineffective. All the more important is the opportunity of public criticism of illegal practices by the services whenever they come to be known. In 1965 on the basis of the criminal law in force at the time, the Federal Court, in the very controversial Paetsch case decision, established the principle that the right of freedom of speech allows the citizen to criticize and attempt to remedy abuses in public life.[36] Accordingly, the right to criticize the government and its services is limited to cases that are actual and provable abuses.[37] Such a guideline is inconsistent with democracy because it places the burden of proof on the citizen who must—while not having access to the information he needs—

32. Heinrich Laufhütte, "Staatsgeheimnis und Regierungsgeheimnis" in *Goltdammer's Archiv für Strafrecht 1974/2*, pp. 52–60.

33. *Achtes Strafrechtsänderungsgesetz*, sec. 94.

34. Ibid., sec. 97.

35. In Germany this subject has its own tradition, which was established by Carl von Ossietzky, a journalist who in 1931 uncovered German-Soviet conspiracies. In spite of the Nobel Prize that he received when he was already imprisoned, Ossietzky was put to death in a concentration camp.

36. Decision of the Federal Court, St. 20, Karlsruhe, November 8, 1965.

37. Arndt, *Landesverrat*, p. 8.

demonstrate that his opinion is based on actual fact. The application of legal sanction following such a principle can be used to reduce citizen involvement to political silence.

The above-mentioned case also had consequences for the Eighth Criminal Law Reform, which states that "facts infringing on the free and democratic basic order, or keeping secrets from allies of the Federal Republic of Germany regarding intergovernmentally agreed upon limitations of armament . . . [are] not state secrets."[38] The amendment has given priority to the public interest in having open discussion of breaches of law and of peace efforts over considerations of external security.[39] Thus one can say that the criminal law in the FRG has reached a stage of development corresponding more closely to the prerequisites of democratic constitutional theory with regard to the free flow of information.

This should not gloss over the fact that in reality the daily flow of information between various branches of the government and the public is still much more influenced by the broad interpretation and extensive application of government secrecy and by stringent sanctioning of any violation according to the Civil Service Law. While only spectacular cases of espionage or controversial press publications bring state secrets to the attention of the individual citizen, the official secret is clearly present in daily contacts with public agencies. It contributes to a widening of the gap between citizen and state.

When civil servants can make important decisions without being accountable and without regard for individual needs and special cases, the state ceases to serve the interests of its citizens and rather becomes an institution whose self-perpetuating interests are paramount and separate from those of the electorate. And if, again and again, a citizen believes that under the shroud of the official secret the principle of equality is not strictly observed, there may be not only lack of identification with the state, but also a hostile attitude and at least the suspicion that governmental actions are tainted by expediency.[40]

Let us leave the question of whether unequal treatment and corrup-

38. *Achtes Strafrechtsänderungsgesetz*, sec. 93, para. 2.

39. Laufhütte, "Staatsgeheimnis und Regierungsgeheimnis," p. 56; Hermann Krauth et al., "Zur Reform des Staatsschutz-Strafrechts durch das Achte Strafrechtsänderungsgesetz," *Juristenzeitung*, no. 19 (October 4, 1968):609–613, 611.

40. Regarding the citizen-administration relationship, see F. Haueisen, "Verwaltung und Bürger," in *Deutsches Verwaltungsblatt*, 1961, p. 833; H. W. Rombach, "Bürger und Behörde," in *Die Öffentliche Verwaltung*, 1963, p. 372.

tion are avoidable in a more open system undecided. In any case, the secretiveness of the political and administrative system, because of a broad interpretation and application of the official secret, hinders the identification of the citizen with the state as a service institution. Official secrets are therefore a major obstacle to the development of both democratic consciousness and democratic behavior in Germany. The results are either alienation or stronger emphasis on the mystical role of the state.

The existence of subservience to authoritarianism under the surface of formal democracy is shown by the apathy of large parts of the middle class toward the problematic function of government in general and toward state secrets in particular. Whenever a government in the Federal Republic of Germany protests against the unauthorized publication of actual or alleged state secrets, or has taken legal proceedings against it, the general public tends to view it as a test of strength between the government and the press rather than as a fundamental and serious problem of democracy. At the outset of such controversies, when the press tries to strengthen its position with screaming headlines, it seems as if it could mobilize the electorate. However, a few years later when the matter comes to a judicial decision, there is no public interest. Even in those cases where the interpretation of the constitution by the Federal Constitutional Court and by the federal courts has far-reaching consequences for the country, only those readers who take the trouble to read the inside pages of their newspaper can find anything about it. This was the case, for instance, in the Spiegel affair as well as in the Paetsch case. A further example is the publishing of secret minutes of the negotiations between USSR and FRG by a German magazine in 1970. The basic democratic dilemma caused by the existence of secrets is realized as a problem only by the intellectual community in this country.

THE INFORMATION MARKETPLACE

Over and above any need for the protection of national security, secrecy is said to be necessary to the increased efficiency of governmental decision-making processes. From this point of view, it seems absurd to inform those who will be affected by a policy at too early a stage because they may interfere with the "efficiency" of the deliberative process. It seems more practical and timesaving and less nerve-racking if those concerned are informed only when the decision in question has "become mature." In effect, apart from the protection of privacy, defenders of official secrets most often find their justification in this very argument. Such a narrow argument for efficiency ignores the difficulties of arriving at a satisfactory settlement of political and administrative proposals, and it is more compatible with an authoritarian regime than with a democratic one.

Given a broader concept of efficiency that would consider the resources that need to be allocated for realizing a policy, particularly for bringing about the necessary consensus, a restrictive information policy has proved to be all the more impracticable and counterproductive the more actively citizens concern themselves with public affairs. Empirically this thesis is supported by the effect of citizen initiatives, which in Germany often tear up with sharp protest the fine web of administrative agreements and thereby destroy the precarious political consensus painstakingly achieved after years of negotiations. It would therefore be cheaper and more efficient in the long run to include in the decision-making process at the outset all those who are concerned with the problem at hand. This means more openness even at the preparatory stages of the deliberation process. It is in this direction that half-serious experiments have been made, especially in the field of local politics. The experiment in Munich was mentioned above.

On the federal level, consultations with "outsiders" also take place. It is rare for a ministry to prepare a law or a regulation without consulting the associations concerned. However, such consultations with interest groups are conducted on a selective basis, and this distribution of information is not aimed at general publicity. Those not represented by an interest group have no chance of being brought into the inner circle. The selective information policy is concerned with efficiency and to some extent has increased government openness, but current practice goes only halfway toward changing secrecy. It also violates the principle of equality by limiting access to government to powerful groups. What is still required, given the insufficient capacity of the government for building a consensus, is the opening up of the political and administrative processes, and this should, from a normative theoretical point of view, be accomplished now.

But in the context of current conditions in Germany, this normative and theoretical requirement seems to be an illusion. For one thing, the public is not yet prepared to participate in decision making. The increasing complexity of politics and administration makes this development technically impossible. Participation in the process of decision making requires a high degree of communicative competence, which an ordinary citizen or a poor interest group cannot be expected to have. Even within the political and administrative system the participants face a language problem, which diminishes their political effectiveness and impedes intercommunications between their fields of duties.[41]

The information strategy that the political and the administrative system has developed to cope with increasing complexity is limited to a consideration of what is viable from a predominantly technical point of view or of what is demanded by interest groups threatening to employ negative sanctions. From the policy-output point of view, a two-fold danger arises out of this form of simplification: on the one hand, the reduction of efficiency in a purely technical sense because important interdependencies are neglected, and on the other hand, the inadequate consideration of interests and social needs because of a distorted input structure. Both dangers can lead to a serious problem of legitimation.

Further augmentation of the complexity of politics because of increasing internationalization and a growing emancipation from authoritarian leadership could intensify the legitimation problem in the future, particularly with regard to the ability of parliamentary governments to cope with social problems without being drastically changed. If the individual member of Parliament no longer succeeds in retaining an expert view of important political issues, how could he successfully play his part as mediator between governmental actions and civic interests?

These difficulties as well as other imperfections in the free flow of information change the nature of the dilemma of government secrecy. The transition from an authoritarian to a democratic regime, from the guarantee of state order to the guarantee of social service efficiency, coupled with the growing influence of advisory bodies and interest groups, are making traditional concepts of government

41. Though a number of papers on the sociology of language barriers have been published in the Federal Republic (for example, Bernhard Badura and Klaus Gloy, eds., *Soziologie der Kommunikation* [Stuttgart: Frommann-Holzboog, 1972]), the results of communication difficulties caused by growing specialization in political-decision processes have hardly been analyzed at all.

secrecy more and more obsolete, no matter how hard their defenders may try to protect them. Instead of absolute secrets we face a new danger called *technocracy*. Technical terminologies and limited competence obstruct the indispensable free flow of information between government, Parliament, and citizens in democratic systems.

Attempts to overcome these growing difficulties are scarce. The information service of the federal government, for example, rarely furnishes new information to the expert public, which is well informed anyway. For the layman, the government reports are not worth reading because of their minuteness and technicality.[42] Besides, their contents often crave for acclamation: They aim at approval, not critical discussion.

In the future, politicians and political scientists will have to be far more concerned with information problems than hitherto. It is more difficult to foresee, however, the roles that will be played by the different parts of the present institutional framework. Will it be the task of the mass media to solve the interpretation problems? In order to do so they will have to acquire sufficient means to employ researchers with technical and journalistic training without becoming financially dependent. In the future will governments themselves supply the critical information of general interest that would be necessary for the control of their actions? Surely not. Will Parliament take over this task through the development of research services and the improvement of the office aides of members of Parliament? Would the resulting professionalism of Parliament be compatible with its traditional role of representation? In the Federal Republic of Germany today probably no one knows the answers to these questions.

42. *Forschung und Öffentlichkeit*, Struktur eines Kommunikationssystems am Beispiel des Bundesforschungsberichts IV (Bonn: Institut für Kommunikationsplanung, June 19, 1972).

14

France

YOHANAN MANOR

In matters of information and secrecy, the French case provides us with a long-term perspective. Government withholding of information in France is done for the usual reasons: The matter is considered to be genuinely secret; premature disclosure of motives and actions would be disruptive; or the government simply does not trust the public at large.[1] But there are also reasons quite specific to France and closely related to some features of the political and administrative culture.

THE CULTURAL CONTEXT

Students of French politics have emphasized the high degree of individualism of the French people and its decisive importance in their approach to politics.[2] Individualism and atomism are among the characteristics mentioned by Hoffman to describe what he called the "French stalemate society,"[3] with the resulting reluctance of the

1. B. Chapman, *The Profession of Government* (London: Allen and Unwin, 1958), p. 321.
2. F. Goguel and A. Grosser, *La Politique en France* (Paris: Colin, 1964), p. 18 ff.
3. S. Hoffmann et al., *In Search of France* (New York: Harper, 1963), p. 11.

French for face-to-face discussions that could enable the parties involved to compromise. Michel Crozier remarks that "coming to terms, bargaining, compromising, dealing and trying to adapt to the demands of other people are not methods praised and accepted by the French."[4] Crozier's remarks refer to present-day France, Hoffman's to the France of the Third Republic, and both echo Tocqueville's observations about French individualism made over a century ago.[5]

This feature, however, coupled with a pronounced inclination for formal egalitarianism and uniformity, has had a deep influence on French political attitudes, with far-reaching results concerning collective action and collective discipline.

The French relate to political parties much more in terms of ideologies and metaphysical conceptions than in terms of programs and concrete actions.[6] In France, political struggles tend to look like religious wars. The inclination for abstract philosophical and moral theories seems to have been nurtured by French governments that preferred to have people discuss general matters rather than have them question the concrete actions of its agents.[7]

These cultural features made it much more difficult for the French to practice democracy without interruption. Hence the temptation to regard despotism as a salvation from the negative and corrosive effects of these features and the inclination to reject it as a threat to individual liberty. Moreover, because of the multiplicity of political parties, the weakness of the executive, and the imbalance between the executive and the legislature, democracy degenerated into obstruction (the old Parliaments under the monarchic regime) or into anarchy and standstill (*Gouvernement d'Assemblée*). In this oscillation between liberalism and despotism a "newcomer" did emerge: the State concept, which was to appear as the indisputable substitue for the various abhorred political regimes.

The concept of the State as a distinct entity is viewed by many

4. M. Crozier, "Pour une Théorie de l'Action Administrative," in J. M. Auby et al., *Traité de Science Administrative* (Paris: Mouton, 1966), p. 776.

5. A. de Tocqueville, *L'Ancien Régime et la Révolution* (Paris: Gallimard, 1964), p. 176.

6. Goguel and Grosser, *La Politique en France*, pp. 23–26; H. Greard and G. De Loys, *La France depuis 1945* (Paris: Cours de l'Institut d'Études Politiques, 1968–1969), p. 15.

7. Tocqueville, *L'Ancien Régime et la Révolution*, p. 136.

French students as a specifically and originally French innovation that played a central role in the development of their administrative and political systems.[8] Not only was the State the supreme arbitrator of social and political conflicts, ensuring order, stability, and continuity, it was also considered the main driving force in society; not only the governor, but also the propeller.[9] Thus, there is on the one hand a positive attitude with regard to the State and its embodiment, public administration, and constant expectation for its interventions and actions. After any disaster, the French response is first of all to "remake the State,"[10] and these were de Gaulle's exact words when returning to power in 1958.[11]

Some of the preeminence and the mystical majesty of the State is attributed also to its administrative machinery. It is not subject to common law, but is regulated by a special jurisdictional framework of administrative law with exceptional status. Similarly, on the local and regional level, there is no truly local government, but rather local administrations (*collectivités locales*), under the tutelage of central authorities.

But on the other hand, the basic attitudes of hostility and defiance against authority have been maintained. There is a tendency to restrict the State's actions, mainly as they affect private life, the family, individual freedom, and property. Hence Boutmy's assertion that in France there are only two parts in the political equation: the individuals and the State.[12] However, the State has gradually increased its power, making the government machinery the real sovereign in France. And this general process has been greatly enhanced by the imbalance in the political system.

The enlarged role of the State and the power of its public administration have led to an entrenched legitimacy of the whole governing process and have affected the attitudes of the French regarding information and secrecy. The basic attitude is that it is not

8. G. Burdeau, *L'État* (Paris: Le Seuil, 1970), p. 32 ff.

9. Leroy Beaulieu, *L'État Moderne et ses fonctions*, 4th ed. (Paris: Alcan, 1911), p. 17.

10. J. Mandrin, *L'Anarchie* (Paris: Table ronde de Combat, 1967), p. 15.

11. See also de Gaulle's speech before the *Conseil d'État*, 28.2.1960: "France has existed thanks to the State. France can make herself only through it. There is nothing more important than Legitimacy, the Institutions and the State," in *Citations du Président De Gaulle*, choisies et présentées par J. Lacouture (Paris: Le Seuil, 1968), p. 31.

12. E. Boutmy, quoted in P. Legendre, *Histoire de l'Administration* (Paris: Presse Universitaire de France, 1968), p. 50.

so important to know exactly what the State (i.e., the government) is doing, or how, as long as it remains within the limits assigned to it, does not encroach upon individual liberties, and treats each citizen in the same mechanical, impersonal, and equal way. The French administrative system is rather closed and is perceived and accepted as such. The privacy of the *bureaux* is respected, just as each citizen would sharply reject inquiries into his private life. Relations with the closed world of bureaucracy are strictly formal, official, distant, and anonymous. In the famous French Declaration of Citizens' Rights, there is no right to know nor right to demand information about government affairs.

There is no strong demand for the dissemination of government information. Individuals, groups, and organizations lack the incentive to ask for information that may be useful for their activities. Collective action being almost exclusively the field of public administration, many reforms formulated in the silent secrecy of the *bureaux* have been carried out with a notable public ignorance and apathy of public opinion, and often even without the knowledge of the Parliament.

Because of their conception of the State's quasi-monopolistic responsibility in the field of collective action, the French have not until recently considered internal administrative information to be of wider interest. Indeed, much valuable material has been meticulously collected and stored by the administrative system without being used by people outside the *bureaux*, especially in the social and economic fields. The administration was thus *une grande muette*.[13] The notion that such documentation, especially in social and economic fields, is "an essential constituent for functional modern democracy"[14] is a somewhat new perception.

French individualism and the conception of the State have also given administrative muteness some status of legal as well as ideological legitimacy. The legal aspect will be studied in the second section of this chapter. Ideologically, secrecy enjoys the blessing and general acquiescence of the public as part of a myth, in which a strong central government is needed to save Frenchmen from themselves and to overcome their seeming inability to produce relatively stable political regimes. Having endowed the State with much power, the French expect its concrete expression to be clothed with majesty,

13. Legendre, *Histoire de l'Administration*, p. 371.
14. Pierre Mendès-France, *Le Monde*, November 24, 1967.

aloofness, mystery, and secrecy. Both civil servants and citizens share this perception.

In the field of foreign affairs secrecy has been practiced very seriously, under every regime and despite criticism.[15] In the domestic field secrecy, ruse, political police, and even violation of privacy are all quite old traditions in France. One can recall Fouché's actions, the political control exerted by the prefects, and more recently, the special unit in the Ministry of the Interior, of the *Renseignements Généraux* (general intelligence), with its antenna in the departments. A former minister of the interior, Jules Moch, called them the "meteorologists of public opinion."[16] It is worth remembering that ruse is a substitute for the use of violence in the exercise of power and that secrecy is a sine qua non condition of ruse.[17] Taking into account the French political culture, resorting to ruse seems to be a necessary precaution because the use of power may lead to violent reaction, uprisings, and dislocation of social order.

Thus secrecy is viewed as a legitimate antidote to some "shortcomings" of French political culture. In the study of French history, it is quite striking to note the emphasis that is put on the role of dissimulation, manipulation, and secrecy in the successful achievements of great French leaders—Louis XIV, Cardinal Richelieu, Napoleon Bonaparte, and de Gaulle. In *The Edge of the Sword*, de Gaulle, knowing his people, found it necessary to restate what had been well known even before Machiavelli, and emphasized the role of secrecy and dissimulation.

On the part of public administration there is a notable reluctance to diffuse information. The French style of administration reinforced the "natural" tendency of the government for distance, remoteness, esotericism, formality, and closeness. Until recently, there was no policy for public information; citizens were considered as administrees, almost as incorrigible individualistic adversaries to be manipulated and distrusted. Withholding information was therefore a necessary, wise step to forestall undesirable, unexpected moves. Besides, the need to cooperate with the citizens, or at least to create the necessary conditions for this, was not perceived at all. The State

15. Condemned by the *Constituante* 1789–1791, and by the new Republican regime in 1848, "nothing is to be secret among a free people" (Mably). In Legendre, *Histoire de l'Administration*, p. 239.

16. R. Backman and C. Angeli, *Les Polices de la Nouvelle Société* (Paris: Maspero, 1971), p. 22.

17. J. Freund, *Qu'est-ce que la Politique?* (Paris: Le Seuil, 1968), p. 60.

and its administrative system were a substitute for the lack of ability for collective and cooperative action. The administrative style was matched to the French culture and was not likely to change it.

But this low propensity to diffuse information can also be attributed to the difficulty of circulating information within the system itself. The main reason for this is the administration's stratification as well as its vertical partition. Hence the additional difficulty for public administration to communicate with its environment. As stressed by Crozier, under such circumstances only a deep crisis will force the system to overcome stratification and partition—both of which are obstacles to the internal flow of information.[18]

An original way to overcome the limitations of this administrative system was to confer a very special status on some categories of high civil servants, the *Grands Corps*.[19] They enjoy high prestige and relatively far better access to all bureau information, although this was not attained with ease. The creation of the *École Nationale d'Administration*, and the subsequent quasi-monopoly conferred on it in enlisting, training, and forming the members of these *Grands Corps*, have increased the relative ease of access to information within the bureaucracy.

THE LEGAL FRAMEWORK OF INFORMATION AND SECRECY

The legal framework of information and secrecy in France is based upon two postulates: first, that man may give up certain of his rights only to preserve other rights through the State, and at the same time the State cannot prevent the exercise of personal rights without destroying its own basis; second, that the State can limit the exercise of personal rights only if this is absolutely necessary for the preservation of the rights of other citizens.[20]

18. M. Crozier, *Le Phénomène Bureaucratique* (Paris: Le Seuil, 1963), p. 260.

19. The *Grands Corps* are the various groups of higher civil servants, each having its specific status. One can distinguish between the Technical Corps, which have gained supremacy and monopoly over engineering fields including the development of physical infrastructures, and the other General Corps in charge of directing and supervising all the systems of public administration: the *Conseil d'État*, the *Cour des Comptes*, the *Inspection des Finances*, the *Corps Diplomatique*, and the *Corps Préfectoral*.

20. G. Burdeau, *Les Libertés Publiques* (L. G. D. J. Pichon, 1966), pp. 59–60.

The rather extensive freedom of speech and the notion of *secret professionel* are concrete expressions of this individualist doctrine. Article 11 of the 1789 Declaration of Human and Citizens Rights— a document that was incorporated in the preamble to the Constitution of 1946 as well as in the one of 1958—established freedom of expression and speech. There is no text denying this fundamental right to the civil servants, as it was restated by the French government before the National Assembly.[21] Article 378 of the Penal Code lays down heavy penalties for the violation of the *secret professionel,* and there is a long list of professions that have been explicitly subjected to this article. But courts have restricted the enforcement of these penalties to the disclosure of confidential information received from the public for the protection of privacy, and not to other information in the hands of public servants.[22]

The combination of a liberal interpretation of freedom of expression and a restricted enforcement of the *secret professionel* might have led to a greater degree of openness in French public administration, denying it the legal means to forbid the disclosure of information not pertaining to professional privacy. In reality, the situation is quite different. The 1789 Declaration of Human and Citizens Rights and the "General Principles acknowledged by the laws of the Republic" have had, at least until recently, an inspirational value mainly. The actual legal framework for public liberties, and among them the people's right to know, has been formulated through rules enacted by the administrative system. In France, public administration is controlled by an independent judicial system within the bureaucracy. The supreme court of this special system is the *Conseil d'État.* The protection of public liberties is entrusted mainly to this administrative body, and less to the civil courts or to the Constitutional Court.[23] The result is that the right to know is in practice governed by a tight network of administrative rules, which tends to favor the interests of the bureaucracy.

21. *Journal Officiel,* Debats Assemblée Nationale, October 5, 1952.
22. S. Salon, *Delinquance et Répression disciplinaire dans la fonction Publique* (Paris: L. G. D. J. Pichon, 1969), p. 88–89.
23. According to the Constitution of 1958, one of the tasks of the *Conseil Constitutionnel* is the judicial review of the status of laws already adopted by the National Assembly but not yet promulgated. Within these severe limits, the *Conseil Constitutionnel* has decided recently to attach a supralegal value to the principles of the 1789 Declaration and to the "General Principles." Cf. R. Errera, *Les Libertés à l'abandon,* 3d ed. (Paris: Le Seuil, 1975), p. 129.

What information is the civil servant entitled to publish?

The first legal barrier against the disclosure of political and administrative information by civil servants is the duty of *discrétion professionelle*, violation of which entails disciplinary penalties. It forbids civil servants to disclose official data, information, and documents[24] that have come to their knowledge during their official duties "contrary to the regulations." This expression in the French context does not mean "forbidden by regulations," but "not allowed expressly by the regulations."[25] Prohibition is the general rule, and everything learned during the service is to remain secret.

The civil servant is not completely silenced by this duty. He can evaluate and decide if it would be wise to reveal the facts and how it will affect the "good" running of the office. The first famous "Case Jannes" tends (at least indirectly) to prove that the disclosure of information concerning administrative practices cannot be considered as a breach of *discrétion professionelle*.[26]

The obligation not to disclose official information to unauthorized persons holds also for insiders. A civil servant is released from this duty only with regard to his superiors, colleagues, and successor, within a specific category of high civil servants,[27] or if there are specific provisions releasing him from this duty. Also, his minister could exempt him from this duty, a very important step that allows testimonies before committees of the Parliament.

Another measure is the duty of *réserve* (circumspection, caution), which is not the result of a legal and specific disposition but rather the result of court decisions and precedents.[28] The duty of *réserve*, recently called forth by the late President Pompidou after the

24. J. Grosclaude, "L'Obligation de Discrétion Professionelle du Fonctionnaire," *Revue Administrative* 20 (1967):131; J. Ribbs, "Information des Citoyens et Secret administratif," *Gazette du Palais*, June 15–16, 1973, p. 166.

25. Grosclaude, "L'Obligation de Discrétion Professionelle du Fonctionnaire," p. 129.

26. Mr. Jannes was an engineer at the ministry of posts and telecommunications who was denied the benefit of a special extra salary distributed (annually) for good services. The *Conseil d'État* has annulled this decision in seeming to accept the argument of Mr. Jannes that the deprivation was due to one of his reports denouncing deficiencies in the acquisition of equipment. *Conseil d'État*, December 23, 1966, Sieur Jannes.

27. A. Plantey, *Traité Pratique de la Fonction Publique* (Paris: Librairie Générale de Droit et de Jurisprudence, 1963), p. 299.

28. It appeared also in subordinate legislation, for the first time in 1958, in the regulations concerning the judges—Ordinance, December 22, 1958.

Aranda scandal,[29] refers to some kind of balance, caution, and "style" in the ways a civil servant expresses his opinions.[30] In a narrow sense it is aimed at preventing slander, but it has also been used to prevent criticism and dissension within the bureaucracy. This wider interpretation, although not adopted by the *Conseil d'État*, was quite vigorously claimed by Malaud, the State secretary in charge of the Civil Service:

> Civil servants are not, as such, to question a decision of their administration publicly, even if it seems to them awkward, unfortunate, detrimental, or even illegal. The right to contest administrative decisions, which has to be protected as one of the foundations of democracy, cannot be within the competence of the public servant, but within that of the administree.[31]

In summary, civil servants are obliged to keep silent. They can legally divulge some kinds of information, but it is a very subtle art that requires dexterity. This outlet is not within the range of everybody and is extremely risky to use, at least publicly.

What information is the public entitled to obtain?

Outside public bureaucracy, publicity is the rule, secrecy the exception. The meetings of the two assemblies are open to the public. Each assembly may decide to meet in secret committee at the request of the premier or by a decision of its members, and also to decide whether or not to publish reports of its committees and commissions.[32] Similar procedures exist in the judiciary field. Quite strikingly, this is not the rule for administrative justice. According to the precedents established by the *Conseil d'État*, "the publicity of the audience is not required before administrative jurisdictions, provided that there is

29. Mr. Aranda was a former member of the cabinet of Mr. Chalandon, then minister for equipment, in charge of contacts with the press. In September 1972, in a letter to the newspaper *Le Monde*, he threatened to publish embarrassing documents if the French government were to sell to Libya Mirage jets. *Année Politique*, 1972, p. 62.

30. J. Y. Vincent, "L'Obligation de Réserve Des Agents Publics," *Revue Administrative* (1973):145.

31. *Le Monde*, February 1, 1973.

32. Article 33 of the 1958 Constitution.

no legislation or subordinate legislation which prescribes the respect of this rule (of publicity)."[33]

The decree of 1970 concerning the accessibility to national archives and departmental documents states that "the documents previous to July 10, 1940, transferred by administrations, public services, and public enterprises to national and departmental archives are transmitted to the public."[34] This is not really a declassification rule after a period of thirty years, since it does not apply automatically to documents dated later than July 10, 1940, or to earlier documents that have not been transferred to the archives. Such documents are not available, whatever their classification unless there are special provisions for their explicit transmission to the public.[35] Members of Parliament do not have the benefit of special provisions. The ordinance providing for the creation of parliamentary investigation committees does not mention any duty of civil servants to help these committees in their work.[36]

This nondisclosure-of-documents rule has been frequently confirmed by the precedents judged by the *Conseil d'État*, although in a few cases this institution and lower administrative courts have accepted the argumentation of complaints and required the *bureaux* to submit the documents to the claimants. When the *bureaux* refused to transmit the required information, all the *Conseil d'État* could do was to annul the decision concerned, because it could not force the *bureaux* to submit the documents themselves.[37] This rather excep-

33. *Conseil d'État*, Brillaud, June 25, 1948; Dlle Delaunay, July 13, 1967.

34. The decree of November 17, 1970, is more progressive than the previous one (July 21, 1936) on this matter. The first one provided for the compulsory transfer of administrative documents to the archives, but only after the "recognition of their uselessness" by the *bureaux*. Moreover, some bodies were not obliged by the provisions of this decree (foreign affairs, defense, colonies, *Conseil d'État*). Many other bodies obtained similar exemptions later on.

35. Documents are classified according to four categories: *Diffusion restreinte, Confidentiel Défense, Secret Défense, Très secret*. The criteria for this classification have been loosely defined in a circular of the *Ministère des Armées* (1966). In the last years a new type of classification has been introduced de facto, without seemingly any juridical basis, by adding the word *politique* instead of *défense* (for instance, *confidentiel politique*). Classified documents transferred to the archives according to the 1970 decree can be transmitted to the public only after special authorization. G. Braibant, "Publicité des Documents Administratifs," in *Revue Administrative* 25(1972):150.

36. Ordinance, December 17, 1958.

37. *Conseil d'État*, May 2, 1954 (Barel case).

tional position adopted by the *Conseil d'État* shows its inclination toward more openness. This inclination is rather modest. For instance, the *Conseil d'État* forbids officials in "public establishments" (such as councils of universities or boards of public corporations) to refuse the transmission of information concerning the association to its members provided these members can show a need to know.[38]

In spite of these drastic limitations still enforced, this change may open the way to a broader interpretation of the right to know.[39] It is not a mere coincidence that a similar evolution is to be noted in the field of private law, which has been no more liberal and permissive. A recent case judged by the *Cour d'Appel de Paris* has recognized the right to know of consumers and their organizations.[40]

Means of communication: press, radio, and television

The Press Law of July 29, 1881, is still in effect today. It provides for the liberty of every human being to publish without restriction except because of *force majeure*.[41] There is no a priori control, no censorship, and no administrative procedure in France to sanction possible breaches of law by the mass media. These matters are left for the courts only. The right to publish information is limited in only few cases (protection of defense secrets, prohibition to publish court procedures involving minors, and so forth). In exceptional situations the government can actually limit these rights and use administrative or judicial seizures. Administrative seizure is to be authorized by the administrative judge when he has been convinced that there is no other way to prevent the disruption of public order. Judicial seizure can be used only to gather evidence of a breach of law,[42] and the *Conseil d'État* has contested the practice by which the

38. G. Braibant, "Publicité des Documents Administratifs," p. 151.
39. This new tendency is manifested in a report about the "public access to administrative documents" prepared by the committee on documentary coordination (*Documentation Française,* November 1974).
40. *Le Monde,* December 23, 1974.
41. B. Voyenne, *La Presse dans la Société Contemporaine* (Paris: Colin, 1971), p. 101.
42. G. Belorgey, *Le Gouvernement et l'Administration de la France* (Paris: Colin, 1967), p. 143.

government tends to use judicial seizure against a newspaper and to stop, by this means, its publication.[43]

However, in 1960 the French government prepared a draft statute to amend the Press Law and to strengthen the hand of the government in its confrontation with the press. At this time the methods used by the French army to reduce the "rebellion" in Algeria were under sharp criticism. Article 38 of the new draft was to state that the publication of "any document, information or piece of intelligence having a secret character is forbidden whatever is its purpose." Heavy penalties were to be inflicted on people "trying to discredit the actions of the army," and the seizure of newspapers was to be legalized.[44] With the change of policy in Algeria, the draft was dropped.

In practice, the government has substantial means at its disposal to deal with the mass media. The periodical publications receive impressive help from the State in the form of direct and indirect postal subsidies, cheap paper prices and tax reductions.[45] Advertisements that count for about 45 percent of the income of the press depend to a great extent on important financial groups that are linked in one way or another with the government, or at least are sensitive to governmental considerations. Moreover, one of the most important advertising firms, the Havas Group, is a public enterprise. This group as well as the French National Press Agency, the new agencies for television and radio, and the S.O.F.I.R.A.D. were all controlled by the minister of information, and now by a special service in the prime minister's office, the *Délégation Générale à l'Information*.[46] The mission of this *Délégation Générale* is not to inform the public

43. Such as the case of the newspaper *Temoignage Chrétien*, judged by the *Conseil d'État* in 1966. Other means can lead to the same "legal strangulation" of a publication by preventing or drastically hampering its distribution, for instance, by absolving the distributors or vendors of newspapers from the obligation of participating in their sale. For instance, the case of the review *HARAKIRI*; see *Le Monde*, November 25, 1970.

44. Errera, *Les Libertés à l'abandon*, p. 42.

45. Voyenne, *La Presse dans la Société Contemporaine*, p. 99.

46. The *Délégation Générale* has taken the place of the various interministerial committees in charge of the government's public image. A representative of each *cabinet ministériel* and journalists of the Agency for Radio and Television attend to these committees under the direction of the minister or state secretary in charge of information.

directly, but to "inform the people in charge of information, about the actions of the government and to comment on them."[47]

It is no wonder that under such circumstances subtle conditioned reflexes are quickly learned by the mass media in France. They are not muzzled; newspapers are very critical of the government and its policies, but there are well-known barriers that are not crossed.[48] The result in France, as in many other Western countries, is the emergence of mutual dependency and exchange relationships between mass media and the government.[49]

Therefore, in spite of the legal framework, which enables public servants to judge the wisdom of releasing information, and of the notably liberal status of the press in France, the secrecy of the documents and information held by the *bureaux* remains the rule. This is reinforced by the very limited right of citizens to demand and get information from government and from various public bodies and organizations.

THE POLITICAL MARKET OF INFORMATION

A traditional scheme reflecting both the cultural features of the French as well as the legal framework previously presented is still dominant in the information marketplace. A second scheme has developed only recently—since World War II—and seems to contrast with the previous one. It may be mainly a response to new patterns of behavior, having as yet no legal expression, although one may find various hints in this direction.

47. *Le Monde*, February 21, 1974, prime minister's declaration at Lyon.

48. An instructive example is the transmission to the government of the results of a Gallup Poll indicating a majority against the government proposition submitted to referendum (the regional reform of 1969) by "courtesy" and before publishing them. See M. Barnier, *La Chute du Général* (Paris: Édition Speciale, 1969), p. 195. By contrast, the independence of *Le Canard Enchaîné* is quite deviant, one of the likely reasons being that it is maintained by its sales; cf. Voyenne, *La Presse dans la Société Contemporaine*, p. 125.

49. I. Galnoor, "Government Secrecy: Exchanges, Intermediaries and Middlemen," *Public Administration Review* 35 (January–February 1975):38–39.

The Traditional Scheme

In the previous sections we saw how cultural features and legal rules tend to legitimize the reign of secrecy. This does not mean that there is no "market" for public information or that this market is confined to the public bureaucracy.

There is a political market for information to which direct access is limited by and large to the political class, including the opposition, provided that they will not use such facilities contrary to the accepted unwritten rules of the game. The rules require members to preserve limited and discriminatory access and to keep the public at large out of it. Jacques Lantier has noted humorously that the very mention of "confidential" or "secret" on a report means that it is worth circulation within political circles.[50]

One can find some confirmation of this in examining the programs of the various political parties, all of which profess internal democracy and participation as central themes. Participation was a leitmotiv of some of the Gaullists—for instance, the followers of E. Faure—the liberals, the centrists, as well as the Giscardists. But when these bodies address themselves to the link between democracy, participation, and information openness, what they stress is the necessity of pluralism through mass media, and not the general people's right to know.[51] A similar approach has also been adopted by the Socialist and the Communist parties in their *Programme commun de Gouvernement,* with special reference to the necessity of shielding information from the dominance of the "money powers."[52] Sometimes the necessity to insure better information flow from public administration is stressed, but in no case are there propositions to establish citizens' rights to information or the need for more openness in government.[53] Quite symptomatically a recent survey conducted by

50. J. Lantier, *Le Temps des Policiers: 30 ans d'abus* (Paris: Fayard, 1970), p. 73.

51. J.-P. Colli, *La France et sa Réforme* (Paris: Denoel, 1972), p. 127.

52. *Programme Commun de Gouvernement du Parti Communiste et du Parti Socialiste,* June 27, 1972 (Paris: Éditions Sociales, 1972), pp. 163–164. However, in a recent "Declaration of Liberties," the French Communist party has stated explicitly that the right of citizens to have access to documents and administrative files, except in cases stated by law. (*Le Monde,* May 12, 1975).

53. C. N. Hardy, *Imaginer l'Avenir: Propositions libérales établiés par le Club Perspectives et Realités* (Paris: Grasset, 1972), pp. 112–115.

the Trade Union Federation of the Magistracy revealed that the political parties are in favor of maintaining the rule of the *Réserve*, although opposition parties are in favor of a more restricted interpretation. Only the reformists are ready to acknowledge the public servants' right to mention publicly defects they observe in the course of their work, which they cannot correct through the usual internal channels.[54]

Even opposition parties seem to demand more guarantees in the diffusion of ideas, and not the reformation of the restricted access to information. They adopt a position very similar to that of other bodies, which, like the "notables" in the old days, act as intermediaries between citizens and the *bureaux*. This pattern was also nurtured by the bureaucracy, especially on the regional and local level, since it has contributed to its power.

The second feature of this restricted market is that it is partitioned but also unified in a special way. It is formed from a set of submarkets, each being somewhat closed with relatively few possibilities for external communication and access. These submarkets are molded by the structure of public administration, and they are geared to its internal divisions and stratifications, as well as to its clients and social environment. The information channels built into these structures are not hermetically sealed. Some people within the bureaucracy, such as the members of the higher civil service (the *Grands Corps*), are able to pass from one relatively closed market to the other, or at least to get information quite easily. In a sense it is because of them that the restricted and fragmented market of information is also unified. A similar structure is to be found on the local level, especially on the level of the *Départements*.

These groups of higher civil servants embody the State. Membership is usually the culmination of the administrative career, and the status confers preeminence and independence, and ensures liberty of internal control. Because of their position in the highest echelons of the hierarchy, members of the *Grands Corps* have full access to the information of the specific market to which they are attached. They also get information from the other sectional markets despite the fact that these corps are often in positions of bitter competition. Communications are facilitated by the fact that since

54. "Quelle Justice, dans quelle société," in *Justice* no. 23 (February 1973): passim.

World War II, Corps members are recruited and trained mainly within the *École Nationale d'Administration* (*ENA*). One central purpose of *ENA*, as stated by its founder, Michel Debré, is to "pull down the partitions between the different administrations and between the administration and the public."[55] The first is achieved through the socialization process of these civil servants; the second by the democratization of the recruitment.

Another institution that contributes to homogeneity among members of the *Grands Corps*, high civil servants, and other members of the political class is the unique French institution of the *Cabinet Ministériel*. It is a team of persons politically or personally attached to a particular minister, higher civil servants in the ministry, and members of the *Grands Corps* not specifically attached to the ministry.

Members of the administrative super elite have fairly free access to information in the various subdivisions of the bureaucracy. Interest groups, private and public enterprises, and even political parties invest remarkable organizational resources to "capture" and secure access to members of this super elite.

The last feature of the information market is, despite what has been said so far, the existence of a special information sector of which every part of the political class tries to gain exclusive control or to use it for its political benefit. It relates to the collection of domestic information of possible political value regarding groups, parties, factions, or individuals, which is done by the *Renseignements Généraux*. Similar information, which may be used for a similar object, was also collected under the control of the army, under the pretext of national defense.[56]

The main result of this first scheme is that in France the problem of getting information amounts to the problem of gaining access to and establishing connections with the higher civil service, and especially the *Grands Corps*. Access may seem a bit easier for politicians belonging to the same social classes, since the new system of selection and training inaugurated with the *ENA* did not change the social

55. *Promotion*, special issue dedicated to the twentieth anniversary of the *École Nationale d'Administration*, no. 83 (1967). For a detailed presentation of the *Grands Corps*, see E. Suleiman, *Politics, Power and Bureaucracy in France* (Princeton: Princeton University Press, 1974), chapter 10, "The administrative super elite."

56. Backman and Angeli, *Les Polices de la Nouvelle Société*, pp. 22–29.

distribution of the members of the *Grands Corps*, who are still "recruited from the highest social strata"[57] and from the administrative elite.[58]

What was described by Suleiman[59] as a spectacular achievement of the U.D.R. Gaullist party in enlisting the high civil service to its interests is but a regular resumption of the attempts made by each governing group to ensure its connection with the administrative elite. Similar attempts were made by the Radicals and the Socialists as well as by other political formations not in power, each in its own way. The higher civil service seems to be quite responsive to these attempts, especially those coming from groups in power. Although the administrative elite is eager to enter this game of seduction, it does not follow that they must also give up independence, a capital carefully preserved by all members of the *Grands Corps*. Rather, connections with multiple political groups other than those in power is considered an asset and a useful device for independence.

The accusations of technocracy that have often been voiced in French politics against the higher civil service, and especially against the ambitious ones graduating from the *ENA* (the "young wolves"), come from both the opposition and the parties in power. One remembers Chaban-Delmas's bitter remarks that what is "ruining the government is that it relies more on technocrat officials than on politicians."[60] This difficulty in getting compliance from the administrative elite indicates the tendency of the *Grands Corps* to promote their own influence by excluding outsiders, sometimes even their political masters.

However, despite the great rigidity of the channels, or perhaps because of the difficulty in circulating information in this highly sectional and hierarchical system, there are often leaks. In such a system, information is a very expensive commodity. Hence the system's need to find arrangements for the dissemination of information. The weekly *Le Canard Enchaîné* owes a great deal of its credibility to its ability to be systematically fed with important leaks. These leaks are different from the leaks intentionally disseminated by the

57. Suleiman, *Politics, Power and Bureaucracy in France*, pp. 71, 86.
58. C. Debbasch, *L'Administration au Pouvoir* (Paris: Calman-Levy, 1969), p. 84.
59. Suleiman, *Politics, Power and Bureaucracy in France*, p. 361.
60. *Le Point*, March 19, 1973.

bureaucracy and aimed at conditioning the attitudes of the public and preparing it for some changes.

Some of these leaks are "unintentional": information that percolates out to the public reflecting infighting among the administrative elite or between some part of it and the political class. One example is the disclosure by the newspaper *Le Monde* of December 3, 1974, of a special report of General de Boissieu, chief of staff of the army. Submitted to the minister of defense, the report dealt, among other things, with the probable consequence of a new May 1968 on the army and expressed in the report opinions quite different from those of the minister of defense.

Another type of leak is of information released mainly to discredit a rival rather than to provide the public with knowledge and to enable it to form an opinion. A good example of this is the publication by *Le Canard Enchaîné* of Chaban-Delmas's income tax returns, contrary to the rule of professional secrecy, a disclosure with which the then finance minister and political rival for the presidency Giscard d'Estaing was not considered by some newspapers to be uninvolved.[61]

Sometimes information is divulged to the public as a protest against the personal detrimental effect of the rules of the game, for instance, Modiano's book *Lettre Ouverte aux Gaullistes Trahis*, where he reveals questionable and suspicious maneuvers implicating many leaders of the majority.[62] Revelations of this kind do not have real political impact, perhaps because of the intensive personal involvement.

A last type is leaks organized by members of the administrative elite as a collective protest. This is a somewhat new phenomenon and is to be related to a developing new scheme. For instance, the project of Mr. Mir, the commanding officer of the *Compagnies Republicaines de Sécurité* (C.R.S.), aimed at creating special units to maintain public order and to transform them into a superpolice, was probably disclosed to the public by police officers.[63]

The system has developed various devices to reduce the practical impact of leaks. The first device is to divert public attention to minor, insignificant actors, as in the Ben Barka case, where only

61. *Année Politique*, 1972, p. 7.
62. Ibid., p. 73.
63. Backman and Angeli, *Les Polices de la Nouvelle Société*, p. 73.

rather low-ranking officials were publicly implicated and penalized.[64] The second is to use articles of criminal or civil procedure established to protect the basic rights of individuals to prevent the diffusion of nondesirable information. Quite a famous case is the Dega affair, where an income tax supervisor was jailed a month before the elections, probably after he had threatened to disclose compromising documents, and remained in jail for over a year without trial.[65] A last device is well known in many countries but was recently used so roughly and without cosmetics that it deserves to be mentioned. After publication by *Le Canard Enchaîné* of the contents of tapes made by the *Groupe Interministériel d'Écoutes* (a special unit in charge of spying and tapping telephone communications), an MP who tried to enter this center and speak to its director, General Caillaud, was refused on the grounds of "national defense secrets." The same argument was also used by the government to deprive the Senate Investigation Committee from getting all the information it demanded about tapping.[66]

One can note the quick self-regulating response of the system to "accidental" distortion. However, this traditional scheme has not succeeded in preventing the development of another one.

The Newly Evolving Scheme

This new scheme is characterized by two main efforts: to promote transparency and to circulate information within the social system. The term *transparency* refers to the clarity of administrative processes. This approach was first inaugurated by Prime Minister Mendès-France in 1955, when he decided after receiving a report on administrative efficiency prepared by an investigative committee to promote the creation of special offices to inform the public. The purpose was to prevent a deterioration in relations between the citizens and the public administration.[67] Although mainly public

64. Lantier, *Le Temps des Policiers*, p. 63.
65. *L'Express*, January 8–14, 1973.
66. *Année Politique*, 1973, p. 59. Soon after his access to the presidency, President Giscard d'Estaing ordered the cancellation of these practices of tapping.
67. F. Aubry, "Conditions, Moyens et Limites d'une Politique d'Information au Niveau Départemental," *Revue Administrative* 25(1972):67.

relations oriented, this approach may also contain some modest element of a new doctrine establishing the right of the citizen to information. In the last years new services have been created to provide information, even by telephone, to the public, and officials and public servants have to identify themselves. This effort has quite remarkably spread not only to other public institutions (such as the Paris Municipal Police, the hospitals, and town halls), but also to other associations. For instance, the French Communist party opened its cells to public scrutiny.

Although it may be viewed mainly as an attempt to recapture public attention and to "integrate the administrees into administration" as a "mechanism to promote conformity,"[68] it also reflects a timid change in social habits, as exemplified by the publication of citizens' income tax rolls and by the Dujardin affair (1974). In this case a judge, probably influenced by the new developing moods in society, agreed to open his office to the investigational survey of a journalist—a real change in French behavior. However this change is very timid. Income tax rolls are open only to people who belong to the same tax territorial region, and they are not to be photographed for evidence. Moreover, Judge Dujardin was temporarily suspended by the minister of justice.[69]

The second feature of this newly evolving scheme is a notable effort to circulate information to relevant actors, especially in the economic sphere. Since World War II a substantial improvement has occurred, especially under the efficient guidance of the *Commissariat Général au Plan* (the General Planning Commission). It has developed with the regular publication of national accounts and exchange of information that evolves from the various committees attached to the *Commissariat*. This new process has led to the coining of new concepts such as *concertation* (concerted action) and *contrat de programme* (programs undertaking), which probably reflect deeper changes in the fundamental attitudes of the French people and which cannot just be considered as a modern avatar of the traditional role of public administration in diffusing valuable information. This circulation of information, initiated by circles in the administration, has tended to create new habits—that is, the habit of cooperating,

68. J. Ellul, *The Political Illusion* (New York: Vintage Books, 1967), p. 160.
69. *Le Point*, December 9, 1974.

negotiating, and demanding the necessary information—that are diametrically opposite to previous fundamental attitudes.

We are therefore inclined to view these trends not just as improved manipulations by the bureaucracy. Assuming that the administrative system cannot continue to run the country alone, and that cooperation and some kind of participation is a necessity, then secrecy and the established patterns of behavior in the information marketplace are going to change, too. These are the components of a newly evolving scheme to be related to deep changes in French society.[70] These changes may entail the shy appearance of new values of cooperative and associational efforts of the general interest not being confused with the interests of the governing group—in short, of more effective democratic processes.

In the meantime, no doubt, the first scheme will remain dominant. The second scheme is as yet marginal and may remain so for the foreseeable future. But who knows? As in the past, the French people may well create surprises.

70. Yohanan Manor, "La France Est-elle une Société Bloquée?" *Res Publica* 14, 4(1972):805–811.

15

Denmark, Norway, and Sweden

ERIC S. EINHORN

INTRODUCTION

What do citizens of the Scandinavian democracies know about the activities of their government? How much do they want to know and how much should they know of the complex political and administrative decisions and compromises that keep their welfare-state machinery running smoothly? These issues are not only important to politically aware Scandinavians; they rightly attract the attention of those concerned with public policy and political participation in pluralistic societies. At least three sources for this interest are apparent. First, the Scandinavian states are universally identified as prime examples of the advanced welfare state. Expansion of the public sector has occurred in all Western democracies, but together with the Netherlands, the Scandinavian states represent the most extensive and rapid development accompanied by enormous tax burdens.[1] One would therefore expect widespread public interest in what the state is doing with these resources and how well the collective responsibilities are being executed. Both the need and the right to know should be a major political concern.

Second, the Scandinavian states have an unusual degree of social

1. Figures calculated and obtained from the Organization for Economic Cooperation and Development, *Economic Survey, Norway* (Paris: OECD, March 1974), pp. 28–30.

and cultural homogeneity. Denmark and Sweden are by West European standards remarkably free from regional, ethnic, and religious divisions. There have of course been important regional differences on economic and occasionally political issues, and center-periphery strife could flare up again. Norway also lacks politically important ethnic minorities, but center-periphery and cultural issues have been and remain more pronounced. The emotional struggle over the two forms of the Norwegian language has been documented, and the question still reflects significant regional and cultural divisions.[2] Most recently, the national referendum in which Norwegians rejected membership in the European Economic Community demonstrated the gap between urban and rural values.[3] Nevertheless, the bicultural problems have in recent years been far more latent in areas of civil rights and public administration than, for example, in Belgium or Canada.

Finally, the three Scandinavian democracies provide examples of how government secrecy questions are handled in countries with consistently high political participation. The forms of political activity continuously change, and unconventional types of political organization frequently appear. High levels of voting in recent parliamentary elections (just under 90 percent) demonstrate that politics remains very much alive. Extensive and intensive political participation continues to test public institutions by making numerous and at times impatient policy demands and by requiring a constant flow of information.

This essay will therefore analyze government secrecy in Scandinavia with reference to the extensive state social service policies, to political institutions that enjoy broad social support, and to political cultures that call for extensive participation by individuals and groups. While similarities between Denmark, Norway, and Sweden will be evident, important differences both historical and current will become apparent.

2. Cf. Einar Haugen, *Language Conflict and Language Planning* (Cambridge: Harvard University Press, 1966).
3. 53.5 percent of the vote cast in September 1972 rejected EEC membership. Although nearly 60 percent of the Oslo voters were in favor of membership, the number of "ayes" fell to 38.9 percent in central Norway and to 28.3 percent in the far north. Cf. Henry Valen, "Norway: 'No' to EEC," *Scandinavian Political Studies*, eds. Stein Rokkan, Helen Aareskjold, and Helga Hernes, vol. 8 (Oslo: Universitetsforlaget, 1973), pp. 214–226.

ACCESS TO PUBLIC DOCUMENTS AND RECORDS

Each of the Scandinavian countries has legislated the conditions and restrictions for public access to government documents and records.[4] Despite different historical traditions, they each recognize that public access regulations are an important policy area that must strike a balance between the public's right to know and the requirements of extensive and candid political communication. There are also the interests of national security and personal privacy to be considered. The current rules for access are summarized below. In the following section, attention is given to the political considerations that seek to balance open discussion and participation in policymaking with a pluralistic political culture that demands confidential negotiation and compromise. These political considerations should be kept in mind when evaluating the open records legislation.

Sweden

Swedes can trace their current open documents law back to 1766, when a liberal freedom of the press act was put into force. The latest public access law dates from 1937 with several more recent amendments. The basic legal principle is that all governmental papers are open to all persons unless explicitly closed by provision of the act. Moreover, a system of appeal and review has been established in cases where access is denied.[5] The law covers all public authorities: national, county, and municipal. Swedish legislation and practice recognize that the public interest may demand confidentiality, but restrictions are clearly specified. Defense and foreign policy matters

---

4. This section draws heavily on both the analysis and public documents in the definitive work of Stanley V. Anderson, "Public Access to Government Files in Sweden," *The American Journal of Comparative Law* 21, 3 (Summer 1973):419–473, hereafter cited as Anderson I. A summary of the research is also available in Stanley V. Anderson, "Some Essential Characteristics of an Effective Public Records Law: Sweden and the United States," *Administrative Law Review* 25, 3 (Summer 1973):329–333. Additional information was provided by the Swedish Department of Justice and the Swedish Information Office in New York City.

5. Anderson I, pp. 423–424. Anderson has translated the Swedish legislation, pp. 450–463. The current Swedish text is reprinted in Sven-Hugo Ryman and Erik Holmberg, *Offentlighetsprincipen och Myndigheterna* (Lund: Ohlsson, 1973), pp. 73–87.

are the most generally restricted. There has been some recent debate on the extent of secrecy in national security affairs, and the time limits are fifty years or more.[6] Section 4 of the Secrecy Act of 1937 broadly defines the areas of defense policy that may be classified, and the government's right of prior censorship has recently been upheld, though not without considerable controversy. Efforts to publish compromising information on the Swedish Intelligence Service (Informationsbyrån—IB) were partially frustrated when the security police raided the homes of several Radical Left activists. Although the criminal penalties were mild, notice was served that defense secrets would be protected. The fact that IB was active in neighboring Finland helped to promote political controversy. While the case may not be a Swedish Pentagon Papers affair, it renews concern about the limits of national security secrecy. The ensuing parliamentary investigation and discussion may redefine the limits.[7]

Swedish regulations also allow secrecy for the records of cabinet meetings, parliamentary committee meetings and correspondence, and draft papers of administrative organs. Should the Riksdag choose to meet in closed session, an extremely rare procedure, these records would also be secret for fifty years.[8] Normally, an administrative authority is not permitted to pass restricted documents to another authority except where cooperation is established by legislation or executive order. In matters of dispute, the cabinet is the final level of adjudication. This restriction does not generally apply to courts, however, which have broader rights of access in connection with trials. Even courts are restricted in seeing foreign and defense policy documents without cabinet permission.[9]

The parliamentary ombudsmen have exceptional powers of access in order that they may carry out their broad duties of review and protection of the public interest. There are presently three coequal ombudsmen to inspect the civil and military administration, and they have been recently supplemented by an antitrust ombudsman, a consumer ombudsman, and a press ombudsman with more specialized duties. Their unique powers permit redress of grievances even in those cases where the public would not normally have access to ad-

6. Anderson I, p. 453.
7. Det Nordiska Rådet (Nordic Council), *Nordisk Kontakt*, 1973:14, pp. 957–959, and *Nordisk Kontakt*, 1974:1, p. 60.
8. Ryman and Holmberg, Secrecy Act of 1937, section 2, p. 50.
9. Ibid., pp. 30–32.

ministrative and even private records. The ombudsmen are responsible only to the Parliament.[10]

Despite the detailed regulation, disputes over whether a specific document should be available can arise. In Sweden, as in Denmark and Norway, administrative and judicial courts as well as the ombudsmen can resolve such disputes, but the final responsibility would be with the cabinet and ultimately the Parliament. Battles over "executive privilege" are precluded by parliamentary government, at least in theory. If a committee of Parliament demands a document and it is backed in that demand by a parliamentary majority, the failure of a government to present the material would be a matter of confidence. A government seeking to resist the will of Parliament would have to dissolve that body and turn to the electorate for the final judgment. In practice, of course, such dramatic confrontations do not occur.[11]

The average Swedish citizen rarely exercises his right to see public documents, but the press has frequently seized the opportunity. Many governmental agencies anticipate routine press review by exhibiting the most important documents on a daily basis.[12] Once the press has exposed a matter, pressure for further inquiry and redress must come from political and interest groups as well as public opinion. Publicity may deter abuse and promote reform, but it is only the first step.

Norway

Norway inherited a tradition of administrative secrecy during the centuries of incorporation in the Danish realm, and it is only in the

10. The Swedish Institute, *Fact Sheets on Sweden: The Swedish Ombudsmen* (Stockholm: The Swedish Institute, FS 71 eOdc, 1973). The press ombudsman is not a public official but rather appointed and paid for by the Swedish Press Association.

11. While only the Constitution Committee (*Konstitutionsutskott*) of the Riksdag has the legal power to investigate the actions of ministers and to see relevant ministerial and cabinet papers, any member of Parliament may question a minister. The minister's answer is not required, but this again might result in a motion of no confidence if the questioner were backed by a parliamentary majority. Such confrontations are exceedingly rare. In addition, other parliamentary committees requesting information and documents in connection with their work have not been refused in recent years. Information supplied in memorandum from the Swedish Justice Department, Stockholm, October 2, 1974.

12. Anderson I, p. 426. Cf. Walter Gellhorn, *Ombudsmen and Others* (Cambridge: Harvard University Press, 1967), p. 228.

last decade that the demand for increased public access has been realized. The principle of openness in administration was among the recommendations produced by a Royal Commission in its 1958 report. The Wold Commission, as it was known, also recommended the establishment of a parliamentary ombudsman based on the Swedish and Finnish models. While the latter was indeed established in 1962, there was no action on public access until parliamentary pressure in 1964 forced the Labor government again to appoint a commission to reconsider the matter. Its report came in 1967, during the four-party nonsocialist coalition government, and this time the recommendation was against significant liberalization of public access. The positive recommendation of 1958 was followed by inaction, but surprisingly the negative report in 1967 spurred a positive response. In 1970, a public access law was passed, but its cautious provisions reflected the concerns of the Royal Commission about possible abuse.[13]

The new legal guidelines provided by the Ministry of Justice could be interpreted as highly restrictive in the case of third parties to an administrative matter, but the judiciary committee, in drafting the final legislation, demanded that administrative journals and registers be open to the public. Without such materials, finding specific documents becomes impossible. Moreover, the provisions are not retroactive to earlier papers.[14]

As with Sweden, the Norwegian law restricts access to a wide range of politically sensitive documents. Draft proposals, working papers, and minutes of the cabinet are closed. Similarly restricted are matters touching foreign and defense policy as well as sensitive economic matters. Moreover, when specific documents are restricted an entire case may be withheld in order to prevent a misleading picture of the case. Although access denials are to be justified and an appeals procedure is established, the government enjoys substantial latitude in determining new categories of restriction.[15]

The powers of the Norwegian ombudsman, although not as extensive as in Sweden, contain substantial investigatory duties that reduce the restrictiveness of the public access laws in practice. The Norwegian

13. Ibid., pp. 432–435.
14. The full text of the Norwegian Law on Publicity in Administration (no. 269, June 19, 1970) is reprinted in ibid., pp. 468–470. Cf. sections 4–6 and 13.
15. Ibid., sections 5–9. Excluded documents may remain secret for up to forty years depending on the case, and discretion lies with the cabinet.

Parliament (Storting) also has substantial powers of review both through the questioning of ministers and the work of the committees. When specific documents have substantial political importance, no government can ignore the parliamentary repercussions.[16]

Denmark

Denmark has a long tradition of official secrecy, and as in Norway, a modest public access law was adopted in 1970 after a lengthy period of study and reappraisal. A commission on public administration was divided nearly evenly in 1950 on the need for greater access to public documents. The new Danish Constitution of 1953 was silent on the matter. but a year later a parliamentary ombudsman was established on the Swedish model but with more restricted powers. In 1956 another study of publicity was initiated. In its report almost seven years later, a narrow majority (eleven out of twenty) voted against public access. One of the commission's recommendations on increased public access for parties to an administrative case was adopted in May 1964. The nonsocialist parties demanded even greater public access, however, and when these parties formed a majority coalition government in January 1968, a revised law on publicity was submitted. After compromise, the 1970 Act on Public Access was adopted with broad support including the opposition Social Democrats.[17]

Various commentators have suggested that perhaps the most positive feature of the public access law is the guaranteed parliamentary review scheduled for 1974–1975. The other provisions are even more restrictive than the Norwegian act. Specifically, persons seeking public documents must identify a particular case before they may gain access to registers and journals. Professor Anderson succinctly concludes that "the new law provides an opportunity for

16. An example would be in 1963 when a public investigatory commission substantiated some accusations of mismanagement of the state-owned coal mines in Spitsbergen. When the Labor government found itself in a minority, it resigned. Unlike Sweden and Denmark, Norway has no provisions for dissolution of Parliament except at specified four-year intervals.

17. Ibid., pp. 436–439. The December 1962 report contained a draft bill on public access despite the majority recommendation against its adoption. Cf. Niels Eilschou Holm, *Offentlighedsloven* (Copenhagen: Juristforbundets forlag, 1971), pp. 15–19.

scrutiny of documents in notorious cases, but provides no opportunity for uncovering potentially notorious cases."[18] This disadvantage may be mitigated by the increased attention to administrative abuse appearing in the daily press and the work of the ombudsman. In the past decade a growing number of papers have set up "hotlines," whereby citizens with administrative problems can get assistance from journalists. Agencies for whom public access has not yet become a habit are less likely to brush off newspapers and run the risk of adverse publicity. There is of course a possibility of abuse by such investigatory journalism, but given the newness of publicity legislation and the lack of real time limits upon responses to access requests, the impact of newspaper inquiries is likely to be greater than private citizens.[19]

An additional control on resistance to public access is the parliamentary ombudsman. His intervention on behalf of those denied access can prevent an excessively conservative application of the law and help to set guidelines for other agencies. Initial experience indicates that agencies quickly produce documents when the ombudsman intervenes on behalf of an individual.[20]

While it is difficult to anticipate the upcoming review, it is important to emphasize that broad areas of public policy are beyond the scope of the current legislation. Sections 1 and 5 exclude access to documents of the Parliament and parliamentary committees, the cabinet and other ministerial meetings, intragovernmental correspondence on proposed legislative and budgetary matters, foreign and national security affairs, and the principal judicial organs.[21] Oversight of these matters remains political, and blatant violations of secrecy are punished.[22]

18. Ibid., p. 440.

19. Eilschou Holm, *Offentlighedsloven*, pp. 106, 116–119.

20. This is illustrated by two cases where the ombudsman secured access to documents of the Disability Insurance Appeals Court (Ankenaevnet for Invalidsforsikringretten), which appear in Folketingets Ombudsmand, *Betretning for Aret 1972* (Copenhagen: Statenstrykkontor, 1973), pp. 110–112, 152–154.

21. There are, of course, many borderline cases. For example, an administrative organ corresponds with a parliamentary committee; that correspondence may be subject to public access. Cf. Eilschou Holm, *Offentlighedsloven*, pp. 26–30, 68–86. Time limits on secret documents range from fifty to eighty years.

22. Following Denmark's accession to the Common Market, section 5, paragraph 6, which excludes foreign policy and foreign economic policy documents from the public access law, could be broadly interpreted and abused. Here, again, the controls would have to be political.

Despite national variations, therefore, each country has sought to delineate between documents open to the public and those closed for a generation or longer. The central theme running through the complex legislation and the accompanying guidelines is that they are to regulate relations between administrative authorities and the private citizen. Recognizing the problems of individual redress of administrative abuse, the Scandinavian countries have given the ombudsmen substantial powers to assist citizens and to undertake their own investigations. Not only does this spare the aggrieved citizen time and expense, but it also reminds the busy administrator of the need to remember due process. The current public access legislation, despite its limitations, is not the last word on balancing the right to know with the business of government. Scandinavian political and administrative processes make the flow of information and the control of state activity part of daily political life.

COMMUNICATION IN A PARTICIPANT POLITICAL CULTURE

The preceding section focused on the legal aspects of public access to governmental documents and information, but attention must also be drawn to the political issues involved. As suggested in the introduction to this chapter, questions of governmental secrecy in the Scandinavian countries are especially interesting because of the wide scope of public policy and the pluralistic sources of political participation. Moreover, political events unfold in an environment of emotions and attitudes that are both complex and of crucial importance. We must seek to trace what Almond has called "particular pattern[s] of orientation to political actions" by analyzing a nation's historical traditions, beliefs, goals, and symbols—that is, its political culture.[23]

The evolutionary development of Scandinavian parliamentary democracy and its generally gradualist approach to political and social change make it difficult to outline shifting attitudes on participation and governmental secrecy. In Sweden the trend toward open records and administrative safeguards may be traced back to explicit policies of the eighteenth and early nineteenth centuries.

23. Almond is cited by Lucien Pye, "Introduction: Political Culture and Political Development," in *Political Culture and Political Development*, eds. Lucien W. Pye and Sidney Verba, (Princeton: Princeton University Press, 1965), p. 7.

Parliamentary supremacy and universal suffrage were not securely established in Sweden, however, until just after World War I. In Denmark some scholars dimly perceived the origins of the modern welfare state in the social relief legislation of 1792 and 1802 when the kingdom was in the firm grip of the absolutist and secretive royal bureaucracy.[24]

Nevertheless, national differences between the Scandinavian countries have become politically less significant in recent decades, and policy and institutional changes in one country have influenced attitudes in the others. In his study of the values and interests that connect as well as divide groups and parties in modern Sweden, Dankwart Rustow described the essential pattern of Scandinavian political pluralism.[25] "The essence of democracy," Rustow later generalized, "is the habit of dissension and conciliation over everchanging issues and amidst everchanging alignments."[26] In brief, Scandinavian politics is coalition politics. Coalition in representation, administrative structure, and policy interests affects the balance between the need for confidentiality and the right to public information.

The Consequences of Coalition Government

The necessity for coalition government has been most dramatically demonstrated in Denmark. Not since the final breakthrough of parliamentary government in 1901 has a single party held a parliamentary majority. The number of parties has varied from four to twelve, but the result has always been government by explicit or implicit coalition. Moreover, since World War II a majority coalition has ruled for only eleven years; otherwise minority governments have had to weld together parliamentary majorities on an issue-by-issue basis.

Recent trends in Norway seem to be similar. In the interwar period, Norway had ten minority governments, but after 1945 the Labor (Social Democratic) party won absolute parliamentary majorities.

24. This provocative but not definitive thesis is expounded by Jørgen Dich, *Den Herskende Klasse* (Copenhagen: Borgen, 1973), pp. 18–21.

25. Dankwart A. Rustow, *The Politics of Compromise* (Princeton: Princeton University Press, 1955), passim, especially chapters 7 and 8.

26. Dankwart A. Rustow, "Transitions to Democracy: Toward a Dynamic Theory," *Comparative Politics* 2, 3, (April 1970):363.

The experience of earlier coalitions made it possible to secure opposition backing for certain policy areas such as defense and foreign relations. After 1961, Labor's majority disappeared, and all subsequent governments have been implicit or explicit coalitions.

The continuity of Social Democratic government in Sweden is legendary. Excepting only a brief hiatus during the summer of 1936, the Social Democrats governed from 1932 until 1976. Nevertheless, there, too, coalition and compromise have been vital. The only extended period of Social Democratic majority was from 1945 to 1951. Coalitions have been varied, and in recent years the Danish and Norwegian examples of seeking broad parliamentary support on an issue-by-issue basis has been followed.

The coalition imperative has been frustrating for politicians seeking a clear mandate for decisive action. Channels of communication must be kept open between the major parties and interest groups. In order that this communication be effective, confidentiality has become an accepted part of the policy-making process. Public debate and public access to administrative documents have had to coexist with closed doors and "quiet" domestic diplomacy.

Administrative Structure

The strong central administrations of the Scandinavian countries have not excluded flexibility and compromise in policy planning and execution. A long tradition of professional and honest career civil service has given these countries an edge in meeting the administrative demands of advanced industrial society. Political accountability remains a fundamental principle of public administration despite the changing forms of control. As described in the previous section, the Scandinavian countries have established elaborate institutions to prevent and correct administrative error and abuse. Public access laws are seen primarily in this regard; they make citizens and the media agents of administrative review. The final court remains the Parliament with its power to inquire, question, and, if necessary, censure abuse of power or dereliction of duty. Admittedly, few cases are resolved at the highest level. Administrative courts and the ombudsmen are the daily watchdogs, but administrative issues are not only legal concerns, they are also political.

The pattern of professional and expert leadership is repeated in the nongovernmental interest organizations. Sweden has been termed the *organized society* by many observers, and the description holds for Denmark and Norway as well. Nowhere outside of Scandinavia do so many citizens seem to be tied together by a web of organizational links that include trade and professional unions (for nearly all of the work force), producers' organizations, voluntary societies, and political movements. While it is true that many formal organizations declined in both membership and participation during the past decade, spontaneous action associations have sprung up on behalf of nearly every cause and group imaginable.

The continuous and extensive interaction between public administrators and leaders of interest organizations fostered by national and local political leaders not only shapes new policies but also oversees the execution of established programs. During normal times this interaction is informal and discrete. Confidentiality prevails at such meetings in order to promote frank discussion and mutual trust. Energetic journalists may call the public's attention to a matter, a question may be raised in Parliament, but deliberate efforts at public information on daily developments are limited. A crisis will disrupt this rhythm. The biannual collective bargaining sessions between the central employers' association and the trade union federation have frequently become deadlocked, and lengthy but obviously closed sessions between labor, management, and the government seek acceptable compromises.[27] In sum, the parallel administrative structures interact on both routine and critical matters. Formal communication between them would be covered at least from the public agency side by the public access statutes as discussed above. Verbal but no less vital exchanges present a much greater challenge that can be met only partially by the press.

The Policy-Making Process

The synthesis of the multiparty parliamentary situation with its demands for flexible coalitions and the elaborate web of governmental

27. The most extensive studies on interest organizations in Scandinavia have focused on Sweden. While there are national differences, the overall pattern of interaction may be generalized from Nils Elvander, *Intresseorganisationerna i Dagens Sverige* (Lund: Gleerup, 1968), especially chapters 5, 7, and 9. Cf. also Nils Elvander, "Interest Groups in Sweden," *The Annals of the American Academy of Political and Social Science* 413 (May 1974):27–43.

and nongovernmental organizations is a participatory policy-making process. However, studies in policymaking suggest that the key stages in the process, when influenced by individuals and when groups may be most likely to affect the outcome, are not always open to public view. The veil of secrecy need only obscure briefly in order to exclude influence on policy or to reduce it to an appeal for reconsideration and reform.

There are significant organizational differences between the executive administrative structure of Sweden on the one hand and Denmark and Norway on the other. Swedish ministries are small agencies for planning, review, and control while the daily administration is left to quasi-independent executive agencies and boards.[28] Danish and Norwegian ministries resemble the British pattern where both political leaders and permanent civil servants interact continuously in both daily operation and policy innovation. In practice, however, it is possible to speak about a policy-making pattern increasingly common to the three states. Policy initiatives come normally from the cabinets and rarely originate in the Parliaments. Policy proposals are submitted to extensive and often lengthy investigation by either formal governmental commissions or direct input from interest groups or both. Parliamentary scrutiny is careful, and with either minority governments or thin majorities the most important compromises are worked out in the legislative committees. Finally, governments seek the broadest possible backing (that is, votes) for the final agreement. In recent years, however, very important policy innovations have been adopted by one-vote majorities.[29] Especially in the second and third stages, public information is most vital to deciding the policy options and compromises, but committee proceedings are usually confidential.

The most important means of investigating the need for policy change have been official governmental commissions, which are usually translated as Royal Commissions. The composition of these commissions has varied, but membership is drawn primarily from the civil service, members of Parliament, and less frequently from interest organizations and academic institutions. In Sweden the trend

28. Cf. Hans Meier, "Bureaucracy and Policy Formation in Sweden," *Scandinavian Political Studies, IV/1969*, ed. Oluf Ruin, (Oslo: Universitetsforlaget, 1969), pp. 103–116.

29. Examples are the Swedish Supplementary Pensions (ATP) in 1960 and the Danish legislative program for housing in 1973.

away from direct participation by MPs and representatives from organizations has been significant.[30] The latter are often contacted nevertheless by the commissioners and can also comment on proposed legislation through the *remiss* procedures. This means that proposed legislation is submitted for comment to all groups likely to be affected by its content. The number of Royal Commission reports, particularly in Sweden, has remained at about seventy-five per year, and the topics covered are almost limitless. There have been recent complaints about the number of commissions and the cost of their investigations, but they do produce an impressive mass of information and data on all aspects of public policy. All are readily available to the public, but their technical nature keeps readership quite limited. The press, of course, is the vital interpreting link between the complex reports and the interested public.

Closely related to official investigations are the efforts of parliamentary committees. The standing committees rarely undertake independent studies but are often involved in the efforts of the Royal Commissions. Their real influence, however, is during the legislative process after the government has presented its proposals and supporting data and after the initial response of interest organizations. Although the committee system varies in each of the countries, there are some common traits. The meetings of the committees are closed, with each member pledged to confidentiality. In fact, the work of most committees concerned with domestic policy is pieced together by the experienced parliamentary press corps. In Denmark, for example, the practice at present is that while the brief minutes of committee hearings and the documents collected by the committees are closed, the committee chairmen usually keep the press informed about developments. Members of committees exercise considerable freedom in reporting their statements in committee sessions but are not supposed to quote their colleagues. Committees and their chairmen in making their public report to the Parliament may decide which documents are to be made public. In those committees concerned with foreign policy and defense, however, secrecy is more strictly enforced, frequently with the sanction of law.[31] The com-

---

30. Meier, "Bureaucracy and Policy Formation in Sweden," pp. 107–109.

31. Correspondence of July 30, 1974, to author from Dr. Kristian Hvidt, parliamentary librarian, Copenhagen, Denmark.

mittees are therefore something of a gray area as far as the public's right to know is concerned. Since the crucial parliamentary compromises are hammered out at the committee stage, the meetings cannot be wide open. This enables parties and members to speak freely and to change their positions without public embarrassment. Nevertheless, without some information it is impossible to build support for the compromise and to allow the pressure of public opinion to nudge party groups. Committee meetings are not, however, held for the explicit purpose of public information as in the American case.

The Scandinavian policy-making process, therefore, goes through three basic stages: open input in the study of problems and proposals, quiet and even secret compromise in legislative committee, and finally open terms that must be approved by a parliamentary majority and accepted by the electorate. Ironically, the effectiveness of this process and even its openness requires confidentiality. It is in this light that the overall significance of governmental secrecy for political communication must be appraised.

THE PROSPECTS FOR OPEN GOVERNMENT

The Scandinavian countries distinguish between publicity in policy drafting and in policy execution. Their decision-making processes accept advice and information from a large number of interest groups. This requires the confidential adjustment of interests, the aggregation of political support, and, above all, effective communication. There have been fears that the close and discrete communication between state and interest organizations might circumvent the safeguards of constitutional democracy. The danger appears to be greatest when there are special ties between powerful interest groups and specific political parties: the labor unions and the Social Democrats, farmer groups and Agrarian parties, and management and industrial organizations and the Conservative parties. Evidence generally indicates that such interest groups jealously guard their prerogatives in promoting the interests of their constituents. Although pressure groups have at times been persuaded to moderate demands in the public interest, they do not like political parties to force them continuously to yield ground for parliamentary or electoral tactical reasons. The differences between interest groups and their would-be political partners have often been openly aired. Moreover, interest organizations serve as indispensable conduits of information about the needs of vital groups in the society and the goals of the political leadership. Studies indicate that this communication role may be a crucial component of the governmental secrecy question.[32]

Precisely because the Scandinavian social service states are committed to such extensive public policies, the need for detailed information by both the "provider" and the "consumer" is great. There is evidence that some of the recent dissatisfaction with the "welfare state" and its cost, which has given birth to several powerful protest parties, may be in part the result of poor information. Similarly the unexpected high costs of new or expanded public programs may indicate that administrative agencies are inadequately informed. It is clear, however, that reducing governmental secrecy may not be enough. Additional steps must be taken to guarantee an adequate flow of accurate information.

The Swedish case illustrates that even the most liberal public access provisions require an effective and energetic press. All three states are committed to maintaining healthy national and regional newspapers. Sweden and Norway give direct subsidies to the press, and Denmark is considering similar steps. Mass media such as television and radio offer additional opportunities for public information. The establishment of quasi-governmental broadcasting organizations with exclusive rights creates severe problems for vigorous critical journalism. The desire to prevent outright political bias in radio and television can easily inhibit investigative journalism. Even a casual observer will notice that foreign and international political issues are treated more critically and candidly than many domestic questions. The matter of political objectivity and bias is a continuous point of contention in the Scandinavian countries. Few critics contend, however, that the state broadcasting systems have been directly harnessed for state propaganda as has been alleged with the ORTF in France.[33]

The most sensitive issue in the area of governmental secrecy remains national defense and security. In each of the countries there has been substantial consensus among the main political parties about

32. Cf. Elvander, *Intresseorganisationerna*, passim, especially chapter 14, pp. 272–301.

33. Several articles analyzing the Scandinavian press appear in Per Torsvik, ed., *Scandinavian Political Studies, 3/1968* (Oslo: Universitetsforlaget, 1969).

the general direction of foreign and security policy since 1945. During the 1960s, however, critics of Danish and Norwegian policies (NATO membership in particular) became louder if not especially more numerous. As elsewhere the issues were vaguely but emotionally tied to the student revolt, the Indochina War, and the whole "counter-culture." The national security agencies were often the target of protest, and several Leftist groups sought to "bring the war home" through exposure of alleged misdeeds. As indicated above in the most recent case in Sweden, secrecy remains the rule in defense and foreign policy matters. In fact, much of the most important information is available through public documents and independent surveys for those seriously seeking concrete information. Moreover, the restrained foreign policies of the Scandinavian states have not given much substance to the conspiracies imagined by some critics. There has been no significant challenge to these restrictions on unauthorized access. It is unfortunate for scholars that secrecy is still imposed on foreign policy materials that date back many decades.

Although seeking increased public information, the Scandinavian countries have become aware of the complex but crucial question of limiting information and its dispersion when the interests of individual citizens so require. Since they are small, highly organized, and extensively surveyed societies, the age of instant computerized information retrieval could seriously undermine personal privacy and liberty. Administrative requirements such as centralized personal registration numbers can make abuse quite simple. Accordingly, there has been even more attention in recent years to protecting and restricting such information banks. In July 1974, the Swedish laws on protection of privacy were substantially strengthened and a state computer inspection board has been established. The right of individuals to see and challenge personal information in private data banks complements their current right to review their public dossiers.

The Scandinavian countries have been seeking ways to increase public access without destroying the confidentiality necessary for a working multiparty political system and an innovative public administration. How the letter of the law is applied is crucial to the latter group, especially in Norway and Denmark where the legislation is so new and the tradition of secrecy so ancient. As initial steps toward more open administration, the cautious legislation of 1970 may be wise. While most would accept the necessity of some secrecy in government, drawing the line is an elusive task. By recognizing that the secrecy question is only part of a larger issue—political communication—it is possible to find a workable compromise. And the pursuit of workable compromise has been the hallmark of modern Scandinavian politics.

PART III

A Comparative Perspective

16

What Do We Know about Government Secrecy?

ITZHAK GALNOOR

A few simple definitions may help us to begin to answer the question posed as the title of this concluding chapter.

Definition 1: "Secrecy" is a result of a deliberate act by A (who holds information) to keep B (who does not) from knowing something (the secret) at a given point in time.

From this definition it follows that (a) secrecy is applied *to* and not embodied *in* information; (b) its application is time constrained; (c) for secrecy to occur, B does not necessarily have to know who A is, or that there is a secret; (d) secrecy in itself is not good or bad, right or wrong; and (e) it is *deliberate*; hence intentions could be used as a basis for evaluation. The emphasis of intentional withholding of information eliminates cases of accidental secrecy and of problems inherent in the communication network itself such as noise or information overload.

When A are private individuals or entities, their right to conceal (that is, to privacy) is generally acknowledged. But when A are leaders and public officials (that is, government), the question is: Who is B?

Definition 2: "Government secrecy" in democracies is a result of a deliberate act on the part of those who govern to keep the governed from knowing something at a given point in time.[1]

Assuming that we are dealing with a democratic system, Definition 2 restricts B to those whose participation is a necessary condition of democracy, that is, the public, the people. Thus the definition excludes all cases in which secrecy is not aimed at the public qua public. If B is less, or more, than the total body politic in a certain country, we are confronted with a different aspect of government's information policies and not with the secrecy dilemma of democracies to be discussed below.

Definition 3: "Government's privilege to conceal" (GPTC) is a measure aimed at protecting a public interest, which on balance is judged to be more important than other public interests.

This definition refers to the fact that in democratic countries there is an axiom, or laws, or established practices legitimizing government's privilege to deliberately conceal certain information from the public. This privilege appears under different names and is applied in many ways (crown, state, or executive privilege; confidentiality; discretionary power; classification rights; censorship; rules of nondiscovery in courts; and so on). The common denominator is the assumption that it is beneficial, under certain circumstances, for the people not to know what government is doing on their behalf.

On the other hand, in democratic countries there is also an axiom, principle, or laws concerning the "people's right to know." In order for the polity to respond to the preferences of its citizens, the citizens should have the right to participate. In modern democracies, at least, there is another link: In order for citizens to exercise their right of participation, they need information about how the polity is in fact responding to their preferences (namely, what government is actually doing). Thus the sequence turns into a circle with two "freedom" loops, one of participation and the other of obtaining information, as in Figure 1.

1. As noted by Carl Friedrich, government propaganda is by and large identical to government secrecy. *The Pathology of Politics* (New York: Harper & Row, 1972), pp. 175–209. It can be defined as a deliberate act on the part of those who govern to manipulate the governed to know something. For purposes of brevity, we shall restrict the discussion to "secrecy" only.

FIGURE 1. THE INFORMATION-PARTICIPATION CYCLE

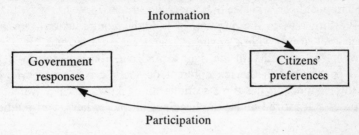

Information

Government responses   Citizens' preferences

Participation

The right to know (the information loop) is often considered an extension of the freedom of the press, but it is much more fundamental than that. Freedom of the press is either an aspect of the participation loop or a tool for citizens to exercise their freedom to obtain information. Hence:

Definition 4: "The people's right to know" (PRTK) is a prerequisite for citizens' participation in that it enables them to secure the facts about government activities in order to formulate their preferences.[2]

The dilemma of secrecy in democratic societies is the contradiction stemming from the fact that the axioms presented in definitions 3 and 4 are in practice and in theory mutually exclusive. Government secrecy must be justified as a deliberate act to protect the public by withholding information. Yet one important public interest that government may be expected to protect is the ability to find out what government is doing to advance the public interest. We need publicity in order to find out whether secrecy is justified. Conversely, the right to know as a basis for formulating preferences means that sometimes people may wish not to know. But, again, we need information in order to signal our government *which* interest is on balance more important. Matters become further entangled because, in exercising their privilege to conceal, those who govern may be motivated by reasons other than protecting the public. Likewise, people may want to know for reasons other than their desire to formulate their preferences and influence government. Thus the

2. On the axiomatic level we can ignore the fact that citizens may "form their preferences" without information, or not form them with or without information. Also, we know that participation can be distorted through the blatant use of propaganda and public relations, or through more subtle means such as controlled media and the "symbolic uses of information" (see chapter 4 in this volume).

secrecy dilemma is related to much broader questions regarding the structure and performance of democratic systems.

We turn now to the question of how this contradiction—government (A) armed with a privilege to conceal from citizens (B), and citizens (B) armed with the right to find out from government (A) —is approached in the ten different democratic countries reviewed in this volume. In the three sections that follow, much of what we know is categorized under the headings attitudes, laws, and politics.

ATTITUDES

Classical democratic theory is more concerned with the participation loop (see figure 1) than with the information prerequisite. The primary role of a citizen is not to be a receiver of information, but a sender of demands to be acted upon by government. Government secrecy was not dealt with explicitly because the problem was relatively obscured as long as suffrage was restricted, government was small and uncomplicated, and information technology was underdeveloped. But as the notion of government as a private affair of the ruler changed, publicity and the duty of government to inform started to be regarded as indispensable.[3] Thus modern democratic theory embraces PRTK, at least implicitly, and regards GPTC as a necessary evil imposed upon free citizens as a result of some imperfection in human affairs or in the governing process. For a full analysis of PRTK in democratic theory, see the two opening articles by Bathory and McWilliams (chapter 1) and Bay (chapter 2).

The tacit assumption, especially in modern *liberal* democratic theory, is that a transparent system of government is basically desirable, and only regrettable, temporary measures require tampering with the democratic requisite of free flow of information. Accordingly, GPTC will ultimately wither away, when

1. international peace and mutual trust will do away with the need to guard information pertaining to security and foreign affairs;
2. adherence to the democratic rules of the game and the exist-

3. See Edward A. Shils, *The Torment of Secrecy* (New York: The Free Press, 1956), p. 23.

ence of an enlightened public will enable politicians and administrators to say publicly what they say in closed meetings;

3. the privacy of individuals, groups, and organizations will
be protected by means (mutual trust, for instance) other than the
classification of information.

This theory has been less concerned with the "pathological" aspects
of government secrecy and more preoccupied with restricting the
damage inflicted by the necessity of allowing government to exercise
its privilege to conceal. Many studies, especially of public opinion,
are designed to find out *which* information serves democratic man in
shaping his attitudes, beliefs, and opinions and *how* he uses it. The
availability of the pertinent information is almost taken for granted.
Also neglected are the inherent need of politics to control and
manipulate information and the bureaucratic propensity to withhold
information. There is obviously a gap here between assumption and
practice. Given what we know about political processes, it is impossible to maintain that secrecy will ultimately wither away.

These are the broader issues. For our purpose in this chapter
there are more limited questions:

1. Is government secrecy a function of the prevailing attitude
in a political culture?

2. What are some common variables influencing the degree
of a country's deviation from the democratic principle of the
people's right to know? Can we compare these variables in order
to determine whether a democratic system is more "open" or
"closed"?

Attitudes in the Political Culture

The intuitive answer to question 1 above is "yes," but there is little
empirical evidence.[4] Brian Chapman tries to use Heine's distinction
between European countries whose citizens are temperamentally
"monarchist" v. "republican" in their attitude to government

---

4. In studying secrecy, "political culture" means "the propensities or the
psychological dimensions of the political system." We are interested in the
attitudes, beliefs, and values that motivate citizens' desire to know, to formulate
their preferences, and to influence officeholders. See Gabriel A. Almond and
G. Bingham Powell, *Comparative Politics* (Boston: Little, Brown, 1966), p. 23.

authority.[5] Germany and Great Britain belong to the first category where there is trust and respect for government. France and Switzerland belong to the second where there is mistrust for any political power. Sweden, Denmark, Norway, and the Netherlands lie in between with a special blend of respect and mistrust. If applied to attitudes toward secrecy, one would expect "republican" countries to be more open, yet "republican" France is as secretive as other "monarchist" countries.

The distinction between homogeneous and fragmented political cultures is also of little help here. For instance, Great Britain and France differ greatly in their degree of homogeneity, yet they are quite close in their cultural inclination toward emphasizing government's privilege to conceal rather than the people's right to know.

It seems that a more meaningful illumination of the connection between the political culture and attitudes toward secrecy can be made by comparing democratic and nondemocratic systems, or countries with high and low degrees of modernization and secularization.

More and Less "Open" Systems

The ten countries considered here share several common characteristics. They have all had rather stable political systems over the last three decades (with the exception of the Fourth Republic of France in the late fifties) and their regimes have enjoyed constitutional legitimacy. They are all industrialized countries with many new contact points between government and citizens. They share a long history of democracy (except Israel founded in 1948). Yet despite their accumulated experience with the contradiction between PRTK and GPTC, government secrecy is still perceived as an acute problem in all of them, and in some it has recently reached crisis proportions. Furthermore, the context of such controversies is much broader than the traditional preoccupation with the freedom of the press, the legality of executive privilege, the document classification system, and so forth. Government secrecy is linked to the more general subjects discussed in part I of this book.

Deviation from the idealistic axiom of PRTK is rooted in the

5. Brian Chapman, *The Profession of Government* (London: Allen & Unwin, 1959), pp. 308–322.

specific conditions or factors that determine the "secrecy culture" in each country. We shall assume that in every secrecy culture there is a crystallized attitude toward PRTK and GPTC and, ignoring obvious changes in these countries over time (for example, Germany before 1945 and afterward or France before and after 1958), shall list in table 1 the factors mentioned by the contributing authors as they pertain to the 1970s. In discussing these attitudes we shall not deal with the important distinction between knowledge pertaining to external (security and foreign) affairs, on the one hand, and domestic affairs, on the other.

The higher PRTK is valued over GPTC, the more a democratic system might be said to be "open." If we set aside for a moment the possibility that any system encompasses what Rourke calls "two cultures" operating simultaneously—a culture of openness as well as a culture of secrecy (Rourke, p. 115)—then, schematically, attitudes fall into three categories, from "more open" to "less open." (We do not use "closed" because all these countries are relatively open systems.)

The four countries in category 1.1 can be considered more "open" than the other five because the value of PRTK is more deeply en-

TABLE 1: ATTITUDES TOWARD PRTK AND GPTC

1.1 *Main reasons given why PRTK is valued higher*

U.S.A.	*Sweden, Denmark, & Norway*
pluralism	pluralism
populistic culture	social and cultural homogeneity
"luxuriating publicity" (publicity as a good in itself)	high degree of political participation
suspicion of government, politicians, and administrators	little external pressure
	welfare states

1.2 *Main reasons given why both PRTK and GPTC are valued*

The Netherlands
influence of German bureaucratic tradition and of French centralism
oligarchic as well as populistic culture
pluralist society and tradition of citizen participation
respect for both secrecy and publicity
pragmatic approach to the existence of government

TABLE 1:   ATTITUDES TOWARD PRTK AND GPTC (*cont'd*)

1.3   *Main reasons given why GPTC is valued higher*

Great Britain	France	Federal Republic of Germany
oligarchic political culture	the state as superior arbitrator in society	influence of Prussian state ethos: oligarchy, elite solidarity, loyalty, and discretion
deep respect for privacy	deep respect for privacy	
trust of and deference to government	PRTK not included in Declaration of Citizens' Rights	no tradition of citizen participation
meritocratic tradition		strong legalistic attitudes
	secrecy as an antidote to "shortcomings" in French political culture	traditional principles of civil service supremacy

Canada	Israel
influence of British approach	influence of British approach
oligarchic political culture	external pressures
trust of and deference to government	closed circle of leaders
	no strong tradition of civil rights
	civil passivity
	small and clanish

trenched in the political culture. The five countries in category 1.3 can be considered less "open" because the legitimacy of GPTC is more generally accepted. Also, as we shall point out in the next section, the U.S.A. and the three Scandinavian countries have formal laws favoring PRTK while Great Britain, France, Germany, Canada, and Israel have laws to secure GPTC. The Netherlands can fall in either category, on both grounds, and has been classified as category 1.2, that is, more or less "open."

Summary: Situational Secrecy

There is no empirical proof that the variables listed in table 1 actually influence the degree of openness in a country. There is little in common between the reasons why PRTK is more valued in the

U.S.A. and in the three Scandinavian countries, all of which belong to the more "open" category. While Great Britain, Canada, and, to some degree, Israel belong to the same "British" family of political systems, the other two countries in category 1.3, France and Germany, do not. Furthermore, despite their common Anglo-Saxon culture, the U.S.A. and Great Britain clearly differ in their attitudes toward PRTK. The difficulty in discovering a pattern remains even if we add other democratic countries to the list. Indeed, the traditional typologies of Western democracies do not seem to apply as far as PRTK and GPTC are concerned. Similarly, Lijphart contends that the process of accommodation in Dutch politics must be shielded from publicity. Hence an information gap is considered desirable and secrecy is a most important rule.[6] This linkage between secrecy and the political culture might be extended to some other fragmented societies (France) and to politically segmented Israel, but even by this criterion we cannot go very far. Great Britain is homogeneous and stable, like Sweden, and yet relatively more secretive.

Therefore, it seems that as far as the ten democracies discussed in this volume are concerned, we do not know what causes the inclination toward being more or less "open." Normatively, what we can learn from table 1 is that the differences among democracies regarding "openness" are probably negligible compared to the differences between them as a group and the really closed nondemocratic political systems. We may tentatively conclude that government secrecy is subject to some kind of "situation ethics," in which there are no unified standards and no moral absolutes with regard to the government's right to inform, conceal, or even lie.[7] But "situational secrecy" leaves the important democratic principle of PRTK dangling in the air and does not provide answers for those who are seeking normative solutions to the secrecy dilemma. Instead, the conclusion of this section must be that the contradiction between PRTK and GPTC is not resolved in liberal democratic theory. Let us now turn to the more formal aspects of government secrecy in order to find

6. Arend Lijphart, *The Politics of Accommodation: Pluralism & Democracy in The Netherlands* (Berkeley: University of California Press, 1968), p. 131.

7. For a discussion of "situation ethics" and its relationship to the people's right to know, see William J. Barnds, ed., *The Right to Know, to Withhold, and to Lie* (New York: Council on Religion and International Affairs, 1969), especially p. 26.

out whether the law provides the missing link between the political culture and secrecy behavior.

LAWS

In the ten countries discussed here, as well as in other democracies, the "right to know" is less tangible, less axiomatic, and more controversial than other rights of citizens such as the freedoms of expression, speech, and the press. We may agree with Jeremy Bentham that the "eye of the public is the virtue of the statesman," but we are still left with the question of whether PRTK is an "essential principle" in democracy.[8]

The focus of the legal approach is on the formal measures that will support citizens and officials, respectively, in an encounter over access to information. In this context secrecy becomes a problem of defendant-claimant relationships to be solved whenever the right to gain access to information is disputed. It is a case of the legal right or privilege of the government-custodian (A) to conceal a certain piece of information versus the legal right of the citizen-claimant (B) to know it. In this custodial approach to secrecy, information is regarded as a tangible property: documents, written memoranda, tapes, transcripts, exhibits, and other materials that can change hands or are submittable as evidence in court.

There are two categories of legal provisions. The laws in the first aim at guiding officials in determining what kind of information should become secret and at preventing disclosures of such information to unauthorized persons. Those in the second category aim at establishing the principle that disclosure is the general rule, not the exception, and that whatever the government does is in the public domain unless legally restricted. The provisions in the first category emphasize GPTC and put the burden of proof on the citizen. In the second category the focus is on PRTK and the government's need to justify withholding information. Table 2 classifies the ten countries into these two categories and illustrates the content of the various laws in each category.

8. C. Bay treats PRTK as a human right, while D. Bathory and W. C. Mc-Williams contend that it is part of the political order and not a natural right (chapters 2 and 1, respectively, in this volume). Newsmen tend to view the right to know as an extension of the freedom of the press. See William Safire, *The New Language of Politics* (New York: Random House, 1968), p. 382.

2.1 Laws Establishing the Government's Privilege to Conceal

	Provision	Country	Remarks
2.11	All official information generated in or collected by government is legally secret.	Great Britain Canada Israel France Germany The Netherlands	The Netherlands —only partially
2.12	Disclosure of official information by officials to unauthorized persons (breaching oaths of allegiance) is legally punishable.	all ten countries	In some countries (Sweden) attempts are made to distinguish between "confidentiality," "loyalty," and "secrecy."
2.13	Certain officials, usually the political heads, are entitled to release information or delegate the task to spokesmen.	all ten countries	In Great Britain, Canada, and Israel— part of the principle of ministerial responsibility
2.14	Special laws and regulations aimed at protecting national secrets pertaining to: a. defense, security, and foreign affairs b. internal processes of government c. criminal matters and law enforcement d. citizens' privacy	all ten countries (a–d are defined differently in each country)	Final decision on what constitutes a "national secret" not in the hands of the executive in Scandinavian countries, the Netherlands, Israel; advanced also by court decisions in U.S.A., Germany, and Great Britain

285

	Provision	Country	Remarks
2.15	Special measures	all ten countries	
	a. crown and executive privilege	a. mainly U.S.A., Great Britain, Canada, France	a. appears under different titles in other countries
	b. document classification procedures	b. all ten countries	b. no clear measures for declassification in all countries
	c. time limit on classification	c. 30 years rule in Great Britain and France; 50 years in the Netherlands	c. no legal time limit in other countries
	d. censorship	d. Israel	d. used by other countries during emergency periods
	e. established voluntary arrangements	e. Great Britain (D-Notices), France (*Réserve*), Israel (Editors' committee and censorship application)	e. *ad hoc* voluntary arrangements in all countries

2.2 Laws Establishing the People's Right to Know

	Provision	Country	Remarks
2.21	Open access	Sweden Denmark Norway	In Sweden—a constitutional provision; in Denmark and Norway—a more restricted law enacted in 1970
2.22	Freedom of Information	U.S.A.	Conceptually more ambitious, an attempt to establish the right to know as a principle; practically similar to "open access"

Legal Definitions of the Government's Privilege to Conceal (GPTC)

In formal legislation, GPTC has received much more attention than PRTK. The legal approach toward preventing disclosure in our ten sample countries includes some or all of the five provisions listed in category 2.1 in table 2.

Provisions 2.11 and 2.12 constitute de facto a norm that all government information is secret. The less comprehensive (and less controversial) norms of confidentiality and loyalty turn into full government secrecy because being bureaucratic in the Weberian sense, public organizations try to protect their informational resources. The prominent example of a law that provides that all government information is considered secret unless specifically exempted for release is the British Official Secrets Act of 1911 and its counterparts in Canada and Israel. Section 2 of this act makes unauthorized transfer of information by a government official to any other person a crime. Similarly, the French Civil Service General Regulations require that any knowledge acquired in the course of public service is to remain secret, and the German Federal Civil Service Law defines all public business as "official" secrets. A more relaxed attitude is taken by the Dutch law, which requires officials to maintain secrecy regarding official information "insofar as this follows from the nature of matter or from an order given by a superior" (Brasz, p. 205).

In the U.S.A. and Sweden, public officials are also prohibited from disclosing official information at will and are required to sign loyalty declarations. The main differences between the countries is in the attempt to distinguish between

1. secrecy (protecting state secrets);
2. confidentiality (preserving the intimacy of the internal deliberations process);
3. loyalty (of civil servants to their department and the government in general).

No country has clearly codified these fine distinctions, but the U.S.A., Sweden, and, lately, Germany have made efforts in this direction.

Even where everything official is considered secret, according to provisions 2.11 and 2.12, government is the source of a huge amount of information released for many different purposes. How does government bridge the gap between the initial state of secrecy and the obvious need to release information? Democratic countries try to solve this problem by recognizing the executive's discretion in determining what to release and when, and by creating a formal machinery for this purpose (provision 2.13). This arrangement is supported by the concepts of ministerial responsibility (Great Britain, Canada, and Israel) and the still-prevailing assumption about the separation between politics and administration.[9] Politicians are considered to be responsible for disseminating information and maintaining the people's right to know, while the anonymous administrators are assumed to have only "professional contacts" with the public and are relieved of the task of explaining policies. In any case, the government or the department formally speaks with one voice, and there are officials who have the responsibility of deciding when it is more beneficial to release information than to withhold it. The more routine tasks are delegated to information bureaus and the public relations tasks to special functionaries.

Despite the discretionary powers of top officials (and the actual discretionary power of every civil servant) to determine what information to release, every democratic country has made an attempt to define areas or subjects in which disclosure of information would constitute treason, grave offense, or some other illegal act (provision 2.14). This information, or parts of it, is referred to as state or national secrets, whose disclosure is considered to do damage to an important public interest. Here the prohibition applies often equally to the holder and receiver of the classified information. The definition of those areas varies from country to country, especially regarding defense and the attitude to borderline cases. In most countries the executive defines what is the "public interest." The custodian of the information is entrusted with judging when publication of information is harmful to the state, and he can extend the prohibition to other governing bodies: the legislature, the courts, investigating committees, and so on. France is probably the extreme case in this respect. In other countries, full discretionary powers in the application of this privilege are no longer solely in the hands of the executive, as illustrated by recent court decisions in Great Britain, Germany, and the U.S.A.

9. Itzhak Galnoor, "Government Secrecy: Exchanges, Intermediaries, and Middlemen," *Public Administration Review* 35 (January/February 1975):32.

The definition of exemptions from the laws requiring freedom of inspection of documents in Sweden has served as an example to other countries trying to define more precisely the areas in which special secrecy measures should be applied. The Dutch system of classifying documents tries to distinguish between more harmful and less harmful categories of secrecy. The Israeli Evidence Act distinguishes between evidence pertaining to "state security and foreign relations" on the one hand, and other "important public interests," on the other, and leaves the decision of disclosure in the hands of the courts. Different definitions of what constitutes internal documents, private information, and commercial secrets can be found in each country.

In provision 2.14 the definition of sensitive *areas* aims at declaring certain types of information more secret than others. In provision 2.15 special *measures*—some of them preventive and some punitive—are taken. The system of classifying documents is a logical extension of the legal measures reviewed above. All countries employ such a system and in most the distinctions between security categories—such as "confidential," "secret," and "top secret"—are practically meaningless. Moreover, the tendency is invariably toward overclassification and vagueness regarding declassification.

The severe safety valve of censorship is used only in Israel, as it is the only country among the ten presently in a state of war. Other European countries, as well as the U.S.A., used censorship during World War II. In Canada censorship was imposed on security matters during the confrontation with the Front Libération de Québec in October 1970. In the case of the undeclared Vietnam War, the attempt to apply "prior restraint" to the publication of the Pentagon Papers in the U.S.A. was rejected by the Supreme Court. Voluntary arrangements for preventing undesirable publication and leaks are at work in most countries, but only some are formally established such as the D-Notices in Great Britain.

Legal Definitions of the People's Right to Know (PRTK)

While government secrecy and the people's right to know have occupied much public attention in the last decade, only three countries—the U.S.A., Denmark, and Norway—have sought to follow the Swedish example and codify it in more comprehensive legislation (table 2, category 2.2). There are great differences between the Scandinavian and American laws. The Swedish constitutional provision recognizes the right of every citizen to see official documents and provides various legal and practical arrangements for free access. The laws in Denmark and Norway were enacted only in 1970 and are more restrictive, but they reflect the same attitude: an attempt to express legally the need to balance PRTK with the business of government in a participant political culture (Einhorn, p. 263). In practice they are used predominantly by the press.

The United States Freedom of Information Act, 1966, is more ambitious because it aims at granting any person, group, or organization access to government records without their having to state a reason for wanting the information. It tries to place on the federal agency the burden of proof that withholding is necessary, and it provides a legal channel to the courts for appeals. Yet the experience accumulated in the operation of the American Freedom of Information Act since 1967 illuminates the discrepancy between the democratic assumption about PRTK and political realities. Most observers tend to agree that the Act has not fulfilled its advocates' most modest aspirations.[10] The trouble might be with the act, or with its advocates' aspirations, but there is also a more general point. The free flow of information can be thwarted on practical grounds: Physical access to information becomes technically impossible, there is no file index, or an inspection fee is too high. In the State Department, for instance, a reading room for inspecting documents was prepared, but nobody in the department knew about it.[11] More important was the fact that the act did not cover the whole area of advisory groups and committees. This could have been an unintended omission or, more likely, a reflection on the political information game itself.

The act was passed at the instigation of the press, the American Bar Association, the American Civil Liberties Union, and some academic groups. Federal agencies were opposed to it but went along once President Johnson decided to sign it. Since then, lawyers

10. House Subcommittee on Foreign Operations and Government Information, *Administration of the Freedom of Information Act* (New York: Praeger, 1973).

11. David Wise, *The Politics of Lying* (New York: Random House, 1973), p. 103.

representing corporations and private interests have made the greatest use of the law because they can afford the expensive and time-consuming process of fighting in the courts for their right to know.[12] Rourke notes that the most ironic twist of the American law is the extent to which the Freedom of Information Act has been used to *reinforce* practices of secrecy in the federal government (Rourke, p. 118; see also Brasz, p. 213). The 1974 amendment is aimed at curtailing some of the loopholes in the law, including the secret activities of advisory committees.

It is too early to assess the impact of this reform but perhaps certain aspects of the ongoing debate about amending section 2 of the Official Secrets Act in Great Britain apply to all reforms. Most witnesses testifying before the Franks Committee assumed implicitly that changing the law would make an important contribution toward changing secrecy practices in Great Britain. A different point of view about the relationship between law and political culture was expressed by Professor H. W. R. Wade, in his letter to the Committee:

> The great task facing the Committee, in my opinion, is to create a new official mentality. . . . If the right mentality can be created, the framing of legislation will not present serious difficulties. If it is not created, no legislation is likely to be satisfactory.[13]

Summary: Discretionary Secrecy

As of 1975, only four democratic countries have a law establishing the people's right to know. In the other countries, notably Great Britain, Canada, and the Netherlands, formal recommendations for changing secrecy laws and practices have been made, but not yet implemented. The secrecy dilemma is very much alive as a controversial issue but there seem to be great limitations on the ability to handle it through legal means.

12. Between 1967 and 1971 a total of 922 requests for information were appealed to the courts. Corporations and private law firms: 60%, media: 10%, public interest groups: 9%, nonfederal government agencies: 6%, researchers: 4%, and labor unions: 2%. House Subcommittee, *The Freedom of Information Act*, p. 160. Similarly, in Sweden the right of access is used predominantly by the press.

13. *Department Committee on Section 2 of the Official Secrets Act, 1911*, The Franks Report (London: H.M.S.O., 1972), Cmnd. 5104, vol. 2, p. 417.

The desirable equilibrium between PRTK and GPTC cannot be achieved by statute alone, basically because in a legal sense information is tangible, and access rights must be defined in terms of property rights. But information, unlike property, can "belong" to more than one party without being divided and without the requirement of partnership. Information can be turned into withheld secrets, and secrets into released information without leaving a trace. It could have happened in the American Watergate fiasco if there were no presidential tapes.

The five countries that were classified as less "open" because GPTC is valued higher than PRTK appear also to have laws establishing this privilege. In secrecy laws, the Netherlands belongs also to this category. More revelant perhaps is the strong evidence that the officials in charge of information can exercise a great deal of discretion in deciding what to release and to whom. For instance:

Canada: "Because of the vagueness of the classification system and the practice of discreet sharing of information . . . the public servant is placed in a position of developing his own guidelines" (Doern, p. 149).

Germany: ". . . [the] distinction between bona fide state secrets and self-motivated government secrets is not observed" (Reese, p. 227).

France: "[civil servants] can legally divulge some kinds of information, but it is a very subtle art that requires dexterity" (Manor, p. 242).

Israel: "Despite the culture of secrecy and the laws requiring it, the system is relatively open. The doors are unmarked, but those who know about their existence can use them" (Galnoor, p. 189).

And so, in countries where laws prescribe secrecy, officials find ways to share information, whereas in the few countries where laws prescribe publicity, officials find ways to withhold information. Despite many scandals involving court decisions on executive privilege or the secrecy of classified documents, the cases in which government withholding of information has clearly been cited as illegal are relatively few and far between. There is ample room for government maneuvering within the legal confines of secrecy and publicity on both foreign and domestic affairs. Information leaks are a familiar and recurring phenomenon in democratic countries, indicating that government officials tamper with the free flow of information and occasionally lose control, as demonstrated by the sensitive content of leaks in many countries.

The function of the laws in category 2.1 in table 2 is therefore to legitimize government secrecy whenever an exchange does *not* take place. The laws in category 2.2 reflect a different attitude in the political culture, but it should be emphasized that the people's right to know can easily be countered with government legal privilege to conceal or more often with technical barriers to actual access. It seems that more light simply drives darkness to other corners. Total illumination may require a change of much broader dimensions in the democratic rules of the game. This does not mean that "legality" in itself cannot project a symbolic value of high importance (see Rothman, p. 66), especially in periods of transition and social tension.[14]

If the laws regarding secrecy and access to information are not anchored in the norms of the political culture, their ability to effect the "real" flow of public information is marginal. Legal remedies do not seem to be an independent vehicle for changing the culture of secrecy.

POLITICS

Government secrecy has thus far been treated in terms of attitudes and laws. But secrecy is also part of political communications. Information becomes a commodity in the political marketplace when it bears some relevance to the political system.[15] Furthermore, information that is subjected to government secrecy can be regarded as a *scarce* political resource. In more general terms, government secrecy is the "added value" of the information commodity, and gaining access is a process whereby data become a means of power and influence.

14. Charles E. Merriam, *Political Power* (Glencoe: The Free Press, 1950), p. 13.
15. This approach has been succinctly presented but not developed by Warren F. Ilchman and Norman T. Uphoff, who define information as a "political resource affecting or being affected by the use of authority," in *The Political Economy of Change* (Berkeley: University of California Press, 1972), pp. 67–69.

Keeping the public in the dark could clearly be instrumental in advancing or protecting national interests. For example, government's use of secrecy could be aimed at keeping a certain piece of information from reaching an external enemy, and the only practical way to do this is by withholding the information from its own citizens. However, government's own political interest can also be enhanced by increasing the value of information or, more frequently, by using secrecy to neutralize the cost (negative effect) of damaging information.[16] Thus governments can keep secrets from the public in order to preserve the value of information vis-à-vis foreign rivals, domestic rivals, or the public itself.

Government secrecy (see definition 2) in terms of internal conflicts is different from GPTC (see definition 3) and rests upon using information as a commodity. The political value of information fluctuates according to (a) the number of people who are party to the information and (b) pressures—usually as a result of extraordinary events (the Profumo affair in Great Britain or Watergate in the U.S.A.)—that alter the exchange rate for information. The demand for information is based on the need to know, and the political "price" paid for it is determined by the benefits that the receiver expects to derive. Access to information is gained, therefore, not as a right, but on an exchange basis. The problem of government secrecy in democracies becomes one of providing for fair play. Given a general abstract commitment to the right to know, freedom of the press, and freedom of expression, the actual circulation of information must be governed by the accepted democratic rules of the political game. Group pluralism as a supplement to democratic representation is an important guarantee for a fair interplay of interests.

Politicians, administrators, journalists, pressure groups, spokesmen, and citizens are engaged in an endless process of exchanges and contacts. Government tries to influence individual citizens, groups, and general public opinion through public relations and propaganda.

---

16. President Kennedy's assistant secretary of defense, Arthur Sylvester, was honest enough to state this fact publicly: "News generated by the action of the government as to content and time is part of the arsenal of weaponry that a president has. . . ." Not surprisingly, this statement and another one arguing for the "right of government to lie," which are in contrast to the ideal formulation of the people's right to know, drew explosive reactions from many quarters. Quoted in Thomas M. Franck and Edward Weisband, eds., *Secrecy and Foreign Affairs* (New York: Oxford University Press, 1974) p. 172.

All of them in turn try to influence government through campaigns, votes, and direct pressures. The mass media act as brokers of information between government and the attentive publics and at the same time use information to sell advertisements and make profits. Officials have many opportunities to disclose information in order to cultivate clientele groups and receive valuable information in return. The closer an official is to the policy-making level, the more he has to offer and the more he needs information for support and exchanges.

In the following pages the presentation is divided into two parts: executive secrecy within government (that is, regarding legislative and judicial bodies) and executive secrecy within society (that is, regarding the various active groups—political parties, special interest groups, and the mass media).[17]

Secrecy within Government

The monopoly of the executive on information is only an indirect indicator of secrecy. Secrecy within the executive and rivalry among departments are the source of much government secrecy. However, this important aspect of government secrecy can be mentioned only in passing. Instead, two categories of general indicators are given in table 3 as a rough measurement of secrecy within the governing bodies:[18] first, the extent to which executive privilege (EP) to withhold information from the legislative bodies is legally recognized, normatively accepted, exercised, or otherwise influenced; second, the extent to which EP (or evidentiary privilege) to withhold information from judicial proceedings is legally recognized, exercised, or otherwise influenced.

17. The focus is on the *executive* only and its exchange of information with "domestic rivals" because the executive is the main source of government secrecy and because in all countries reviewed, the ability to exclude establishes it as a formidable gatekeeper of information flow.

18. A third indicator is the amount of secrecy between national and subnational governments as well as the degree of secrecy at subnational levels where "national interests" (security, foreign affairs) cannot serve as justifications for secrecy. Unfortunately, the information available on this subject is scattered and does not permit even calculated speculations. The most detailed treatment of executive privilege in the United States is Raoul Berger, *Executive Privilege: A Constitutional Myth* (Cambridge: Harvard University Press, 1974).

TABLE 3:   EXECUTIVE PRIVILEGE WITHIN GOVERNMENT

3.1   Legislative Access to Executive Information

	3.11 EP recognized legally[1]	3.12 EP accepted as norm[2]	3.13 Direct access to civil servants[3]	3.14 Ombudsmen access[4]
U.S.A.	no (partly)	partly	yes	no
Sweden	partly	partly	no	yes
Denmark	partly	partly	no	yes
Norway	partly	partly	no	yes
Netherlands	partly	partly	no	no
Germany	yes	partly	no	yes
France	yes	yes	no	no
Israel	yes	yes	no	yes
Canada	yes	yes	no	no
Great Britain	yes	yes	no	yes (restricted)

1. In all countries "legal recognition" is a vague criterion. In some, such as the U.S.A., executive privilege (EP) might be constitutionally questionable despite important precedents. Conversely, in Sweden, EP is generally recognized, but Parliament can investigate any action of individual ministers. Only the degrees of difference between the countries should therefore be considered.

2. Same difficulties as in 1. EP as a dominating political norm can also be evaluated on the basis of legislative committees' access to executive information (the U.S.A.) v. lack of full access (Israel, Great Britain).

3. "Direct access" of legislators to public servants such as in congressional open hearings in the U.S.A. (that is, not through the political head of the department).

4. In some countries the comptroller general acts in a capacity similar to the ombudsman in securing information from executive departments (U.S.A.). In

LEGISLATIVE ACCESS

Table 3 ignores important institutional factors that may cause EP to vary from country to country, such as the difference between presidential executives and parliamentary cabinets, the number of parties, the existence of a doctrine of ministerial responsibility, and many more. For our purposes, it is sufficient to point out the patterns of secrecy within government in these ten countries. In all of them, some formal provisions exist for recognizing EP vis-à-vis the legislative bodies (3.11). In those countries where this privilege is debatable or constitutionally questionable, EP is not fully accepted as a

3.2   Judicial Access to Executive Information

3.21 EP recognized legally [5]	3.22 Recognition of judicial discretion [6]	3.23 Administrative court discretion [7]
yes	yes	no
yes	partly	yes
yes	partly	no
yes	partly	no
yes	no	partly
yes	no	yes
yes	no	yes
yes	yes	partly
yes	yes	no
yes	yes	no

others (Norway and Great Britain) there are certain restrictions on his activities, which limit his access to information.

5. "Recognition" is the right of the executive to ask for "special treatment" regarding evidence claimed to be secret.

6. "Judicial discretion" is the right of the court to decide whether evidence claimed to be secret by the executive should be made public or not. In Israel this right is established by law; in Canada, Great Britain, and the U.S.A., by recent precedents.

7. There are great differences between the Swedish and German administrative courts set up mainly to reduce bureaucratic abuse of power, and the powerful French *Conseil d'État*. In the Netherlands and Israel there is no administrative court, only special administrative adjudication within the Supreme Court.

political norm (3.12). This does not imply, of course, that the executive does not exercise privilege, or that the legislative body did not go along with it in the past. The expectation that those countries that do not uphold EP will establish some legal procedures for legislators to question civil servants directly is not fulfilled in the Scandinavian countries and the Netherlands (3.13). Similarly, there is no consistent connection between accepting EP as a legal and/or political norm, on the one hand, and the existence of an ombudsman with access to all information, on the other (3.14). Some countries that accept EP, such as Great Britain, Israel, and Germany, have ombudsmen (of different kinds), while others (France and Canada) do not.

There likewise seems to be no clear connection between the type of political system and the degree to which EP vis-à-vis the legislative bodies is accepted. The two presidential executive systems (U.S.A. and France) and the eight parliamentary cabinet systems differ among themselves in their approach to EP. The three federal systems (U.S.A., Germany, and Canada) are likewise divided in their approach, as are the other nonfederal systems.

In all these democratic countries the constitutional requirement of legislative oversight is supported by formal measures aimed at providing legislative access to executive information. The range of instruments varies from open hearings and direct testimony of civil servants to closed sessions of parliamentary committees with executive officials. However, these measures do not reveal the real nature of the informational relationship (and influence) between the two governing bodies. There seems to be a distinction in table 3 between the category of countries we termed more "open" in their political culture and legal provisions (U.S.A., Sweden, Norway, and Denmark, with the Netherlands joining this group) on the one hand, and the other five countries we termed less "open," on the other. In the first category EP is only partially accepted, whereas in the second it is fully accepted. However, the importance of this distinction in political terms should not be overstated because the differences between the two categories are not clear-cut. The relationship between the executive and the legislature on this question is probably subject to some other political rules.

JUDICIAL ACCESS

Insofar as EP is applied to judicial proceedings, in all countries it is accepted that despite the need for open processes of justice, there are some cases in which the executive is entitled to claim secrecy in the public interest (table 3, 3.21). The questions here are: To what matters does this privilege pertain; who decides when a document or testimony should be excluded from evidence; and, who has the final say—the public official or the judge?

Again, countries differ in their approaches to these questions. Unlike the issue of EP vis-à-vis the legislature, however, the trend here is toward recognizing judicial rather than executive discretion in determining which public interest should prevail in a certain case—the right of the public to see that justice is done or the need to preserve state secrets (3.22). Countries that recognize EP, such as Great Britain, Canada, and Israel, have recently moved in the direction of leaving the final say—including the decision to inspect secret documents in camera—in the hands of the courts. In other countries judicial discretion is not accepted (the Netherlands, Germany, and France), but there is some form of administrative court to deal, among other things, with secrecy matters (3.23). It can be said that as far as the judicial process is concerned, the trend is clearly toward limiting the application of EP.

Secrecy within Society

Our definitions of government secrecy posed the "government" on one side and the "public" on the other in order to analyze the contrast between GPTC and PRTK. We can now modify definition 2 to read:

Definition 2A: Government secrecy is a deliberate act on the part of those who govern to preserve or to add to the value of information that they possess by keeping the governed or parts thereof from knowing it at a given point in time.

We should also reformulate the government-citizens information-participation cycle (Figure 1) to include all the other "informationally active" actors in society.

The intermediaries between the government and the public in democratic systems appear under different names and have different

FIGURE 2. A MORE ELABORATE INFORMATION-PARTICIPATION CYCLE

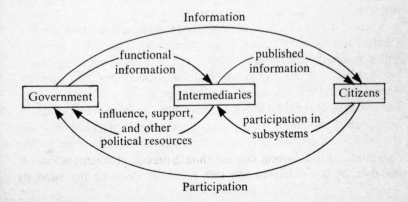

modes of operation. We shall focus our discussion on three of them: political parties, interest groups, and mass media and on what is referred to as "functional information" in figure 2. Also, even though "government" includes legislators, advisory bodies, and so on, we shall again concentrate on the executive only.

POLITICAL PARTIES

To discuss political parties as part of the intermediary network is a simplification of their role in democracies. Nevertheless, parties play structural roles in the political process and must develop access routes to government information. When in power, they need this information in order to offer ideological and operational guidance to their men in government. When in opposition, parties must have it in order to know what to oppose.

Does a political party have a "right" to demand information from the government of the day? Formally, the answer is no, because partisan considerations are not supposed to influence administrators. In reality, however, the question can be turned around: Can the executive carry on between elections without sharing information with political parties? Evidence is inconclusive and varies from country to country, but strong parties can mobilize enough political power to achieve at least a consultative status, similar to the position of other intermediaries such as pressure groups. Table 4 presents three simple variables regarding political parties and the countries subdivided into the "more open" and "less open" categories of tables 1 and 2.

The number of parties (A) does not seem to be related to the degree of "openness." Both the more open and less open categories of countries are internally polarized.

There seems to be a link between (B) internal party discipline (that is, the ability of leaders to keep members, especially legislators, within the party line) and the ability of the political system to retain information in closed circles, especially in those democratic countries where political affiliations are the most important channel of access for members of different elites. In the United States, the low cohesion and weak discipline of the parties makes them far less important in the information marketplace than interest groups and the mass media. In all the other countries, the political system provides for strong or medium party discipline, and the result is the relatively stronger

TABLE 4: POLITICAL PARTIES—NUMBERS, DISCIPLINE, AND POLITICIZATION

	4.1 More open	4.2 Less open
A. Number of Parties*		
Two	U.S.A.	Great Britain
Two and a half		Germany, Canada
Multiple	Sweden, Norway, Denmark	Israel, France, the Netherlands
B. Internal Party Discipline		
Strong and Medium	Sweden, Norway, Denmark	Israel, Germany, France, Great Britain, Canada, the Netherlands
Weak	U.S.A.	
C. Degree of Partisan Politicization of Other Intermediary Bodies		
Strong		Israel, the Netherlands
Medium	Sweden, Norway, Denmark	France, Great Britain, Germany
Weak	U.S.A.	Canada

* According to J. Blondel, *Introduction to Comparative Government* (London: Weidenfeld and Nicolson, 1970), pp. 157–159.

position of the parties as brokers of information. The Scandinavian countries are an exception because, despite their strong party discipline, they are relatively open. However, all the "less open" countries require a higher degree of party discipline. Confidentiality in the political system is supported by internal partisan loyalty and discipline. In many of these countries, party discipline has been weakening, and pressure groups and other associations are becoming more important channels of communication (see Lowi, chapter 3).

It follows therefore that the higher the degree of partisan politicization of other intermediary bodies (C), the higher the prominence of the parties in the communication network. In Israel and the Netherlands, where the divisions between the main parties signify some sort of political subcultures, government is rather closed, but the political system is "functionally open." Lower degrees of politicization in Great Britain, Germany, and Canada strengthen, paradoxically perhaps, the formal aspects of GPTC and make the whole political system less open. The same conclusion, tentative and uncertain, applies to the more open countries: Lower degrees of politicization strengthen the formal aspects of PRTK. It seems that "politicization" works against formal rules, at least those concerned with secrecy.

The demand for strengthening PRTK is not a major plank in the platforms of the major parties in the six "less open" democracies. (It was also not emphasized by the American parties prior to Watergate.) One exception is the attempt of Barend Biesheuvel to advance publicity in the Netherlands while a member of Parliament and his resort to secrecy when he became prime minister (Brasz, p. 209); another is the declaration of the French Communist party in 1975 (Manor, p. 247). Political parties tend to avoid a strong commitment to PRTK for two practical reasons. First, it becomes a nuisance for a party in power. Second, like other participants in the marketplace of information, parties follow the rules of supply and demand and try not to commit themselves a priori to a position that will restrict their ability to use secrecy and publicity.

INTEREST GROUPS

That interest groups are central participants in the information marketplace is self-evident. How such groups function is reported in the articles on the different countries:

Great Britain: "Extra pressures to publicity come from the widening range of nongovernmental agencies involved in policy making" (Seymour-Ure, p. 169).

Federal Republic of Germany: "It is rare for a ministry to prepare a law or regulation without consulting the associations concerned. However, such consultations with interest groups are conducted on a selective basis, and this distribution of information is not aimed at general publicity. Those not represented by an interest group have no chance of being brought into the inner circle" (Reese, p. 231).

Scandinavian countries: "The continuous and extensive interaction between public administrators and leaders of interest organizations fostered by national and local political leaders not only shapes new policies but also oversees the execution of established programs. During normal times this interaction is informal and discreet. Confidentiality prevails at such meetings in order to promote frank discussion and mutual trust" (Einhorn, p. 266).

The Netherlands: ". . . the tendency toward politicization of the government apparatus means that civil servants may with impunity give information to politicians and nongovernment. . . . Organized interest groups make use of that latent openness and find it worth their while to organize efficiently" (Brasz, p. 213).

Israel: ". . . regardless of the legal provisions, truly sensitive information is divulged time and again to selected confidants while 'unauthorized' people regularly gain access to the most confidential sources" (Galnoor, p. 187).

U.S.A.: "Sometimes secrecy can be linked together in the public and private spheres in ways that are mutually advantageous to organizations in both sectors of society but highly detrimental to the rest of the country. . . . [Secrecy] springs in no small measure from the pressures of groups outside the governmental apparatus itself" (Rourke, pp. 124–125).

The articles in part II seem to confirm the assumption that in practice there is no such thing as total government secrecy. Rather, officials have an acute need to share information, and so what is usually kept secret for a while is the *context* of a certain piece of information in the policy-making process.

Unlike what are dubbed "leaks" in journalistic jargon, the exchanges referred to in the above quotations are usually hidden from the public. They are the kinds of bargains in which the exclusion of certain outsiders (notably the public) is a prominent feature. Recent controversies about secrecy—and the pressure toward more openness —seem to emanate mainly from organized interests rather than from a sudden outburst of support for the principle of PRTK. In countries such as Great Britain or Germany, these pressures could perhaps be related to the weakening position of political parties. Where parties are still relatively strong (Israel, France), the influence of "citizens' pressure groups" is negligible. In contrast, Rourke holds organizations such as Common Cause to constitute, together with the mass media, the "antisecrecy lobby" in Washington and to be a new and permanent force of reform in American politics (see chapter 7). In the Netherlands, over the last few years, action groups have joined the information market, specializing in independent compilation of data relevant to policy making. Similarly, the establishment of Information Canada could be described as an attempt to institutionalize the function of citizens' pressure groups by centralizing their sources of information about government policies. The creation of policy advisory bodies in Canada is described (Doern, p. 153) as an instance of government producing both its own critics and a buffer between well-established interest groups and the general public. Finally, the "politics of protest" in countries such as Germany or France have also contributed to the competition over information and to the struggle for more openness in government.

The "active government," to use Shonfeld's term, cannot be expected to carry out its new and complex functions without the involvement of nongovernment groups.[19] Increased activity means touching on new interests or affecting old ones more deeply. This situation is quite a way from the time when government was charged mainly with defense, diplomacy, and justice. The result is an enormously complex network of information, in which groups have nearly a dominant influence on the degree of openness. This "openness," however, is functional and often conditional, and may exclude the public at large.

The Mass Media

Prominent in the information network and deeply involved in all the aspects of government secrecy mentioned so far are the mass media. Information is their forte, and they sit (according to definitions 3 and 4 above) on the very horns of the secrecy dilemma in democracies.

The role of the mass media in determining the actual degree of openness in a given democracy is highly constrained by the cultural, legal, and political variables. This assumption—which stands in contrast to the opinion that mass media's strength, resourcefulness, and professional standards are the most crucial factors influencing government secrecy in a country—is based on four main reasons, which can be only summarized here.

19. Andrew Shonfeld, *Modern Capitalism* (London: Oxford University Press, 1965), p. 389.

First, culture and communication are inherently related, not only because communication media are a major channel of culture in modern society, but because culture has a direct influence on the style and tone of communication.[20] The reasons for the difference between the muckraking tradition of the press in the U.S.A., the attitude of relative deference in Great Britain, and the mixed disposition in Canada are anchored in the general and political culture of these countries. These factors influence the mass media's role and their position relative to other social institutions, including government. The position of the mass media influences, in time, the communication patterns of a system, and as noted by Almond and Powell, "the performance of the communication function does not include all the other political functions, but it constitutes instead a necessary prerequisite for performance of other functions."[21] The mass media in democracies are the most specialized communication institution. While the impact of this expertise is strongly felt in political communication, it is also highly constrained by other variables in the political culture.

Second, all ten countries surveyed have traditionally upheld freedom of the press as the cornerstone of freedom of expression. But crusades by mass media on behalf of the people's right to know or against the government's privilege to conceal take different forms in these countries and this seems to be connected to, or influenced by, their organizational affiliations. The more any channel of communications is publicly controlled, the less it would be interested in the legal protection of PRTK. The privately owned newspapers in the ten countries have been fighting for more openness. Notable among them have been the battle of British newspapers for changing the Official Secrets Act or the strong opposition to government secrecy by the three unaffiliated newspapers in Israel. Likewise, the privately owned television and radio stations in the U.S.A. were, together with the press, a major vehicle in legislating the Freedom of Information Act in 1966 and its amendment in 1974. But radio and television were less involved in similar activities in Denmark, Norway, France, Germany, Great Britain, and Israel, where there is some form of

20. See, for instance, Robert E. Park's definition of communications as a "web of custom and mutual expectations which binds together social entities," in "Reflections on Communications & Culture, *The American Journal of Sociology* 44 (1939):191.

21. Almond and Powell, *Comparative Politics*, p. 166.

state or public supervision. If our assumption that the affiliations of the mass media influence their disposition toward PRTK and GPTC is correct, then the environmental constraints that determine these affiliations, as well as the degree of public control, also influence the behavior of the mass media in the information marketplace.

Third, the information revolution has elevated mass media into a unique position in the information marketplace. Government's power to inform, to withhold, to leak, and to lie is exercised to a great extent through mass media channels.[22]

Yet power creates dependence, and it is possible to assume an even stronger need for symbiotic relationship between mass media and government in the future. Thus, what Lowi calls the "manipulated consensus" (p. 49), is based on the close reciprocal relationship between sources of information (where government is the dominating factor) and channels of communication (where mass media has a near monopoly over other brokers of information). Also, mass media will continue to play the role of the chief supplier of "meaning"—as opposed to raw, undigested facts—in modern democracies (Rothman, pp. 64–65).

Fourth, despite the mutual dependency of media and government, the authors report that in the ten democracies surveyed, the adversary role of media vis-à-vis government has increased lately. In the U.S.A. the watchdog tradition of American journalism seems to have reached some sort of peak in the late sixties and early seventies. Rourke suggests that as a result of Watergate, the press emerged with greater authority to expose wrongdoing in government (p. 123). While no other country has something similar to what Shils calls the American "luxuriating publicity," Reese reports that in Germany the struggle for more openness has been a constant feature in the mass media's campaign since Adenauer descended from power. In the Netherlands, despite the high degree of "latent openness," a committee composed of representatives of the mass media, the universities, and the State Information Services recommended more openness. In Sweden criticism of defense policies instigated protests against the restriction on access to national security information. In Canada and Israel, newspapers have been active in exposures and leaks and have widely publicized political scandals. Similarly, in

22. See Arthur M. Schlesinger, Jr., *The Imperial Presidency* (Boston: Houghton Mifflin, 1973), p. 354.

France a great deal of the political combat within the hitherto closed executive has lately been transferred to the front pages of the press. On Fleet Street, pressure toward more openness has been increasing: There is less of the partisan loyalty that has characterized some of the British national press for a century and more investigative journalism that previously would have seemed too aggressive.

In view of this recent combativeness, it is worth asking: What is the media's role in attacking government secrecy—instigators, participants, or reflectors? Many observers, especially in the U.S.A., tend to regard mass media as the principal actor in the recent anti-secrecy campaigns.[23] It could be argued that despite the media's dependence on government as the chief supplier of information, they try, like any other organization in such a position, to increase their freedom of action. From this point of view, the media's crusade on behalf of PRTK is mainly a fight for their own power. Strengthening the instrument may serve the cause of democratic participation by producing better-informed citizens, but this is a by-product and not the main goal.

Another possibility is to view the media as one of the participants in the politics of confrontation. The fact that in most countries there is an increased use of leaks tends to support this view. Leaks are, by definition, an attempt to cash in on the value of a hitherto classified piece of information. But in publishing leaks, the media are only one side of the bargain and are often manipulated by the source of the leak. Therefore, despite a general increase in the adversary relationship vis-à-vis government, the media or parts thereof continue to play the more traditional double role of mediators in all countries. Like other organizations, the mass media are dependent upon both suppliers and clients. They align with the public (a supplier as well as a client) in advancing the cause of PRTK against government. But they also side with government (a client as well as a supplier) in acquiescing in GPTC.

Still another possibility is that the media's involvement may merely *reflect* the recent social turbulence. The vigorous role played by the media against government secrecy is related to what is euphemistically referred to as "the crisis" of modern democracies. Is the battle for

---

23. From a reporter's point of view, the Pentagon Papers and the Watergate cases seem to confirm this opinion. See, for instance, Peter Schrag, *Test of Loyalty: Daniel Ellsberg and the Rituals of Secret Government* (New York: Simon & Schuster, 1974).

more openness a symptom of ungovernability in the minority of countries that remain democratic? Or is this striving a signal of re-invigorated democratic societies? Such questions highlight the link between politics and the information marketplace, but they are difficult to answer. They require judgments based on ambiguous evidence whose meaning may only be known in retrospect; and the evidence, ambiguous or otherwise, is in a key respect incomplete because mass media are among the most secretive of organizations.

We know that mass media exercise discretionary power in selecting what the people should know and when, but we do not know on what basis the selections are made and therefore how the media serve PRTK. Part of this discretionary power is justified on professional grounds. But an argument for disclosure of how media policy is determined can be advanced by using the same reasoning that the media use in attacking government secrecy. Nevertheless, the possibility that media reflect more than they instigate seems to be the more plausible one. Political turbulence and government secrecy are obviously related in all the ten countries and the mass media tend to reflect (and magnify) this new dimension of the old secrecy dilemma.

Summary: Political Secrecy

The above discussion of the relationship between the mass media and politics could serve as a summary of this whole section on government secrecy and politics. Despite the variance in the ten countries, the similarities of the political aspects of government secrecy are rather great. Politics is changing in these countries, and the politics of information is changing too. These changes, especially in the nature of exchanges between the governing bodies and the active groups in society, bring to the foreground the ever present contradiction between the people's right to know and the government's privilege to conceal.[24] The commodity approach to information,

24. A recent example in Great Britain reconfirms this observation. The cabinet tried to prohibit the publication of the Crossman diaries with the usual secrecy arguments. While the theoretical and legal battles went on, the following occurred: "Human nature being what it is, copies have leaked out with a typically British elitist result. Almost anyone in the know who wants to see it can see it; most television and newspaper offices have it. And yet the public is denied from seeing it" (B.R.C., "Commentary: Opening the Crossman Diaries," *The Political Quarterly* 46 [January–March 1975]:3).

which served as the basis for the analysis in this section, comes close to describing reality, however pleasant or unpleasant. Government secrecy (definition 2) is therefore not based only on GPTC (definition 3). As suggested by definition 2A, exchanges of information and other political commodities seem to determine the actual degree of openness in a given society. Government secrecy is part of the political process rather than an independent phenomenon. If so, all the attempts to treat secrecy surgically and to change it directly through legislation alone are bound to fail.

GOVERNMENT SECRECY: WHAT WE DO KNOW

In comparing the secrecy profiles of ten democratic countries, we discussed attitudes, laws, and politics. Figure 3 presents a highly subjective summary of their relative positions.

In our discussion of attitudes and laws, we noted the difference in the legitimacy of government secrecy. In figure 3 we grouped the ten countries into two clusters: those oriented toward PRTK in their attitudes and laws (Sweden, U.S.A., Denmark, Norway, and the Netherlands), and those oriented toward GPTC (the Netherlands, Germany, Canada, Israel, France, and Great Britain). We can now compare the similarities between the countries in each cluster, in such terms as size, population density, federal v. nonfederal systems, presidential v. parliamentary executives, social homogeneity, political stability, and so on. Without undue elaboration, even a casual survey demonstrates that the characteristics listed above are not significantly related to secrecy or openness. For instance, within the "more open" cluster, the U.S.A., on one hand, and the Scandinavian countries and the Netherlands, on the other, form two distinct groups with regard to most of the above characteristics. More importantly, the U.S.A. is considered to be closer to the Anglo-Saxon political systems of Great Britain and Canada than to the systems of the Scandinavian countries. Even more perplexing are the differences between the five countries in the "less open" cluster discussed in various parts of this chapter.

Neither does there seem to be a clear-cut pattern regarding the impact of security and foreign affairs on attitudes and secrecy laws in the different countries. In the U.S.A. the cold war is often mentioned as the main reason for the increase in government secrecy,

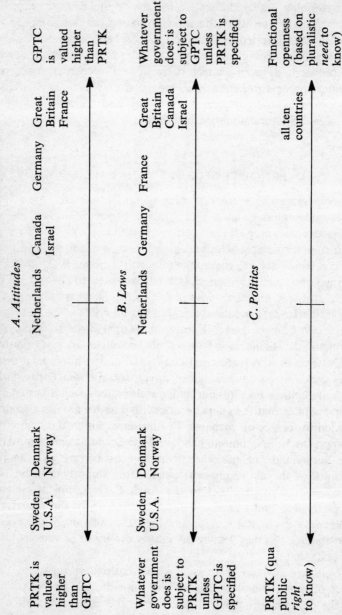

FIGURE 3. RELATIVE POSITION OF TEN DEMOCRATIC COUNTRIES ALONG DICHOTOMIZED AXES OF THREE SECRECY DIMENSIONS

A. Attitudes

PRTK is valued higher than GPTC

Sweden U.S.A. — Denmark Norway — Netherlands — Canada Israel — Germany — Great Britain France

GPTC is valued higher than PRTK

B. Laws

Whatever government does is subject to PRTK unless GPTC is specified

Sweden U.S.A. — Denmark Norway — Netherlands — Germany — France — Great Britain Canada Israel

Whatever government does is subject to GPTC unless PRTK is specified

C. Politics

PRTK (qua public *right* to know)

all ten countries

Functional openness (based on pluralistic *need* to know)

yet the U.S.A. is relatively more open than a country such as France, which is now less preoccupied with external security. While Israel and Germany are higher on the external tension scale, which could explain their legal provisions for safeguarding information, equally secretive are Canada or even Great Britain, which have been far less preoccupied with security since 1945.

Democratic theory has not provided answers to "'situational secrecy," and despite the tacit assumption that secrecy will ultimately wither away, its importance in modern politics has been increasing. Legal remedies aimed at coping with this problem can provide only partial answers because they tend to reflect the prevailing attitudes in the political culture.

As for C (politics) in figure 3, we noted that despite important differences among these ten countries in the ways in which partial interests gain access to government information or in the degree of influence of mass media on politics, they are very similar in the sense that they are *functionally open* societies or democracies.[25] Functional openness (that is, guaranteed access to information by groups that represent recognized interests) is not identical to "populistic openness" (access and influence of the most generalized grouping in society).[26] Even though PRTK is not equally valued or ideally observed in these democracies, pluralistic openness is maintained on a need-to-know basis.

I hope that the reader who has come this far will have acquired some insight into the dynamics of government secrecy in democracies. Our sample analysis of ten countries demonstrates that we cannot draw firm "rules" about the behavior of more "open" or more "closed" democratic systems. We also have difficulties in fixing the "profile" of each country on the basis of the variables presented. Yet, the tentative conclusion—that despite all the differences, these countries are functionally open—seems to provide a clue for further comparative analysis. We began by defining the dilemma of secrecy

25. Robert Dahl lists "alternative sources of information" as one required guarantee for people in a democracy to formulate, signify, and advance their preferences, *Polyarchy* (New Haven: Yale University Press, 1971), pp. 1–4. David Apter defines information and coercion as two functional requisites that can be used and traded off by government to preserve legitimacy, *The Politics of Modernization* (Chicago: University of Chicago Press, 1965), pp. 223–238.

26. For a closely related approach see David Apter's distinctions between less functional and more functional information, *Choice and the Politics of Allocation* (New Haven: Yale University Press, 1971), p. 139.

in democracies as a conflict between the norms of openness and of government's privilege to conceal, and proceeded to define government secrecy as the "added value" of information in political communication. If all the systems discussed here are more or less functionally open, then democracy guarantees at least pluralistic information practices. Moreover, criticisms about government secrecy can in themselves be taken as an indicator of increased openness. Where real secrecy is operative, no one knows that there are secrets to be revealed.[27] As the opposing practices of preserving both the people's right to know and the government's privilege to conceal operate, we know that some balance is essential for preserving democracy. The problem is that the sum of information which circulates as a result of supply and demand in the political market does not meet the normative requirement of democracy. Government, and especially the executive, has a formidable advantage over all other participants. Moreover, the politics of information tends to discriminate against those who are too weak to mobilize adequate resources in order to participate. The recent changes in the political roles played by the various groups in most democratic societies, and their increased political belligerency, are probably the reasons why most of the authors of the chapters in part II predict more openness of government in the future.

Government secrecy has been an important political issue in all the ten countries. New legislation has been the main reform suggested. Three countries (U.S.A., Denmark, and Norway) have followed the Swedish example and enacted open access laws. In three others (the Netherlands, Canada, and Great Britain) there have been official or semiofficial proposals for relaxing the secrecy laws. In Germany and France, despite some pressures, no formal recommendation has been proposed, while in Israel additional legal measures for protecting official secrets (preventing leaks) have been considered. In Sweden, there has been no strong pressure for legal action either way. The other remedies suggested or tried are also closely involved with internal political developments, such as new information services (Canada and France) or responses to the pressures of active groups and the mass media.

---

27. Shils made a similar observation twenty years ago: "Never before has the existence of life controlling secrets been given so much publicity and never before have such exertions been made for safeguarding of secrets" (*Torment of Secrecy*, p. 36).

In observing these developments we can see that the time is ripe for some changes in both the formal and practical aspects of government secrecy. There is a high probability that there will be changes in the internal politics of these democracies—changes that will affect government secrecy. What remains to be seen is the direction and the degree of these changes.

Contributors

ITZHAK GALNOOR is a senior lecturer in the political science department and director of the public administration program at the Hebrew University of Jerusalem.

CARL J. FRIEDRICH is Eaton Professor of Government, Emeritus at Harvard University and a consultant to governments in many countries. His numerous books include *Constitutional Government and Democracy* (1968), *Totalitarian Dictatorship and Autocracy* (with Z. K. Brzezinski, 1969), and *The Pathology of Secrecy: Violence, Betrayal, Corruption, Secrecy and Propaganda* (1972).

PETER DENNIS BATHORY teaches political theory at Livingston College and at Rutgers University, Graduate School of Arts and Sciences, specializing in classical and medieval thought. He is an associate of the Columbia Faculty Seminar on Social and Political Thought and of the Institute for the Study of Civic Values.

WILSON CAREY MCWILLIAMS is professor of political science at Livingston College, Rutgers University. He is the author of *The Idea of Fraternity in America* (1974).

CHRISTIAN BAY is a professor in the department of political economy, University of Toronto. He has previously taught at the universities of Oslo, Michigan State, California (Berkeley), Stanford, and Alberta, and is the author of *The Structure of Freedom* (1958 and 1970).

THEODORE J. LOWI is John L. Senior Professor of American Institutions at Cornell University. His books include *The End of Liberalism* (1969); *The Politics of Disorder* (1971); *Poliscide*, a book on science policy; and *American Government/Incomplete Conquest* (1976).

ROZANN ROTHMAN is assistant professor of political science at the University of Illinois at Urbana, Champaign. She is the author of several articles, including "Stability and Change in a Legal Order: The Impact of Ambiguity" (1972), "Government-Press Relations and the Role of the Media in Watergate" (1975), and a monograph, *Acts and Enactments: The Constitutional Convention of 1787* (1974).

DAVID CURZON is an Australian citizen, and at the time of writing, he taught economics at the Polytechnic Institute of New York. He has a bachelor's degree in physics and a Ph.D. in economics. He has worked for a private firm, for the federal government in Australia, and with NASA in Washington.

FRANCIS E. ROURKE is a professor of political science at Johns Hopkins University. He is the author of *Secrecy and Publicity: Dilemmas of Democracy* (1961) and *Bureaucracy, Politics and Public Policy* (1969). He recently edited a symposium on "Administrative Secrecy: A Comparative Perspective" in the *Public Administration Review* (January–February, May 1975).

BERNARD SCHWARTZ is Edwin D. Webb Professor of Law at New York University.

G. BRUCE DOERN is an associate professor and director of the School of Public Administration, Carleton University. He is coeditor and author of *The Structures of Policy Making in Canada* (1971), *Issues in Canadian Public Policy* (1974), and author of *Science and Politics in Canada* (1972).

COLIN SEYMOUR-URE is chairman of the board of studies in politics, University of Kent, Canterbury, and senior lecturer in politics. He is the author of *The Press, Politics and the Public* (1968) and *The Political Impact of Mass Media* (1974). He has contributed chapters on the press to books by David Butler on the British general elections and served as a research consultant to the Royal Commission on the Press, 1975.

HENK A. BRASZ is professor of public administration in the social science faculty at the Free University in Amsterdam. He served several local authorities and the Dutch Union of Local Authorities in the Netherlands. He is the author of *Changes in Dutch Communalism* (1961) and coauthor of *Introduction in Public Administration* (1975).

JUERGEN REESE studied sociology, political science, and economy, and received his Doctor rerum socialium at the University of Konstanz, West Germany, in 1971. From 1970 to 1973 he worked at the planning department of the chancellery of the federal government. In 1975 he was a postdoctoral fellow at the University of California (Berkeley).

YOHANAN MANOR did graduate work at the École Nationale d'Administration in France and received his Ph.D. from the University of Paris. He is now a lecturer in the political science department at the Hebrew University of Jerusalem. He has written about politics, planning, and administration in France and in Israel.

ERIC S. EINHORN is assistant professor of political science and director of Western European studies at the University of Massachusetts at Amherst. He teaches comparative public policy and international politics. He did research in Denmark on a Fulbright and Harvard Graduate Prize Traveling Fellowship, and has frequently returned to Scandinavia.